Lisa Dumas
October 1989

PENGUIN BOOKS

THE SPANIARDS

Born in 1950, John Hooper was educated at St Benedict's Abbey in London and St Catherine's College, Cambridge. At the age of eighteen he travelled with a television crew to Biafra during the Nigerian civil war to make a documentary for ITV. After graduating with an honours degree in history, he became a reporter for the BBC Radio current affairs and in 1973, when commercial radio was set up in Britain, he joined IRN as its first diplomatic correspondent. After a spell at the *Daily Telegraph*, he went to Cyprus as freelance correspondent for a number of news organizations including the *Guardian*, the *Economist*, the BBC, NBC and Reuter. In 1976 he became the *Guardian*'s correspondent in Spain and Portugal. He is currently its energy and trade correspondent.

John Hooper is married to another Fleet Street journalist, Lucinda Evans.

The Spaniards won the Allen Lane Award for 1987.

JOHN HOOPER

THE SPANIARDS

A PORTRAIT OF THE NEW SPAIN

PENGUIN BOOKS

PENGUIN BOOKS

Published by the Penguin Group
27 Wrights Lane, London W8 5TZ, England
Viking Penguin Inc., 40 West 23rd Street, New York, New York 10010, USA
Penguin Books Australia Ltd, Ringwood, Victoria, Australia
Penguin Books Canada Ltd, 2801 John Street, Markham, Ontario, Canada L3R 1B4
Penguin Books (NZ) Ltd, 182–190 Wairau Road, Auckland 10, New Zealand

Penguin Books Ltd, Registered Offices: Harmondsworth, England

First published by Viking 1986
Revised edition published in Penguin Books 1987
Reprinted 1987, 1988 (twice)

Made and printed in Great Britain by
Richard Clay Ltd, Bungay, Suffolk
Typeset in Ehrhardt

For Lucy

Contents

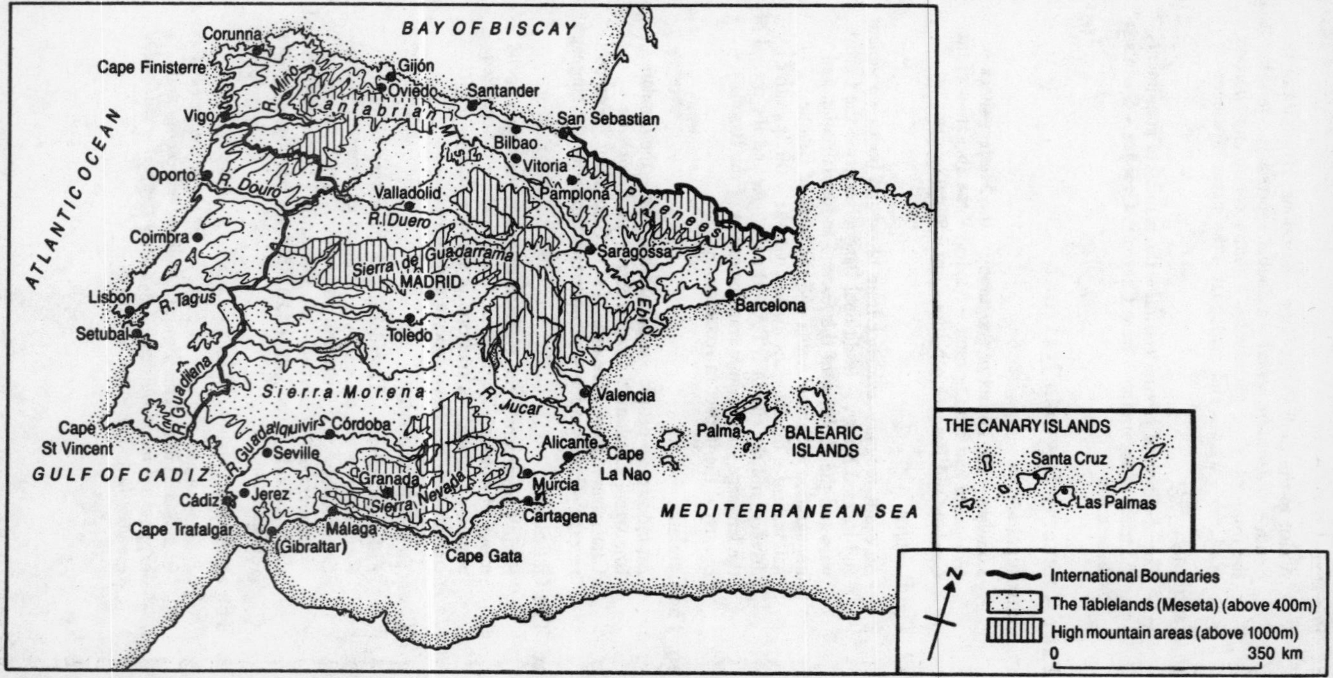

Spain, provinces and regions

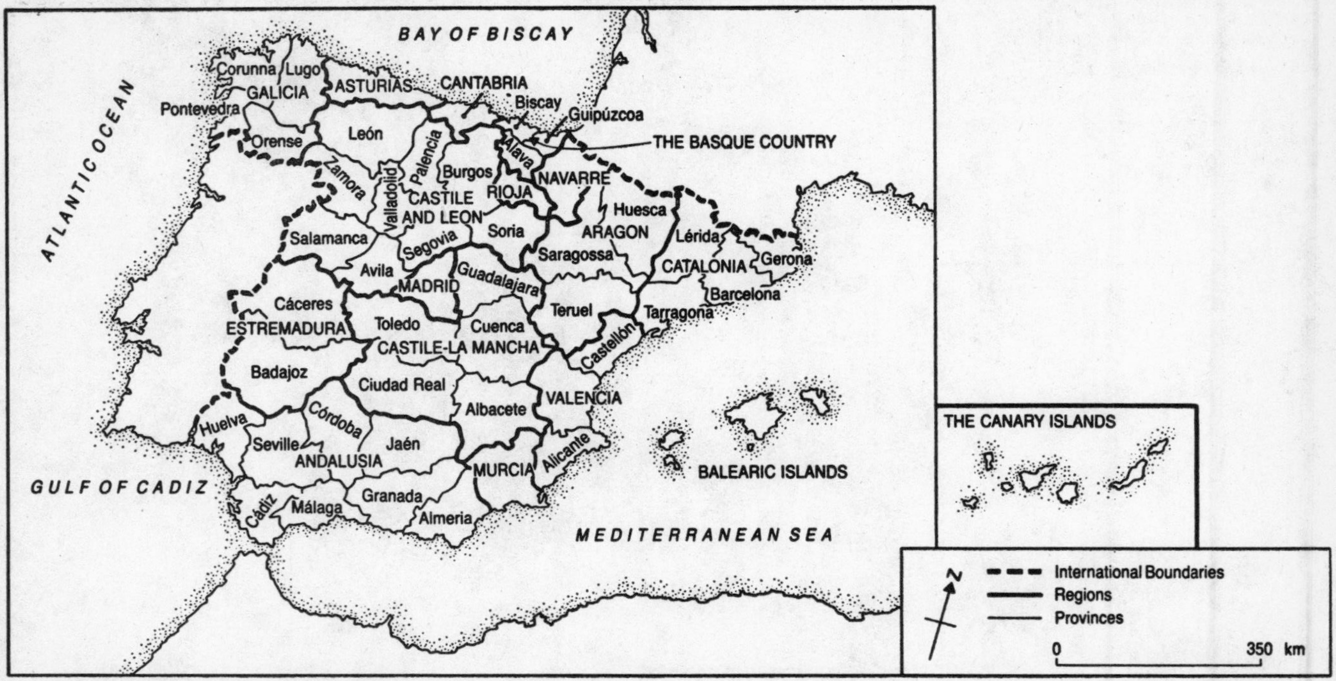

Iberian peninsula, physical features and main towns

Acknowledgements

If, after General Franco's death, the editor of the *Guardian*, Peter Preston, had not agreed to my taking over the paper's coverage of Spain and Portugal at a particularly sensitive moment in both countries' history and if two successive *Guardian* foreign editors, Ian Wright and Campbell Page, had not encouraged me to balance day-to-day news reporting with a periodic look at the social aspects of Spain's transformation, I would not have been able even to contemplate the writing of this book.

A number of my fellow journalists in Madrid, Spanish and foreign alike, helped me to a greater understanding of the country, but two in particular – Kees van Bemmellen of *De Telegraaf* and Marta Ruiz, then of *Pueblo* – were instrumental in opening my eyes to the effects that the political changes were having on the lives of ordinary Spaniards. I was also fortunate enough to be in Madrid at the same time as an unusually inquisitive and perceptive British military attaché, Major Bernard Tanter. I owe to him much of my interest in, and knowledge of, the Spanish army.

In 1978 George Lewinsky, then a producer with the London Bureau of the CBC, commissioned me to make a one-hour documentary on the non-political aspects of Spain's transition. It was the experience I gained during the making of that programme which, more than anything, persuaded me that there was the material for a full-length book on the subject. Nevertheless, it would almost certainly never have been written but for the encouragement I received from my first agent, Aubrey Davies of Hughes Massie.

I am deeply indebted to José Antonio López de Letona, Press and Information Counsellor, and Amado Jiménez Precioso, formerly Press and Information Attaché, of the Spanish Embassy in London, and to Ramón Cercós and Dionisio Garzón of the Prime Minister's Office in Madrid, who arranged an extensive itinerary of interviews for me when I visited Spain to update my material.

With the generosity of spirit that is so characteristic of Spaniards, numerous officials, journalists and others gave up their time to help me gain a better understanding of Spanish society. I would like in particular to mention Francisco Velázquez of the Prime Minister's Office; Anselmo Calleja of the

Ministry of Finance; Alvaro Espina Montero of the Ministry of Labour and Social Security; Joaquín Arango of the Ministry of Education; Pedro González Gutiérrez-Barquín of the Ministry of Justice; Francisco Sosa Wagner of the Ministry of Territorial Administration; Rafael del Río, Director-General of Police; José Luis González Haba, Director-General of the *Instituto para la Promoción Pública de la Vivienda*; Francisco García de Valdecasas of the *Asociación Nacional de Promotores Constructores de Edificios*; Emilio García Horcajo, the *Segundo Teniente Alcalde* of Madrid; Jorge Tinas Gálvez, Director of Environmental Services of Madrid City Council; Father Pedro Miguel Lamet, Editor of *Vida Nueva*; Juan Cruz, Arts Editor, and Antonio Gómez, Rock Critic, of *El País*; Rafael Borras of *Planeta*; Pere Gimferrer of *Seix Barral*; Luis Antonio de Villena, and Lluis Pasqual, Director of the *Centro Dramático Nacional*.

Bill Lyons of *El País*, who must be the only American ever to write regularly for a Spanish newspaper on the Spaniards' own *fiesta nacional*, was kind enough to read through the section on bullfighting.

Much of the anecdotal material in chapter 15 comes from Feliciano Blázquez's *Cuarenta años sin sexo*, Sedmay Ediciones, Madrid, 1977.

Dr Don Tills of the Museum of Natural History in London and the late Professor Antonio Tovar of the University of Salamanca provided me with priceless assistance in preparing the chapter on the Basques, while Professor Aina Moll, Director of Linguistic Policy at the *Generalitat*, helped me to grasp the intricacies of Catalan dialects.

Finally, a note on the spelling of place names. Wherever an anglicization exists which involves a change of spelling, I have used it. Thus, for example, Castilla has become Castile and La Coruña, Corunna. But where the anglicized form merely involves the loss of an accent (as in Aragon or Cordoba), I have stayed with the accented Spanish version.

Geneva
January, 1985

INTRODUCTION

Let me begin by telling you what this book is *not* about. With the exception of the first two chapters, which describe the events and trends that have moulded Spain into the nation it is today, this is not a book about politics or economics. Nor does it concern itself with the political-cum-economic world of industrial relations. There are plenty of experienced foreign correspondents in Spain whose job it is to report on these subjects and it is not my intention to duplicate their efforts.

The aim of this book is to paint a picture of the society which has taken shape in Spain since General Franco's death. It explains, among other things, how well the Spanish are educated, housed and cared for by the state, how many go to Mass on Sunday, what has been happening in the arts and the press since the end of the dictatorship, how Spain's novel system of home rule is working out and how far the change in sexual habits and attitudes has gone.

Spain is in different ways the best known and the least known of the major European nations. Every year more than forty million people go there. Yet the vast majority are holidaymakers who spend most if not all of their time at coastal resorts which are quite untypical of the country as a whole. All but a handful fly directly to and from the *costas*, the Balearic Islands and Canary Islands without ever seeing the everyday Spain of the ordinary Spaniard.

If the average non-Spaniard has any picture at all of the land that lies behind the *costas*, it is of the *meseta* – the vast, arid plain that occupies the centre of the peninsula and which encompasses Old and New Castile, León, La Rioja, La Mancha, Estremadura and parts of Aragón and Navarre. Yet Spain is anything but monotonous. It is above all a country of immense variations in climate and landscape.

Galicia, the north-westernmost region, which sits atop Portugal, is as wet and lush and mournfully beautiful as the West of Ireland.

The dominant colours there are the green of its gorse and the grey of its granite. Like Brittany and Ireland, it gets a lot of rain and much of it finds its way back to the sea along valleys which have subsided over millennia to the point where their seaward ends have sunk below the level of the ocean leaving only the valley sides visible in the form of great promontories. These half-submerged valleys or *rías* are an abundant source of shellfish – crabs, lobsters, oysters and, above all, the scallops which the pilgrims who travelled to Santiago de Compostela in medieval times adopted as their emblem. The dish of scallops cooked with mashed potato and grated cheese which the world knows as *Coquilles Saint Jacques* is by origin a Galician delicacy copied by the French.

Further along the coast, Asturias with its wild countryside and coal mines is more akin to South Wales than anywhere in the Mediterranean. Next door, Cantabria has soaring peaks with villages on their slopes that are cut off for months on end every winter, and deep potholes among which were found the famous cave paintings of Altamira. Much of the farming is pastoral and the sound of cowbells is never far away. You could almost be in Switzerland.

The Basque country also has an Alpine look to it. The typical Basque farmhouse with its broad eaves is virtually indistinguishable from a Swiss chalet. But whereas Switzerland is mountainous, the Basque country – although frequently described in the press and elsewhere as 'mountainous' – is in reality a land of odd-looking, steep-sided, flat-topped hills that tower over the valleys between them. The countryside in most areas is of a uniquely intense shade of green – a green so dark that it sometimes appears unnatural. In fact, it is a result of the rain that pours down in the Basque country day in day out, week in week out, during the winter. But then, Bilbao would be a dismal enough place even without the rain and the constantly overcast skies. To visit it is to take a trip in time back to the industrial North of Europe of earlier this century. Its belching smokestacks, grimy buildings and dogged, pasty-faced inhabitants are the very stuff of Lowry paintings.

In the foothills of the Pyrenees, in Navarre and Aragón, you could almost be in the Highlands of Scotland, but in both regions the landscape changes dramatically as you move southwards away from the French border. In Navarre you go through a stretch of splendid, undulating countryside around the capital, Pamplona, before entering an almost Mediterranean district where there are extensive vineyards. In Aragón you descend gradually towards the vast, flat depopulated Ebro valley and then rise again into the bare uplands around Teruel.

Catalonia and Valencia are perhaps the regions that the majority of people regard as being most typically Spanish, although a lot would, I think, be surprised to learn that a clear majority of Catalans and a sizeable minority of Valencians do not even speak Spanish* as their first language. Nor, whatever they may think, have many of the foreign holidaymakers who have visited Spain's east coast been for a holiday on the Costa Brava. The term 'Costa Brava' means 'rugged coast' and is used by Spaniards to describe the rocky shoreline that begins around Sant Feliú and extends to beyond the French border. Resorts like Lloret de Mar which tour operators habitually describe as being on the Costa Brava are on flat, sandy land further to the south.

Beyond Valencia lies Murcia – hotter, drier, flatter and poorer. But beyond Murcia lies Almería, which is sufficiently reminiscent of Arizona for it to have been used as the setting for a string of Westerns. By the coastal route, Almería forms the gateway to Andalusia – Spain's Deep South. Here again, the contrast between image and reality is considerable. The Andalusia of legend is an undulating expanse of corn fields and olive groves divided up into a small number of large estates. That is indeed true of the more northerly and westerly of the eight provinces that make up the region – Huelva, Cádiz, Seville, Córdoba and Jaén. But Málaga and Granada are hilly – and, in parts, even mountainous – provinces where smallholding has always been the rule rather than the exception. As for Almería, much of it is quite as barren as the Sahara.

The cities of this 'other Spain' behind the *costas* are quite unlike the jerry-built, neon-lit resorts that make up what is virtually a single city – homogeneous in character and appearance – stretching from Lloret to Marbella. Indeed, what is striking about the majority of provincial cities is how old they look. Some have extensive industrial estates and dormitory suburbs on the outskirts, but with very few exceptions – Guadalajara and Vitoria are two that spring to mind – the centres have been dealt only the most glancing of blows by the property developers. Pamplona, Avila and Santiago de Compostela, for example, seem barely to have changed since Spain's Golden Age.

The other thing that strikes the newcomer is the altitude. Most people are ready to accept that Spain is among the hottest and

---

* The use of the word 'Spanish', instead of 'Castilian', to describe Spain's most widely spoken language is unfortunate in that it implies that the others (Basque, Catalan and Galician) are either un-Spanish or less Spanish. It is rather like calling English 'British', but with less justification since vernacular languages are far more extensively used in Spain. Hispanic Latin Americans tend to use the term *castellano* as much as, if not more than, *español*. Within Spain itself, the use of the word *español* rather than *castellano* is a recent phenomenon and one which was encouraged by the nationalistic dictatorships of Primo de Rivera and Franco. The first edition of the *Dictionary of the Royal Academy* to be called 'Spanish' was not published until 1925. Both the 1931 and 1978 constitution referred to the official language of the nation as 'Castilian'. There is now a growing tendency for Spaniards to use the two words indiscriminately. I have followed their example.

biggest countries in Europe, but few would think of it as one of the highest. Yet the average height of the ground in Spain is greater than in any other European nation except Switzerland. If you look at a relief map you will see that with the exception of the Guadalquivir and Ebro valleys, the ground climbs rapidly away from the sea. This gives to the central plain one of its most distinctive characteristics – the almost painful brightness of the light. Not only is the *meseta* a land of huge expanses, but one where you can as often as not see to the furthest limits of those expanses. 'In Spain,' the author and journalist Manuel Vicent wrote recently, 'there is a lot of sun and an excess of light, so that everything is all too clear. It is a country of emphatic claims and denials where historically doubt has been put to the torch – to that sinister clarity.'

This alone has made Spain seem a forbidding place to the foreigner. But then Spain is a difficult country to come to grips with from almost any angle. For a start, it contains several different cultures. What is true of most of Spain need not be true of the Basque country, or of Catalonia or Galicia. Partly for this reason, anyone who sets out to study Spanish history will soon discover that lengthy stretches of it are dauntingly complicated. The culture is not easy to understand either. Some of the country's finest artists and writers – Murillo and Calderón for example – deal largely with themes that are peculiar to their time and place, while a lot of the popular culture derives from traditions – Arab, Jewish and Gypsy – that are alien to the experience of the majority of Europeans. Non-Spaniards appreciate the spectacle of flamenco, but few could tell good from bad. Even the cuisine, with its ardent spices and outlandish ingredients like pigs' ears and bulls' testicles, requires an adventurous spirit. Above all, the Spaniards have spent most of their history cut off from the outside world. Throughout the Middle Ages they were caught up in a more or less self-contained struggle against the Moslems and after a brief period of ascendancy at the beginning of the modern era they withdrew into a brooding isolation which lasted for a century and a half. From 1808 when Napoleon's troops invaded until the end of the civil war Spain was open to the outside world. But with Franco's victory, the shutters were brought down once again.

For as long as Franco was alive, Spaniards were unable to speak openly about their society and much of the information the government provided to outsiders was deliberately misleading. The consequence is that people's ideas about Spain are still based to a great extent on what was written during or about the period leading up to Franco's takeover. The best-known twentieth-century works on Spain – Gerald Brenan's *Spanish Labyrinth*, Orwell's *Homage to Catalonia*, Hemingway's *For Whom the Bell Tolls* and Hugh Thomas's history of the civil war –

all depict a pre-industrial society of huge economic imbalances and violent political conflicts. That Spain has gone forever. There is a new Spain and, I believe, a new kind of Spaniard very different from the intolerant, intemperate figure of legend and history. This new Spaniard is the result of the truly immense changes that have taken place during the last quarter of the century. The most obvious were the political ones that followed General Franco's death. But equally if not more important were the developments which transformed Spain's economy and society while the dictator was still alive and which went all but unnoticed in the outside world.

[illegible]
[illegible]
[illegible]
[illegible]
[illegible]
[illegible]
[illegible]
[illegible]
[illegible]

PART ONE:

THE MAKING OF THE NEW SPAIN

CHAPTER ONE

Economic and social change: from the 'years of hunger' to the 'years of development'

Although Franco's regime was frequently referred to as a fascist dictatorship, the description was never wholly correct. Spain's fascist party, the Falange, was only one of several factions and institutions which rallied to the side of the officers who rebelled against the elected government in 1936 and which thereby earned the right to a share in the spoils when, three years and half a million lives later, their side emerged victorious. In addition to the Falange, there was the army (or rather that section of the officer corps which had sided with the rebels), the Church and the monarchists, including both those who favoured the restoration of the heirs of Alfonso XIII – the King who had left Spain in 1931 – and those who supported the cause of the Carlist pretenders whose claims to the throne had twice provoked civil war during the previous century.

It was not unusual for membership of these 'families', as they have been called, to overlap. There were generals who belonged to the Falange, just as there were devout Catholics who wanted the restoration of the monarchy in some form. But there were also irreconcilable differences, notably between – on the one hand – the Falangists, who wanted to set up a fascist republic and – on the other – the Alfonsine and Carlist monarchists. To ensure that their rivalries did not undermine the war effort and to assert his control over their activities, Franco – who emerged by a mixture of chance and design as *Generalísimo*, or Commander-in-Chief, of the rebel forces – fused the political parties representing these three groups into a single entity with the tongue twisting, catch-all title of *Falange Española Tradicionalista y de las Juntas de Ofensiva Nacional-Sindicalista* (FET de las JONS). This odd coalition, which came to be called the *Movimiento Nacional*, was from then on the only lawful political entity in Franco's Spain. Throughout his rule, there was usually at least one member of each 'family' in the cabinet and the number of portfolios held by a particular faction was usually a good indication of the extent to which it was in or out of favour with the *Caudillo*.*

The army enjoyed a brief heyday in the immediate aftermath of the war, but it was the Falange which later became the dominant influence on Franco. Neither the Church nor the army was capable of providing a programme for running the country and the monarchists of both camps stood for a solution that could only be put into effect if Franco were to give up the position which he had by that time acquired as Head of State. In any case, the Blueshirts (for blue was to Spain's fascists what brown was to Italy's and green was to Portugal's) appeared in 1939 to represent the shape of things to come.

Over the next few years the Falangists took over the *Movimiento* and laid the foundations of Franco's regime. As soon as it became apparent that the Axis powers might not after all win the world war that had begun within months of the end of Spain's civil war, Franco reduced the number of Falangists in his cabinet by giving non-fascists the ministries which had most contact with the outside world. Nevertheless, Falangists continued to hold most of the economic and social portfolios and Falangist ideas dominated the regime's thinking.

This was partly because fascist political philosophy with its emphasis on national economic independence and on agricultural rather than industrial development dovetailed conveniently with the course of action forced upon Franco by events. During the Second World War, Spain had remained neutral while actively favouring the Axis. At the end of the war she found herself in an acutely uncomfortable position. Unlike Britain and France she was not entitled to the rewards of victory. Unlike Germany and Italy she was not at risk from the encroaching power of the Soviet Union. The Allies therefore had no incentive for giving Spain aid and a very good reason for denying it to her. In fact, they went even further than that and actually punished the Spaniards for having been taken over by a right-wing dictator. In December 1946 the newly created United Nations passed a resolution recommending a trade boycott of Spain. Coming on top of the deprivations brought about by the civil war, which had cut real income per head to nineteenth-century levels, the boycott was a disaster – not so much perhaps because of its direct effects, but because it made it unthinkable that Spain should benefit from the Marshall Plan for aid to Europe which got underway six months later.

---

* This was Franco's other title, equivalent to *Führer* or *duce*. In Spain it has – or had – heroic overtones because it is the word most commonly applied to the native chieftains who led the guerrilla war against the Roman occupation.

All the European nations suffered deprivation in the post-war era but Spain, where the late forties are known as the *años de hambre* or years of hunger, suffered more than most. In the cities, cats and dogs disappeared from the streets having either starved to death or been eaten. In the countryside, the poorer peasants lived off boiled grass and weeds. Cigarettes were sold one at a time. The electricity in Barcelona was switched on for only three or four hours a day and trams and trolleybuses in Madrid stopped for an hour in the morning and an hour and a half in the afternoon to conserve energy. But for the loans granted by the Argentine dictator, General Perón, it is possible that there would have been a full-scale famine.

The UN-sponsored blockade was lifted in 1950, but the Falangists' insular and ineffective doctrines continued to hold sway. For this, Spain was to pay dearly. In spite of the Falangists' exaltation of the rural economy, agricultural output fell to a level even lower than at the end of the civil war. Industry, immured from the outside world by a wall of tariffs and quotas, unable to buy the foreign technology it needed to modernize or to seek out new markets for its goods, bound on all sides by government regulations, could only grow at a painfully slow pace. National income did not regain its pre-civil-war level until 1951 and it was not until 1954 that average income returned to the point it had reached in 1936. In the early fifties an attempt was made to ease trade restrictions and stimulate private enterprise, but although it eventually succeeded in boosting industry it opened up a trade gap that rapidly absorbed the country's foreign reserves. In the meantime, bungling in other areas of the economy led to bursts of rip-roaring inflation.

To the villagers in the poorer parts of Spain – and particularly Andalusia which had been the scene of desperate poverty even before the civil war – the deprivations of the post-war era were the final straw. Individuals, families and in some cases entire villages packed up their belongings and headed for the industrial centres of the north – Barcelona, Bilbao, Oviedo and Saragossa – and for Madrid which, with the deliberate encouragement of a regime which feared the economic prowess of the Basques and Catalans, had ceased to be a purely administrative capital. Once they reached the cities the migrants settled like besieging armies on the outskirts. With nowhere else to live, they build *chabolas* or *barracas* (shacks) out of whatever they could scavenge – some breeze blocks off a building site, an unwanted door, a few empty cans and boxes and a sheet of corrugated iron or two to serve as a roof, weighted down with lots of heavy stones to make sure it did not blow away. The shacks were suffocatingly hot in the summer and bitterly cold in the winter. None had running water, so there was no question of sewerage. Since the shanty towns had sprung up without official permission it was usually several years before the municipal authorities got around to supplying them with electricity, let alone the more sophisticated amenities such as garbage collection or access roads. With a grim humour, one of the shanty towns outside Barcelona was nicknamed *Dallas – Frontier City*.

The whole idea of migration to the cities ran counter to the Falangist dream of a populous countryside inhabited by peasant farmers each owning a modest but adequate plot of land. At first the authorities tried putting a stop to the exodus by force. Policemen were sent to the railway stations with orders to collar anyone with a dark complexion and a battered suitcase and put him on the next train out of town. But it was like trying to turn the tide. In any case, migrants already living in the shanty towns saw in it a way of returning home for a holiday courtesy of the government – all they needed to do was put on their scruffiest clothes, travel a few miles out of town and catch a train coming up from the south.

The authorities later turned to a more sophisticated and successful approach, which was to limit the number of shacks by licensing those that had already been built and giving them numbered plaques. Those that did not have a plaque were liable to be torn down by the teams of municipal workmen – the dreaded *piquetes* which usually arrived in the middle of the morning or afternoon when the men of the shanty towns were out working or looking for work. Although the number of licenses had to be increased bit by bit, the system made the building of a shack such a hazardous enterprise that their numbers started to stabilize towards the end of the fifties.

By then Franco's regime was virtually bankrupt. The foreign exchange account was in the red, inflation was heading into double figures and there were serious signs of unrest among both students and workers for the first time since the civil war. It took a long time to persuade Franco, who had no interest in, or knowledge of, economics that a radical change was required. But in February 1957 he reshuffled his cabinet and gave the Trade and Finance portfolios to two men, Alberto Ullastres Calvo and Mariano Navarro Rubio, who were representative of a new breed in Spanish politics – the 'technocrats'. The typical technocrat came from a well-to-do background, had had a distinguished career in academic or professional life and – this was the *sine qua non* – belonged to, or sympathized with, the secretive Catholic 'freemasonry', Opus Dei. The technocrats' philosophy had its roots in Opus's analysis of the dilemma facing the Church, which was that wherever and whenever there was economic progress Christianity lost ground. Accepting that economic progress was inevitable, Opus Dei's view was that if only devout Catholics could take a hand in it at an early stage they could use it to bolster rather than undermine the power of the Church. And in the Spain of the late fifties helping the Church meant saving a regime that could be counted upon to safeguard traditional values. The technocrats believed that they could alleviate the regime's political difficulties by resolving its economic problems – improving the standard of living was seen as a means of delaying the restoration of democracy. In 1966 General Jorge Vigón, who had entered the cabinet as a result of the 1957 reshuffle and was close to the technocrats in outlook, wrote that 'Freedom begins as of the moment when the minimum earnings of each citizen reach $800 per annum.'

It was not until two years after their appointment that the new team began their all-out assault on the economy. Their short-term aim was to tackle inflation and redress the balance of payments. Their long-term objective was to free the economy from the restrictions that had been placed on it by the Falangists. The so-called Stabilization Plan introduced in July 1959 was intended to achieve the first of these goals. Public spending was cut, credit was curbed, wages were frozen, overtime was restricted and the peseta devalued. The Plan achieved what was expected of it. Prices levelled out and the deficit in the balance of payments was transformed into a surplus by the end of the following year. But the cost in human misery was considerable since real earnings were slashed. As a result, many Spaniards set off to find work abroad. Measures to liberalize the economy, and thus achieve the second of the technocrats' goals, were introduced over a longer period beginning at the time of the Stabilization Plan. Spain was opened up to foreign investment, much of the red tape binding industry was cut away, restrictions were lifted on imports and incentives were offered for exports.

The performance of the economy during the years that followed was dramatic. Between 1961 and 1973, a period often referred to as the *años de desarrollo* or years of development, the economy grew at 7 per cent a year – faster than any in the non-communist world except Japan's. Income per head quadrupled and as early as 1963 or 1964 – the exact moment is disputed – it passed the $500 mark, removing Spain from the ranks of the developing nations as defined by the UN. By the time Spain's 'economic miracle' had ended, she was the world's ninth industrial power and the wealth generated by her progress had led to substantial improvements in the standard of living. Spaniards had a better diet. They ate less bread, fewer potatoes and more meat, fish and dairy products. The results are visible on any Spanish street today – the teenagers are noticeably taller and slimmer than their parents. During the sixties, the number of homes with a washing-machine rose from 19 per cent to 52 per cent and the proportion with a refrigerator leapt from 4 per cent to 66 per cent. When the 'boom' started only one in every hundred Spaniards owned a car. By the time it ended the figure was one in ten. Telephones ceased to be the prerogative of offices, factories and a few wealthy or influential individuals and become commonplace in private homes – a fact that had considerable impact on relations between the sexes, which was in turn mirrored in the pop songs of the day. The number of university students tripled and by the early seventies the infant mortality rate in Spain was lower than in Britain or the United States.

It should be pointed out, though, that one reason why the proportionate increases in all areas were so impressive was that the starting points were so low. Even in 1973 income per head was still lower than in Ireland, less than half the average for the EEC countries and less than a third of the average in the United States. Moreover, *pluriempleo*, the practice of holding several jobs, which became widespread in Spain during the boom years, meant that Spaniards had to work harder for their prosperity than other Europeans.

The principal reason why the economy was able to continue growing after 1959 in a way that it did not following the reforms at the beginning of the decade was that ways were found of bridging the trade gap which opened up as soon as Spain's economy began expanding – a consequence of the fact that Spain had to pay more for the fuel, raw materials and capital equipment which she needed to feed her industrial expansion than she could get for the goods and produce she sold abroad. Throughout most of the period from 1961 to 1973, imports outstripped exports by about two to one, but the deficit was amply covered by invisible earnings in the form of foreign investment, money sent back to Spain by Spaniards who had found work abroad and – finally and most importantly – receipts from tourism.

In all these areas, the government had played an important role. It had eased the conditions for foreign investment, provided financial incentives for Spaniards to seek work abroad and, while tourism had been growing steadily throughout the fifties, it was not until 1959 when the government stepped in to abolish the requirement for visas for holidaymakers from Western Europe that the industry really took off. It is equally true, however, that none of these invisible earnings would have been forthcoming in such quantities had the other countries of the West not been enjoying a period of growth and prosperity. It was this which created the surplus funds that found their way to Spain, which made the companies of North-Western Europe thirsty for cheap foreign labour and enabled individuals in North-Western Europe to contemplate holidays abroad. To this extent, Spain's economic miracle was a by-product of the sixties boom in Europe as a whole.

The way that Spain acquired her vital invisible earnings had an immense impact on the country's lifestyle. Oddly spelt names which

Spaniards found difficult to pronounce like Chrysler, Westinghouse, John Deere and Ciba-Geigy began appearing on hoardings and in the press. The young businessmen recruited by the new foreign companies picked up their employers' habits and attitudes and passed them on to their counterparts in Spanish-owned firms. Soon, a new breed of *ejecutivos* began to emerge – clean-shaven, wearing button-down shirts, casual suits and sometimes a pair of black-rimmed spectacles. Their speech, liberally sprinkled with English words and phrases, is known as *ejecudinglish.* The archetypal representative of these Americanized Spaniards, now in their forties, is the singer Julio Iglesias.

Between 1961 and 1973 well over a million Spaniards received assistance to go and work abroad. By the time the boom ended there were some 620,000 in France, 270,000 in West Germany, 136,000 in Switzerland, 78,000 in Belgium, 40,000 in Britain and 33,000 in Holland – a veritable army of Spaniards all sending back about a quarter of their earnings to swell the deposit accounts of their homeland.

Spain's Mediterranean coastline was transformed out of all recognition. It is hard to believe now that when the novelist Rose Macaulay drove along it in the summer of 1947, she 'encountered scarcely any travelling compatriots and saw only one GB car'. Her main complaint was that 'on these lovely shores as elsewhere in Spain the inhabitants stare and point'. Between 1959 and 1973 the number of visitors to Spain leapt from under three million to over thirty-four million. Land by the coast which, because it was usually either rocky or sandy, was generally regarded as virtually worthless and was frequently bequeathed to the least-favoured offspring, suddenly became valuable. On the Costa del Sol, at San Pedro de Alcántara, a plot of undeveloped land next to the beach which changed hands for 125 pesetas per square metre in 1962 was sold eleven years later – still undeveloped – for 4,500 pesetas per square metre.

The material benefits of the tourist boom were considerable – not only for property developers, but also for shopkeepers and the ordinary people of the villages near the coast who became waiters and chambermaids in the tourist hotels. But that is not to say that the tourist boom was an unmitigated blessing. The development took place in an environment which had not changed all that very much since the eighteenth century – a world of thrift and deprivation which had its own strict moral code. Overnight, its inhabitants were confronted with a new way of life in which it seemed as if the men had more money than they could cram into their wallets and the women walked around virtually naked. Accustomed to measuring time in hours, they were all of a sudden expected to think in minutes. They had to come to grips with new concepts like credit cards and complicated machines like dishwashers.

The result in many cases (although, for some reason, less among women than among men) was shock. Not in the metaphorical but the literal sense of the word – the most common symptoms were insomnia, listlessness and breathlessness. In the mid-sixties, the Civil Hospital in Málaga enlarged its psychiatric wing by adding on a ward specifically to cater for young patients. It immediately became known as 'the waiters' ward'. According to a study carried out in 1971, 90 per cent of all non-chronic mental illness in the rural parts of the province of Málaga was among teenage males who had gone to work on the coast.

Tourism, emigration and the arrival in Spain of multinational firms all served to bring the Spaniards into contact with foreigners and in particular with other Europeans, thereby whittling away the xenophobia which had always been a characteristic of the Spanish, and never more so than in the early years of Franco's rule. But Spain did not, as the technocrats had hoped, become a member of the EEC. Her application, submitted in 1962, was ignored although she did manage to wheedle a preferential trade agreement out of Brussels eight years later. On the other hand, her best soccer team – Real Madrid – had succeeded between 1956 and 1960 in carrying off the European Cup five years in a row (a feat which has never been equalled) and in 1968 a Spanish vocalist, Massiel, won the Eurovision Song Contest with a suitably anodyne offering entitled 'La, La, La'. These victories probably made as much of an impression on the average Spaniard as anything on the diplomatic level would have. They showed Spaniards that they could not only gain acceptance in 'Europe' (the Spanish, like the British, often talk about Europe as if it were somewhere else) but also hold up their heads while doing so.

The 'economic miracle' also changed the nature and volume of internal migration. Poverty-stricken villagers from Andalusia continued to flood towards the cities, but they were joined in increasing numbers by migrants from Galicia and the regions of the *meseta* – Castile, León, Estremadura and Aragón. Whereas the typical migrant of the fifties was a landless labourer forced to move by hunger, the migrants of the sixties were just as likely to be craftsmen or shopkeepers whose standards of living had dropped because of the falling population in the countryside or peasant farmers who were still able to make a meagre living from the soil but were lured to the city by the promise of a less arduous and more varied existence. An American anthropologist, Dr Richard Barrett, who carried out a field study in the Aragonese town of Benabarre between 1967 and 1968 noted that the girls there were unwilling to marry the sons of peasant farmers if they intended to stay and work their fathers' land – and to such an extent that young farmers were driven to advertising in the press for brides from the poorer regions of the country. The dream of the girls of Benabarre was to marry a factory worker – or at least a boy who was prepared to leave home in an attempt to become one.

Come the sixties, the original migrants were beginning to move out of their shanty towns and into cheap, high-rise accommodation. Since shack building was by then practically impossible, the new arrivals either had to buy a shack from a family which was moving on to better things or to pay for accommodation in the apartment of a family which had already done so. From the point of view of the first wave of migrants, selling a shack became a way of getting the down payment on a flat. Taking in lodgers was a way of finding the monthly instalments.

While the cities were rapidly becoming overcrowded, the countryside was equally quickly becoming depopulated. In 1971 Dr Barrett returned to Aragón and visited seventeen hamlets near Benabarre. By referring to the 1950 census figures he discovered that during the intervening twenty years they had lost 61 per cent of their population. Four were completely deserted and in some cases the depopulation had taken as little as six years. Today anyone driving through Spain who is prepared for a bumpy ride off the main road will sooner or later come across one of these deserted hamlets. Perhaps the most forlorn of all are those that are almost, but not quite, abandoned – where the last inhabitants, who are too old to leave and too young to die, keep their livestock in what were once their neighbours' cottages.

Before the civil war, the Catalan politician, Francesc Cambó, had described Spain as a country of oases and deserts. Migration made this even more true. By the end of the boom, the table of population density by provinces showed a steady gradation from most to least densely populated, but what was striking about it was the size of the gap between the two extremes. At one end, there was Barcelona with more than 500 people per square kilometre – which makes it as crowded as the industrial centres of North-Western Europe – and at the other end there were eleven provinces with fewer than twenty-five inhabitants per square kilometre – a figure comparable with countries like Bhutan, Nicaragua and Upper Volta. The process of depopulation has gone so far in some parts of the country that it is difficult to see how it can be reversed. In 1973, as the flood of migration began to abate, Teruel became the first province in Spain's history in which there were more deaths than births. Since then, several provinces with elderly populations have joined Teruel. Even if migration from these areas stops altogether, they will continue to lose inhabitants.

The increasingly uneven distribution of Spain's population encouraged an even more unequal allocation of the country's wealth. Any attempt at regional planning while Franco was still alive ran up against the problem that the areas into which the country would have had to have been divided for planning purposes were precisely those whose demands for recognition were anathema to the dictator and whose identity he had been at great pains to erase. The technocrats' answer was a so-called 'pole' policy. The idea is to select a number of towns in underdeveloped or semi-developed regions and offer incentives to firms to set up business there in the hope that the resulting prosperity will spill over into the surrounding countryside. The criteria used for deciding which towns and firms should benefit from the scheme were never made clear and it is suspected that a good deal of corruption surrounded their selection. But the most serious flaw in the 'pole' project was that the incentives were not offered for long enough for entrepreneurs to be confident of success. By and large investment did not live up to expectations and what investment was generated was relatively unsuccessful in creating new jobs. Of the twelve towns chosen as poles only Valladolid fulfilled the hopes placed in it. By the early seventies, it was well on its way to becoming a sizeable industrial centre.

With the exception of Valladolid and Madrid, new business tended to set up shop in the Basque and Catalan provinces, which had become industrialized in the last century, or in places like Oviedo, Saragossa, Valencia and Seville – big cities which had already had some industry before the civil war. In 1975 five provinces – Barcelona, Madrid, Valencia, Biscay and Oviedo – produced 45 per cent of the country's total output. Most of the prosperity was concentrated in the north and east of the country. Of the fifteen peninsular provinces with the highest average incomes, all but two lay along or to the north of the River Ebro. The two exceptions were Madrid and Valladolid. Average earnings in the poorest provinces of Andalusia, Estremadura and Galicia were less than half those in the richest – Madrid, Barcelona and the three Basque provinces. The disparity in wealth was mirrored by a disparity in the provision of amenities and services. There were eighty doctors per 100,000 inhabitants in Jaén but 230 per 100,000 in Madrid.

As the boom progressed, the migrants became potentially one of the most influential classes in Spain, having virtually engulfed the old highly politicized urban working class. Unlike the workers of the thirties, the militancy of whose socialism and anarchism was famed throughout Europe, the vast majority of migrants had very little interest in, or experience of, politics. In rural Spain only a tiny number of people had the time or money to take an interest in political developments outside the village and they were the rural notables – landowners, merchants and professional people who controlled, through their economic influence, the destinies of the labourers, tenants, sharecroppers and smallholders in patron–client relationships. During the periods in which Spain was a democracy, the clients usually voted the way that they were told to by their patrons (which was one of the main reasons why democracy was so widely despised and therefore so vulnerable). The migrants who arrived in the cities during the fifties and sixties were not so much right-wing or left-wing as simply apolitical, although they were highly receptive to the go-getting materialism and individualism which, to a greater or lesser extent, affected every level of society during the *años de desarrollo*. In the shanty towns, acts of great kindness co-existed with an almost total absence of class solidarity and once they had found their way out of those ramshackle purgatories the migrants were understandably reluctant to do anything, such as striking or demonstrating, that might cause them to return. Nevertheless, their initial submissiveness tended to obscure the fact that migration had broken forever the hold that the rural upper and upper-middle classes had once exerted over the rural lower-middle and lower classes. What is more, it was clear – although not at first to the migrants themselves – that their interests were not those of their employers. Indeed, whenever they were pressed in polls and surveys to define their views, the sort of ideal society that their answers implied was distinctly more left-wing than right-wing. By the start of the seventies, they were beginning to become politically more aware and to develop an outlook that was, if not radical, then certainly liberal.

Although the 'economic miracle' changed almost everything about Spain – from how and where people lived to the way that they thought and spoke – one of its paradoxes was that what it changed least was the economy itself. It grew, of course, but its shape and character remained virtually unaltered. When the boom ended, there were still far too many small firms (over 80 per cent of all Spanish companies employed less than five workers) and it was as difficult as it had ever been to get long-term credit. Between them, these two factors ensured that nowhere near enough money was spent by industry on researching new products or training skilled workers. Productivity remained low (half the EEC average), unemployment was comparatively high – certainly much higher than the official figures suggested – and the traditional gap between imports and exports was widening rather than narrowing.

The political effects of the boom were far greater both in number and complexity. The most popular explanation of recent Spanish history goes roughly as follows – the reason why democracy did not take root in Spain in the late nineteenth and early twentieth centuries was that Spain did not have a middle class. The economic 'miracle' was responsible for redistributing the country's wealth and creating a 'new middle class'. Together, these two factors helped to remove, or rather to bridge, the gulf which had existed up until then between the 'Two Spains' and which had been responsible for the civil war. By healing this historic breach in Spanish society between the upper and lower classes, the boom was thus responsible for Spain's relatively smooth transition from dictatorship to democracy.

There is an element of truth in this. Unquestionably, the economic 'miracle' in the sixties helped to smooth the way for the political transformation of the seventies. But the mechanism of cause and effect was a little more complex than is usually made out. In the first place, Spain – as we have already seen – has long had a middle class. But from the point of view of consolidating a democracy, what matters is not so much the existence of a middle class *per se* as the existence of an urban rather than a rural one. What happened during the boom years was that a substantial section of the Spanish middle classes was lured away from the countryside and into the towns for much the same reasons as the working classes. As they moved from one environment to the other they – or more often their children – abandoned many of the conservative attitudes and prejudices which are typical of rural élites everywhere. The idea that the boom helped to level out wealth is quite simply a myth. Apart from a few radical Falangists, Franco's supporters were not ones to worry about redistributing income. The *Caudillo* himself had once cheerfully admitted that the civil war was 'the only war in which the rich became richer'. During the sixties, the technocrats were content to see the gulf between the richest and poorest in society grow even wider. It was not until the seventies, when the illegal trade unions seized the initiative from Franco's worker-employer *sindicatos* and started to flex their muscles, that the gap began to close. Even so, by the time Franco died, the top 4 per cent of households accounted for 30 per cent of total income.

But although the way the cake was cut did not change all that much, the size of the cake grew enormously. Greatly increased buying power enabled just about everyone in society to jump up a class in absolute as distinct from relative terms. To that extent, the 'miracle' did indeed create a 'new middle class' from out of the ranks of what one might call the upper-lower class – mainly craftsmen and peasants. Far more importantly, though, the same process decimated a class which had been destabilizing Spanish society for well over a century – a lower-lower class of landless, unskilled pariahs whose misery and desperation encouraged them to throw in their lot with any messianic demagogue who promised them salvation in this world rather than the next.

On the day following the first general election after General Franco's death, the Madrid newspaper *Diario 16* published an article comparing the number of votes cast for right and left in 1977 and 1936. The percentages were almost identical. Poignantly, the article was entitled 'Forty Wasted Years'. The consolidation since then of a two-party system only serves to underline the point – to the extent that there were 'Two Spains', they survived the *años de desarrollo* intact. What the boom years did was to make both of them wealthier and therefore more content and more tolerant.

The miracle ended with the same dramatic suddenness with which it had begun. The European boom had started to run out of steam towards the end of the sixties and the first people to feel the effects were the emigrants. As the expansion of the other Western European economies began to slow down, the number of jobs available declined and the need for foreign labour diminished. After 1970 the number of Spaniards leaving the country to work abroad dropped off. Soon, even those who were already working abroad began to find that they were no longer wanted. France, for example, offered emigrants an indemnity of 150 times their average daily wage – payable as soon as they reached their country of origin. In 1973 the emigrants began to return and in 1974 the amount of money they sent home started to fall. The same year also saw tourist earnings and foreign investment drop for the first time as Europeans tightened their belts and marshalled their resources. Even so, Spain's invisible earnings would have been enough to cover her trade deficit had it not been for the increase in oil prices following the war in the Middle East. At that time, Spain depended on oil – almost all of it imported – for two thirds of her energy. The OPEC price rises doubled the size of Spain's trade gap and unleashed the inflationary pressures that had been simmering away below the surface of the economy throughout the boom years. During 1974 the cost of living rose by more than 17 per cent. The following year, an estimated 200,000 Spaniards returned from abroad in need of work. Then, on 20 November 1975, General Franco died and for the second time this century Spaniards were left with the unenviable task of restoring democracy in the depths of a worldwide recession.

CHAPTER TWO

POLITICAL CHANGE: FROM DICTATORSHIP TO DEMOCRACY

At first light on 21 November 1975, the day after Franco's death, a detachment of artillerymen trundled three massive cannon into a park on the outskirts of Madrid and began firing a last salute to the late dictator. The sound of the guns echoed through the city all day, heightening the sense of apprehension that had taken hold of the capital and the nation.

For thirty-six years all the important decisions had been taken by one man. His disappearance was of itself enough to justify a feeling of trepidation among supporters and opponents alike. But Franco had also left behind him a perilous gap in expectations between the people and their rulers. It was plain to anyone with eyes to see and ears to hear that Spaniards wanted a more representative form of government. Even among those who had once supported the dictatorship – and their numbers were consistently underestimated by foreign observers – there was a widespread recognition that Francoism had outlived its usefulness. Yet up until his dying day, Franco had restricted the exercise of power to those who had refused to countenance change – collectively nicknamed the *bunker* – or accepted the need for change but were only prepared to introduce it slowly and conditionally – the so-called *aperturistas*. The country's illegal opposition parties, meanwhile, were united in calling, quite unrealistically, for a clean break with the past – what, in the jargon of the times, was known as a *ruptura*. However, since they had no political power, the only way that they could put pressure on the authorities was to call for street demonstrations which invariably turned into riots as soon as the police arrived.

Of the many prophecies circulating on that chilly November morning, one of the gloomiest yet most plausible was that the government would sooner or later be overwhelmed by an outburst of popular frustration. At that point, the armed forces – which had much to lose and little to gain from the introduction of democracy – would step in to 'restore order', possibly in the name of a higher authority. From then on, so the theory went, Spain would settle in to a pattern well known to the Latin American nations (and which was in fact set in Spain during the last century) – phases of limited reform alternating with outbursts of savage repression.

If Spain were to avoid such a fate it was clear that much would depend on the role played by the young man who had succeeded Franco as Head of State. Franco had always implied that he was a monarchist at heart. Ever since 1949, in fact, Spain had in theory been a monarchy, even though Franco ensured that he was made acting Head of State for life and given the power to appoint his own successor. It was no surprise therefore that, six years before he died, Franco should have named as his 'heir' a member of the royal family. But instead of selecting the legitimate heir to the throne – Alfonso XIII's son, Don Juan – Franco chose a young man over whom he had been able to exert enormous influence – Don Juan's son, Juan Carlos.

Juan Carlos was hardly someone in whom Spaniards who aspired to a modern, democratic state could have much faith. Ever since the age of ten, when he had come to Spain for his education, the young Prince had been projected through the media as a loyal son of the regime – passing with distinction his *bachillerato* (including a compulsory paper on the Formation of the National Spirit), going on to attend all three military academies and doing a sort of internship in the administration. In recent years he had rarely been seen except in Franco's shadow – standing behind the old dictator on platforms and podiums at official ceremonies. On such occasions he invariably looked a bit gormless – an impression which was reinforced by the awkward way in which he delivered speeches. The overall impression was of a nice enough chap but with not enough intelligence or imagination to question the conventions of his background.

Few people can have been so universally misjudged as Juan Carlos, for his rather gauche manner belied a penetrating and receptive mind. To the *Caudillo*, Juan Carlos was the son he never had. The young Prince fully reciprocated his affection – to this day he will not permit anyone to speak ill of the old dictator in his presence – but he had formed the opinion long before Franco's death that Spain could not and should not continue to be governed in accordance with the principles laid down by his mentor. Starting in the sixties, Juan Carlos made it his business to get to know as many people from as many walks of life and of as many shades of opinion as possible. By then, he was living in a small palace near Madrid guarded by police. Several of the people he wanted to meet had to be smuggled in either by the Prince's secretary or by friends. Some entered in the boots of cars. Javier Solana, then an activist in the clandestine opposition and later the Socialist Minister of Culture, went in on the pillion of a banker's motorbike wearing a crash helmet that obscured his features.

Whether Franco knew or guessed what his protégé was up to will probably never be known, but he certainly restricted the freedom and influence that Juan Carlos would enjoy after his accession. On the day after he had been named as successor, the Prince was made to take an oath in front of the members of Franco's rubber-stamp parliament. Kneeling down, with one hand resting on the New Testament, he swore loyalty to Franco and 'fidelity to the principles of the *Movimiento Nacional* and the fundamental laws of the realm'. In a speech afterwards he hinted broadly at his true beliefs. 'I am very close to youth,' he told the ranks of elderly timeservers in front of him, 'I admire and I share their desire to seek a better, more genuine world. I know that in the rebelliousness that worries so many people there can be found the great generosity of those who want open horizons, often filled with unattainable dreams but always with the noble aspiration to a better world for all.' Nevertheless, in a country where keeping your word has always been a concomitant of preserving your honour the public oath he had just sworn meant that his freedom of movement would henceforth be severely restricted. If the apparatus of Francoism were going to be demolished it would have to be done according to the rules that Franco had himself devised. This in turn meant that whoever was in charge of the government would need to be both firmly committed to the restoration of democracy and extremely knowledgeable about the structure of the dictatorship – an apparently impossible combination.

For most of his rule, Franco had been Head of Government – in other words Prime Minister – as well as Head of State. But in June 1973 he relinquished his grip on the premiership and conferred it on one of the few men he ever really trusted – Admiral Luis Carrero Blanco. Franco evidently hoped that Carrero – a formidably able politician – would still be in the saddle when Juan Carlos succeeded to his throne. Carrero's assassination by Basque terrorists six months later was thus immensely helpful to the young Prince, because it allowed him a degree of manoeuvre which he would never have enjoyed had the Admiral still been around. The best man Franco could find to take over from Carrero was a supremely uncharismatic lawyer, Carlos Arias Navarro. Arias was the most cautious kind of *aperturista*. Dimly aware that the nation was clamouring for democracy yet temperamentally and ideologically committed to dictatorship, Arias was incapable of moving with any determination either forwards or backwards. Even before the *Caudillo*'s death he had begun to cut a helpless figure, yet not one for which anyone felt much sympathy. Juan Carlos himself had little time for Arias and their relations became still worse after Arias tried to resign during the delicate period just before Franco's death in protest at the Prince's decision to hold a meeting with the armed forces ministers without first telling him.

However, under the constitutional system devised by Franco, the monarch could only choose his Prime Minister from a list of three names drawn up by the Council of the Realm, a seventeen-man advisory body consisting almost entirely of Franco diehards. Knowing that he stood no chance of getting a suitable candidate from the Council, the King reluctantly confirmed Arias in office after General Franco's death. In the eyes of the public it did him no good at all. Whenever young demonstrators took to the streets during the early days of King Juan Carlos's reign, their favourite chant was:

España, mañana
Será republicana

(Spain, tomorrow
Will be republican)

In January 1976 Arias outlined a programme of limited reforms. But it did nothing to reduce the level of violence on the streets. In March five workers were killed in Vitoria when police opened fire on a crowd of demonstrators. The following month Arias made things worse with a broadcast to the nation in which he seemed, even more than before, to be harking back to the past. In May the government pushed through the *Cortes* (parliament) a law making it possible to hold meetings and demonstrations. The month after that, the centrepiece of Arias's programme – a bill for the legalization of political parties – was passed by parliament. But hours later the same assembly threw out the legislation needed to put the bill into effect. It was eventually rescued, but the incident showed that Arias could not even carry with him his old friends and colleagues in the Francoist establishment. On 1 July the King called him to the Palace and told him that things could not continue like this. Arias, who had never enjoyed being Prime Minister, seized the opportunity to tender his resignation and the King accepted at once.

It was realized that the country had reached a turning point in its history. Arias's cabinet contained three men with modestly progressive reputations – Antonio Garrigues at the Justice Ministry; Manuel Fraga, the Interior Minister; and José Maria Areilza, the Foreign Minister. Even the most conservative *aperturistas* had been dismayed by the effects of Arias's dithering and could be persuaded of the need for a firm policy of some kind. Most commentators were convinced that if the King, who was entitled to call for up to three lists, was prepared to hold out he could ensure that the name of at least one of these ministers would turn up.

When the King's choice eventually became known, the reaction was of stunned disbelief. The man he had chosen to succeed Arias was one Adolfo Suárez who, at forty-three, was the youngest member of the outgoing government. Everything about Suárez except his youth seemed to be at variance with the spirit of the times. He had spent his entire working life serving the dictator in a variety of posts of which the most important and recent had been the General Secretaryship of the *Movimiento Nacional* – a post which entitled him to an *ex officio* seat in the cabinet. Not surprisingly, he filled his first government with men of his own age whom he had met on his way up through the state apparatus. A report in the liberal daily, *El País*, on the composition of Suárez's first cabinet listed the main characteristics of its members as 'an average age of forty-six, a classic Catholic ideology and good relations with certain banking institutions'. On the same day the newspaper carried what was destined to become a notorious commentary by one of Spain's leading historians, Ricardo de la Cierva. His response to the King's choice of Suárez and Suárez's choice of ministers had been the same as that of most democratically minded Spaniards and was summed up by the headline – 'What a mistake! What an immense mistake!' The period immediately following the change of government, the King has since admitted, was the worst of his life – 'Nobody trusted me. They didn't even give me a twenty-day margin to see if I had made the wrong choice.'

His choice of Suárez was not, as some observers had suspected, simply a matter of taking the best name on offer from the Council of the Realm. It was the culmination of months of assiduous conspiracy. During the last months of Franco's life, Juan Carlos had asked a number of politicians and officials for their opinions on how the country could best be transformed. One of the most detailed and realistic appraisals came from Suárez. The more the future King considered him, the more that Suárez seemed to fulfil the apparently contradictory requirements of the Prime Minister whose job it would be to change Spain from a dictatorship into a democracy. He had an intimate knowledge of the workings of the administration, yet he accepted that its reform could not be partial or gradual. What is more, he had enough personal appeal to be able to survive once democracy had been restored – he was from an inoffensively middle-class background, he was strikingly handsome, immaculately dressed, affable and thoroughly versed in the use of the media, having been Director-General of the state television and radio network. Unknown to Suárez himself, he had only one serious rival by the time Franco died – José María López de Letona, who had been

Minister of Industry during the late sixties and early seventies. It was at the suggestion of the King's former tutor and close adviser, Torcuato Fernández-Miranda, that Arias included Suárez in his team. Soon afterwards, the King made up his mind that Suárez was indeed the man for the job. He tried to forewarn him while they were watching a football match between Saragossa, which at that time had a young chairman, and Real Madrid, which was still run by the venerable Santiago Bernabeu. The King expressed the view that older men had to make way for younger ones 'because the life of the country is changing fast in every respect'. Suárez, who was perhaps too engrossed in the game, failed to take the hint. After Arias resigned, Fernández-Miranda, whom the King had manoeuvred into the chairmanship of the Council of the Realm, wangled Suárez's name on to the list of candidates as a makeweight. He received less votes than either of the other two and the members of the Council were as astonished as everybody else when the King chose him.

Suárez recognized that he would have to move with great speed. By November, three months after the swearing in of his government, he had laid before the *Cortes* a political reform bill which would introduce universal suffrage and a two-chamber parliament, consisting of a lower house, or Congress, and an upper house to be called the Senate. His resoluteness caught the old guard in disarray. They had no leader and no alternative and only the most purblind could believe now that the nation did not want reform. In parliament, the role of the redoubtable Fernández-Miranda, who was also the Speaker of the *Cortes*, was once again decisive. He arranged for the bill to be sped through its committee stages so that there was no chance for it to be watered down. Outside parliament, it was made clear to the members of the *Cortes* – many of whom were now old men looking forward to a comfortable retirement or a remunerative sinecure – that the way they voted on the bill was bound to affect such matters as who sat on which committees and whether the administration turned a blind eye to certain untaxed accounts. Finally, the entire proceedings were to be broadcast on radio and television and each of the deputies was to be called upon by name to stand up and say either *si* or *no* to reform.

By the time the bill came to be debated in the *Cortes*, it was widely expected that the government would win. Even so, when the vote eventually came to be taken on the evening of 18 November, it was difficult to believe that it was happening. As one by one the members of the *Cortes* – generals and admirals, ex-ministers, bankers and local bigwigs – stood up to endorse a measure that would put an end to everything that they had spent their lives supporting, it became clear that the majority in favour of reform was going to be much, much bigger than anyone had imagined. In fact the vote was 425 to 59 with thirteen abstentions. It was the night that Spaniards began to realize that the long nightmare of Francoism really had come to an end. On 15 December the political reform bill was overwhelmingly endorsed in a referendum. Of the votes cast, the 'yes' votes totalled 94.2 per cent and the 'no' votes only 2.6 per cent. It was conclusive proof of the extent to which support for Franco's system of government had dwindled.

The speed of events dumbfounded not only the Francoists, but also the opposition. Even before Arias's resignation, some leading figures within the opposition had begun to speculate openly about the possibility of a *ruptura pactada* or negotiated break. But, divided among themselves and mistrustful of the new Prime Minister, they failed to take up an offer from Suárez of talks until after the referendum. By that time Suárez was beginning to acquire considerable prestige as the man responsible for engineering the return of democracy, whereas the opposition politicians – most of whom had misguidedly called for abstention during the referendum campaign – had suffered a humiliating rebuff when more than three quarters of the electorate turned out to vote. At the talks which began between the government and the opposition after the referendum on how best to hold the elections foreshadowed by the political reform bill, the government had the advantage of wielding both the moral and the real authority. Further reform measures came thick and fast. Early in 1977 the cabinet endorsed a procedure for the legalization of political parties more agreeable to the opposition than the one devised by Arias's cabinet. The Socialists were legalized in February and the Communists in April. In March the right to strike was recognized, trade unions were legalized and the following month the *Movimiento* was abolished. Since by that time the government and opposition had agreed on how the elections should be conducted and votes counted, a date was set – 15 June.

The problem for Suárez and the members of his administration was that while they now enjoyed tremendous popularity they did not belong to any of the political parties that were shaping up to contest the election. The point on the political spectrum that appeared to have most appeal for the voters was what at that time passed for the centre – the frontier between those who had worked for the old dictatorship and those who had worked against it. To the right of it were the most progressive *aperturistas*, including Suárez and his ministers. To the left of it were the most moderate opposition parties – a plethora of Christian Democrat, Social Democrat and Liberal groups, some of which amounted to little more than dining clubs. The mood of the moment was reconciliation and it was clear that whichever party could embrace supporters as well as opponents of Francoism would stand a good chance of winning the election.

The first serious attempt to create such a party was made in November 1976 when a group of *aperturistas* from inside as well as outside the government launched the Partido Popular. It was headed by José María Areilza, whose fellow-minister in the first government of the monarchy, Manuel Fraga, was busy forming the more conservative Alianza Popular (AP). In January the Partido Popular absorbed another *aperturista* group and changed its name to the Centro Democrático. From then on, like a snowball rolling down a hill, it gathered to it one after another of the minor opposition parties. As it became apparent that the Centro Democrático was the coming force in Spanish politics, Suárez approached some of its most senior figures with a deal – he would lead them into the forthcoming election, thus virtually assuring them of victory, if they would agree to two conditions. First, they must ditch Areilza, the only member of the party who could have seriously challenged the Prime Minister for the leadership. Second, they must accept into their ranks the ministers and officials whose help Suárez would need if he were to continue ruling the country. They agreed, and in March Suárez joined the party, which was subsequently renamed the Unión de Centro Democrático.

The UCD emerged from the election as the biggest party, but with only 34 per cent of the vote and 165 of the 350 seats in the lower house. By far the largest opposition party was the Partido Socialista Obrero Español (PSOE), which won 121 seats with some 29 per cent of the vote. The PSOE had been gaining strength ever since 1972 when control of the party had been wrested from the PSOE's ageing and increasingly out-of-touch exiled leadership by a group of young activists inside Spain led by a lawyer from Seville, Felipe González. González was even younger than Suárez and, in a different way, just as attractive both in manner and appearance. During the run-up to the election he had managed to appear responsible and realistic while remaining aggressively anti-Francoist. Neither Alianza Popular on the right, nor the Spanish Communist Party (PCE) on the left, did as well as they had expected, winning only sixteen and twenty seats respectively.

Since the UCD lacked an overall majority in the lower house, it looked as if Suárez would have to negotiate individual *ad hoc* alliances with the parties to either side of him in order to win a majority for each of the items in his legislative programme. Instead, he opted for a comprehensive agreement. The Moncloa Pacts, named after the Prime Minister's official residence, where they were signed in October, covered not only a substantial part of the government's legislative programme but also such matters as prices and incomes, government spending and regional policy. The worst thing about the Pacts was the effect that they had on public opinion. Spaniards were all in favour of reconciliation but after so many years of contrived unanimity they were equally hungry for debate. Yet here were the four main party leaders, who only a few weeks before had been ridiculing one another's programmes on the electoral hustings, apparently seeing eye to eye to the extent that they were able to come up with a comprehensive plan for running the country. There was a widespread feeling that the politicians, having taken the electors' votes, were now deciding what was good for them. The Pacts created a mild feeling of scepticism about democracy in Spain which lodged itself in the body politic like a tumour where it remains to this day contracting and expanding according to circumstances. The great advantage of the Pacts was that they allowed the politicians to concentrate on the most important task before them – the drawing up of a new constitution.

Since the beginning of the previous century, Spain had had eleven constitutions and the main reason why none had worked was that each had been drafted and imposed by one particular group with little or no regard to the views of anyone outside it. As far as the Constitution was concerned the case for consensus was unanswerable. The work of preparing one was entrusted to a parliamentary commission representing all the major national parties and the more important regional ones. The document which they produced – and which was passed after amendments by the *Cortes* in October 1978 – was exactly what one would expect of a committee made up of people with very different political outlooks. It is far too long, often vague and sometimes contradictory. But it is nevertheless something in which all the major parties have a vested interest and which they have so far shown no sign of wanting to amend let alone replace. The new Spanish Constitution is arguably the most liberal in Western Europe. Spain is defined as a parliamentary monarchy, rather than just a constitutional monarchy. There is no official religion and the armed forces are assigned a strictly limited role. The death penalty is forbidden and the voting age fixed at eighteen. In December the Constitution was overwhelmingly approved by the public in a referendum. Then, early in the New Year, Suárez dissolved what had in effect been a constituent *Cortes* and called another general election for 1 March. It produced a result almost identical to the previous one.

The 1979 general election signalled the end of a period in which politics had been concerned almost entirely with great issues – should Spain be a republic or a monarchy? Should it remain a dictatorship or become a democracy? And if it was to be a democratic monarchy, what sort of constitution should it have? From now on, the most important problem was how to ensure that the transition from dictatorship to democracy was reflected in people's daily lives. Divorce and abortion were still forbidden and the administration, the army and the police, the judiciary, the health and welfare services, the state broadcasting network and the schools and universities were all imbued with the spirit of a totalitarian regime. A thoroughgoing reform programme was needed to sweep away the authoritarian institutions and practices that had survived in every corner of society. But it soon became apparent that Suárez and his party were incapable of meeting the challenge. To some extent, this was a consequence of the Prime Minister's own personality. All politicians are a blend of ambition and conviction. In Suárez's case, however, the element of belief seems to have been limited to a single premise – that democracy is preferable to dictatorship. Once the transition from one to another had been completed he appeared to have no aspiration to inspire him nor any ideology to guide him. By contrast, the problem for the UCD was an excess of aspirations and ideologies, many of which were in conflict with one another. The parties which had formed the basis of the union ranged on the conventional European spectrum from a point just to the left of centre quite a long way to the right. By the summer of 1980 a gap that was to prove unbridgeable had begun to open up between the Social and Christian Democrats within the UCD over the government's plan to legalize divorce. As for the men and women who had been inserted into the union at Suárez's insistence in early 1977, it was not what they differed over but what they had in common that proved to be the problem. Having come up through the old Francoist administration, most of them found it genuinely difficult to see the need to do more than tinker with Franco's legacy and true to their political origins their first impulse, whenever an apparent misdemeanour or injustice came to the surface, was to cover up rather than investigate. Within the party, they found it difficult to come to terms with the idea that in a democratic institution policy initiatives can come from the rank and file as well as from the top brass.

It was only in the very last months of Suárez's premiership that he began to reveal – or perhaps discover – his true sympathies. But far from making things better, it only made them worse because the Prime Minister was seen to be siding with the most liberal wing of his party and to lead a coalition as diverse as the UCD from anywhere but close to the centre was virtually impossible. Not surprisingly, therefore, the revolt against Suárez's leadership, when it came, was mounted by the Christian Democrats. But it drew considerable strength from the discontent in every sector of the party over lack of consultation. In January 1981 Suárez resigned from the premiership and in recognition of his services the King bestowed on him the highest honour in his gift – a dukedom.

One of the least satisfactory aspects of Spain's new constitutional arrangements is that an unusually lengthy period is allowed to elapse between governments. It was during the uncertain month between

Suárez's resignation and the swearing in of his successor, Leopoldo Calvo Sotelo, that all Spain's nightmares came true.

From the very beginning, the most serious threat to democracy had come from the predominantly reactionary officers of Spain's armed forces. In 1978 a conspiracy was found to have been hatched in a Madrid café and on more than one occasion the UCD's defence over-lord, Lieutenant-General Manuel Gutiérrez Mellado, was openly insulted by fellow-officers. By early 1981 a group of senior officers had persuaded themselves that the country faced political and economic turmoil and that the unity of Spain, whose preservation had been entrusted to the armed forces by the Constitution, was at risk from the government's regional policy.

On the afternoon of 23 February, a lieutenant-colonel in the Civil Guard, Antonio Tejero Molina, marched into Congress with a detachment of his men and proceeded to hold almost every politician of note in Spain at gunpoint for the best part of twenty-four hours. Tejero was what he appeared to be – a naïve fanatic. But he was merely the puppet of more senior officers – in particular, the commander of the Motorized Division at Valencia, Lieutenant-General Jaime Miláns del Bosch, and a former military instructor and personal secretary to the King, Major-General Alfonso Armada. The coup was cut short mainly because of Juan Carlos's quick wits and steady nerve. Using a specially designed communications centre which he had had installed at the Palace at a cost of ten million pesetas to enable him to talk directly to the country's eleven captains-general, he assured them that Tejero's action did not – as the plotters were claiming – have his backing. Any captain-general who showed signs of wavering was commanded to obey.

The abortive coup persuaded the incoming government to try to appease the military. The army was given a token role in the trouble-some Basque country and plans for reform in a number of areas were either diluted or abandoned. Within the UCD it initially had the effect of forcing the warring factions to close ranks. But the truce was short-lived and as soon as the government had to face an important policy decision the familiar divisions reappeared. Each time during the eighteen months between the coup and the next general election in November 1982 that Calvo Sotelo tried to shift the balance of his programmes to left or right in an attempt to accommodate a rebellious faction on one wing of his party he would invariably provoke defections from the other. In this way, the UCD spawned a Social Democratic Party (which linked up with the PSOE), a Christian Democratic Party (which linked up with the AP) and even a Liberal Party. In 1982, the Duque de Suárez delivered what many saw as the *coup de grâce* to the party he had founded, when he himself left it to found the Centro Democrático

Social (CDS). By the time a general election was called, the UCD had lost a third of its deputies in Congress. The loss of its support in the country was even more dramatic and this was in part because of the coup. The Centrists had topped the poll at two elections by selling themselves rather in the same way as you might sell a contraceptive – by persuading the electorate that they represented 'the safe way' to democracy. If, voters reasoned, you got a coup even with the UCD in power, what was there to lose by going for broke with a party that had a much more genuine commitment to reform? The door was thus open at last for Felipe González and the PSOE.

Ever since the 1979 election González, like Suárez but with greater success, had been trying to drag his party towards what the polls indicate is the political fulcrum of Spain – the centre-left. At one point he went so far as to resign the leadership in an eventually successful bid to force his supporters to drop Marxism from the party's definition of itself. At the 1982 election he stood on a platform of exceptional moderation, which was partly so as not to alienate the mass vote, but also partly because he was afraid that anything more radical might upset the generals. To that extent there is still a degree of pretence about Spanish politics that you will not find in the other countries of Western Europe. Nevertheless, if one is to put a date to the end of the transition then it must be 28 November 1982, because the fact that the armed forces were prepared to accept González's victory showed that it was possible for power to be transferred from one party to another without bloodshed – and that, ultimately, is the test of a democracy.

The Socialists won 201 seats, giving them an outright majority in Congress. To the PSOE's left, the Communists' share of seats fell dramatically and humiliatingly from twenty-three to five. On the right, the Alianza Popular emerged as by far the biggest opposition party with 105 seats. But the UCD, which had run the nation for five years, picked up only eleven. And as for Suárez – the mastermind of the transition, the man who had led the nation for much of its eventful journey along the path from dictatorship to democracy – his Centro Democrático Social won precisely two.

The resurgence of the CDS four years later, when it increased the number of its seats in Congress to twenty, was one of the few points of note in an election that confirmed the Socialists' grip on power. They retained their overall majority, albeit reduced. The 1986 election, even more than the 1982 one, showed that – in spite of their conflicting reputations for diehard traditionalism and violent radicalism – the Spaniards today are a nation with a deep-seated bias towards moderate reform. The political coloration of the new Spain is a very pale, but remarkably uniform, pink.

PART TWO:

A Changing Society

CHAPTER THREE

A MODEST MONARCHY

The tone of King Juan Carlos's reign was set before it began. Some months before Franco's death, the Prince – as he then was – decided that when he took the throne he would not move into the residence of his ancestors, the eighteenth-century Palacio de Oriente in Madrid, but remain in the house where he had lived since 1961.

The Palacio de la Zarzuela, a few miles to the north-west of the capital, is no bigger than many a company chairman's home. The drawing-room can only just take a hundred people standing so the grander official receptions have to be held in the Palacio de Oriente. Yet the Zarzuela houses not only the Royal Family itself but also the offices of the Royal Household and the living quarters of some of the people who work for it. The King and Queen's personal staff is small – two valets, two maids, a couple of waiters and a chef. The Household proper is headed by the Marquis of Mondéjar, Don Nicolás Cotoner y Cotoner, a retired cavalry general who has known Juan Carlos since the mid-fifties when he became one of his military instructors. He has been its head since 1969. The Royal Household comprises a Security Service (staffed by policemen), the Royal Guard (composed of soldiers), the Military Household (which helps the King carry out his duties as Commander-in-Chief of the armed forces) and finally the Secretariat whose officials arrange his audiences, receptions and visits, help him to keep abreast of events and deal among other things with the prodigious number of petitions which the King receives from his subjects and which he is constitutionally bound to pass on without prejudice to the relevant ministry. Apart from the Zarzuela, the King and Queen also have the use of the Palacio de Marivent, a former museum overlooking a bay just outside Palma de Mallorca, where they spend August and some of their weekends during the summer. During the winter, the Royal Family occasionally goes skiing at Baquiera Beret – a resort in Catalonia –

or shooting, sometimes with the novelist and journalist Miguel Delibes who lives in Old Castile. But in spite of pressure from the aristocracy, they have not re-established any sort of court. The Spanish monarchy costs about half as much as Britain's and less in fact than any in Europe.

The modesty of their claims upon the nation reflects a realistic assessment of the position in which the King and Queen find themselves. They know that if they are to earn the respect of the Spanish people and ensure the survival of the monarchy they need to be seen to be putting in more than they take out. Unlike, say, the British Royal Family, they cannot rely on an underlying current of goodwill. This was vividly demonstrated after the abortive coup in 1981. For the first week or so everyone was full of gratitude for the way the King had responded. But the public's admiration for him was gradually undermined by a reluctance to believe that General Armada, who had been one of Juan Carlos's few confidants, would have acted without the King's complicity. The most popular version was that he pulled out when he saw that the plan was not going to work, leaving Armada and the rest to face the consequences. This is not, I think, fully appreciated abroad – that a large number of Spaniards believe that their sovereign was involved in a plot to overthrow democracy. I personally believe that they are wrong, but there are perfectly understandable reasons why they should be so ready to suspect. One is that, with only a few exceptions, Spain's Bourbon monarchs, of whom Juan Carlos is the latest representative, have been a pretty incompetent and feckless lot. Another is that Juan Carlos himself was helped to the throne by precisely that section of the monarchist camp which was most prepared to collaborate with the dictatorship.

The Bourbons came to rule Spain, not by invitation but through a war – the so-called War of the Spanish Succession – which broke out among the European powers over who should inherit the Spanish throne after the previous, Habsburg, monarch had died without an heir. The war not only split Europe. It divided Spain too. A sizeable number of Spaniards – principally the Catalans, the Valencians and the Aragonese – took the side of the Bourbons' opponents and when the war was over they were punished for having picked the wrong side. It was a Bourbon, moreover, who abjectly surrendered to Napoleon's forces in 1808 and although his son was restored six years later his descendants never really lived down the fact that a monarch had shown himself to be less patriotic than his subjects. During the 123 tumultuous years that followed, dissatisfaction with the monarchy twice reached such a pitch that the ruler of the day was forced to leave the country. The first occasion was in 1868 when an alliance of liberal generals and admirals got rid of the nymphomaniac Queen Isabel and the *Cortes* invited a member of the Italian Royal Family to take her place. But he abdicated soon afterwards, ushering in a brief and disorderly period of Republican rule. After the failure of the First Republic the Spaniards decided that there was nothing left to try and restored the Bourbons in the person of Isabel's son, Alfonso XII. It was his son, Alfonso XIII, who lost the throne once again.

In 1923 he connived at the seizure of power by a group of senior officers led by the flamboyantly eccentric General Miguel Primo de Rivera. By putting up with Primo de Rivera's dictatorship the King flouted the very constitution from which the restored monarchy derived its legitimacy and tied its standing to the success or failure of Primo de Rivera's experiment. After seven years, the experiment failed. The King survived for slightly more than a year until he allowed the local elections of 1931 to become a trial of strength between pro- and anti-royalists. As the results came in from the towns and cities, which were the only areas where a fair ballot had been held, it became clear that the King's opponents were going to sweep the board. A republic was declared in the Basque industrial centre of Eibar and it seemed certain that unless Alfonso stepped down there would be bloodshed. On the evening of 14 April he issued a statement in which he carefully avoided abdicating but said that he did not want to be held responsible for the outbreak of a civil war. 'Therefore,' he added, 'until the nation speaks I shall deliberately suspend the use of my royal prerogative.' That night he left Madrid for exile. Spain became a republic but the tensions between right and left that had been articulated for a brief period as support for and opposition to the monarchy merely re-surfaced in other guises and the internecine conflict that Alfonso had been at pains to avert broke out five years later.

Alfonso died in Rome in 1941, a few weeks after his failing health had persuaded him to abdicate. His eldest son, also called Alfonso, had already given up his claim to the throne in 1933 to marry a Cuban woman. He died in a car crash five years later without leaving any children. Shortly after his renunciation, his brother Jaime who was next in line, but being deaf was thought incapable of assuming the responsibilities of Kingship, also renounced the succession. He subsequently married and had two children, Alfonso and Gonzalo. The legitimate heir was therefore Alfonso XIII's third son and fifth child, Juan, Count of Barcelona. Don Juan, as he came to be known, had left Spain with his father in 1931 and gone to the Royal Naval College at Dartmouth. In 1935 he married another Bourbon, María de las Mercedes de Borbón y Orléans, Princess of the Two Sicilies. The military uprising against the Republic the next year seemed to the young Prince as if it could be the means by which he might recover his throne and that he ought to be a party to it. A fortnight after the start of the rebellion he crossed secretly into Spain to join the Nationalist forces, but the rebels – reluctant to risk the life of the heir to the throne – put him back over the Pyrenees. Perhaps they were sincere in their motives, but it was nevertheless a singularly convenient decision for General Franco who, later that year, was proclaimed Head of State.

Once the war was over the *Caudillo* showed no intention of giving up the Headship of State to Don Juan. The principal reason was of course that he thoroughly enjoyed the exercise of power, but it is only fair to point out that had he, say, become a mere Prime Minister under Don Juan, he might have wrecked the tenuous alliance of forces that had won the war – the accession of a monarch, any monarch, would have upset the anti-royalist Falange, while the accession of one of Alfonso XIII's sons would have alienated the Carlists. Equally, Don Juan's subsequent disenchantment with Franco, although it had its roots in the *Caudillo*'s refusal to surrender power, grew in conviction as the Count, who saw the monarchy as an instrument of reconciliation, had to stand by while Franco used his power to humiliate his former opponents.

The Law of Succession to the Headship of State, which the *Cortes* passed in 1949, restored the monarchy in name but made Franco acting Head of State for life and gave him the right to name his successor 'as King or Regent'. Spain became, in the classic phrase, 'a monarchy without a monarch'. The law split Don Juan's followers down the middle. To some – the more liberal – it proved that Franco intended hanging on to power for as long as he could and that the only sensible course was to side with the proscribed opposition. To others – the more conservative – it showed that the only way the monarchy would ever be restored was through Franco's offices and that if the royalists were to get their way they would have to collaborate with Franco's regime. The sometimes bewildering changes of tack by Don Juan over the years that followed, which succeeded in antagonizing the majority of both pro- and anti-Francoists, can to some extent be explained by the conflicting advice he received from 'purists' and 'collaborationists' on his ninety-three-member Privy Council. Shortly after the Law of Succession was passed, for example, his representatives entered negotiations with the exiled Socialists and Communists. These negotiations ended in the so-called St Jean de Luz Agreements whereby, if Franco fell, there would be a referendum to decide the form of state. Yet before they were signed Don Juan had met Franco on board his yacht to discuss the dictator's suggestion that Don Juan's sons should be educated in Spain.

Don Juan's heir, Juan Carlos, had been born in Rome on 5 January 1938. He was Juan and Mercedes's third child. They already had two daughters, Pilar and Margarita. In 1942 the family moved to Lausanne in neutral Switzerland and it was there that Juan Carlos began school. In 1946 when his parents moved to Portugal, so as to be as close as possible to Spain, they made arrangements for Juan Carlos to stay as a boarder at the Marian Fathers' school in Fribourg. Franco's offer put the Count of Barcelona in an extraordinarily difficult position. On the one hand, he was being asked to surrender control over the upbringing of his son and heir to a man he mistrusted. Moreover, to do so would give credibility to the dictator's claim to have restored the monarchy. On the other hand, Franco undoubtedly had a point. If the monarchy were ever to be restored it would have to have a credible representative and if Don Juan were to die before the *Caudillo* his son would need to be up to the challenge. As it was, Juan Carlos – who had never seen Spain – spoke Spanish with a pronounced French accent. After several weeks' deliberation Don Juan decided to accept Franco's offer and on 8 November the ten-year-old Juan Carlos and his younger brother, Alfonso,* boarded the Lusitania Express at Lisbon for a train ride across the featureless Estremaduran countryside into history.

The first few years of the Princes' stay in Spain, during which they studied in Madrid and San Sebastián, saw something of a reconciliaton between the Count and the *Caudillo*. But after Juan Carlos passed his *bachillerato* in 1954 it became clear that the two elder men had very different ideas about his higher education. Don Juan wanted him to go to a foreign university where he would receive a liberal 'European' education. Franco, on the other hand, wanted him to study at a military academy before entering a Spanish university. In December 1954, Don Juan and General Franco met once again, this time at a hunting lodge near the Portuguese border and Franco once more won the day. The following autumn Juan Carlos began a four-year military training – two years at the army college in Saragossa to be followed by a year each at the navy and air force colleges under the overall supervision of General Carlos Martínez Campos, Duque de la Torre. In 1959 Juan Carlos passed out as a lieutenant in all three services and returned to his parents' home in Estoril. Franco had decided in consultation with the Duke that the next phase of Juan Carlos's education should take place at the University of Salamanca and it was only after his rooms had been chosen and his tutors selected that Don Juan seems to have realized the implications of his son being sent to an institution that had remained intellectually fossilized for centuries. He refused to sanction the idea and the Duke

* Like his namesake in the previous generation, Alfonso died in tragic circumstances. In 1956, at the age of fifteen, he was shot while playing with a loaded gun at the family home in Estoril. Juan Carlos, who was with him at the time of the accident, was profoundly affected. Childhood friends say that the incident turned him from a bit of a bully into an altogether more thoughtful, sensitive boy.

resigned his post. Don Juan and General Franco returned to the hunting lodge in March 1960 and this time it was the Count who got his way. The Duke's place was taken by a panel of six eminent academics who specially designed a two-year liberal studies course for Juan Carlos. He was to take the course in Madrid and would be taught by the academics on the panel and the lecturers and professors they selected.

His engagement to Princess Sofía was announced while he was at university. They had met seven years earlier on board the Greek Royal Family's yacht during a cruise in the Aegean and it was on board a smaller boat that they very nearly split up later. 'I once went sailing with him when we were still engaged,' Sofía later recalled, 'and I shall never understand how I was able to marry him after that.' The Princess – eldest daughter of King Paul and Queen Frederica of Greece – was born on 2 November of the same year as Juan Carlos. Like him, her earliest memories were of exile and, like him, she had been packed off to boarding school – only in her case she went later but stayed longer. On 14 May 1962 Juan Carlos and Sofía were married at the Catholic cathedral in Athens before a constellation of Kings, Queens and Presidents. Over the next few years, Sofía gave birth to three children – Elena in 1963, Cristina in 1965 and Felipe, who was born on 30 January 1968.

After university, Juan Carlos spent a few weeks in each of the ministries seeing how they worked. In December 1962 Franco had celebrated his seventieth birthday and the question of who should succeed him appeared increasingly urgent. But it was not easy to see how he could put into effect his apparent intention of restoring the monarchy.

The Carlists were a spent force. In the first place, their claim to the throne was now exceedingly tenuous. The original pretender's last direct male descendant, Alfonso Carlos, had died in 1936 without leaving a son. His closest male relative and therefore the successor to the Carlist claim was none other than Don Juan, so to keep alive the cause Alfonso Carlos had before his death adopted as his heir a remote cousin, Prince Javier de Borbón Parma. In spite of this, in 1958, several leading Carlists publicly acknowledged Don Juan's entitlement to the pretendership. Javier subsequently abdicated in favour of his son, Carlos Hugo. Eight years older than Juan Carlos, Carlos Hugo was young enough to be an eligible successor to the throne and in 1964 he enhanced his credentials still further by marrying Princess Irene of the Netherlands after a runaway romance. But the Carlists' dream of a return to absolutist monarchy seemed even to Franco to be impracticable in the latter half of the twentieth century and throughout his rule the Carlists never had more than a token presence in the government.

The problem was that the other branch of the family was represented by a man whom he neither liked nor respected. In view of

Franco's disdain for Don Juan, an increasing number of Don Juan's more reactionary supporters, who had always felt that it would be better if Franco were to outlive the Count so that he could hand over to a King brought up under the dictatorship, began to toy with the seemingly outlandish notion that, even if the Count outlived Franco, Juan Carlos might succeed to the throne. The most committed proponents of the 'Juan Carlos solution' were the Opus Dei technocrats who had been responsible for initiating Spain's economic 'miracle' and whose popularity with Franco was rising at about the same rate as the GNP. Their patron was Franco's old friend, Admiral Carrero Blanco.

A lot of Spaniards, though, were convinced that – given the problems – Franco would never bring himself to name a successor. The Falangists, in particular, hoped that he might fudge the issue by bequeathing power to a regent. The man they had in mind for the job was another old friend of Franco's, Lieutenant-General Agustín Muñoz Grandes. A lifelong Falangist, he had led the Blue Division – Franco's contribution to the Axis war effort – and served as a minister in two cabinets. In 1962 Franco appointed him Deputy Prime Minister, the first time he had created such a post.

Muñoz Grandes's elevation thoroughly alarmed royalists of all hues and it was at about this time that the technocrats and Admiral Carrero Blanco launched a campaign, which came to be known as *Operación Lucero*, aimed at promoting Juan Carlos's candidacy both to Franco and to the nation. In retrospect, it can be seen that Franco needed very little persuading – at about this time he remarked to Juan Carlos that he had 'more chance than your father of becoming King'. Selling Juan Carlos to the country was a more difficult task. The technocrats had considerable influence in the media, business and the universities but the Falange – through their control of the *Movimiento* – held sway over much of local government. Whenever Juan Carlos and Sofía visited the provinces, as they did a lot at about this time at the prompting of their supporters, they were often met with either total indifference – or rotten fruit. Juan Carlos, who had been jeered by Falangists in the streets of San Sebastián when he was at school and had had to face a demonstration by Carlists when he was at university, knew how to cope. He subsequently recalled how when he was being shown round once by a local bigwig 'I sensed that something was going to happen – something disagreeable naturally. We were walking along, with me on the alert, looking out for the place where I thought the trouble might occur, when suddenly I took one step forward and two steps back and a tomato imprinted itself on my companion's uniform.' For Sofía, it must have been quite a trial.

The extent to which Juan Carlos sympathized with the ulterior motives of *Operación Lucero* remains a mystery. As late as January 1966 he told a visiting correspondent: 'I'll never, never accept the Crown as long as my father is alive.' The first public indication that the plan was succeeding came the following year when Franco summarily dismissed Muñoz Grandes and gave his job to Carrero Blanco. The accession of Juan Carlos now began to look like more of a probability than a possibility. Feeling that regency was a lost cause, a number of Falangists reconciled themselves to the idea of a monarchy and began promoting the candidacy of Alfonso de Borbón-Dampierre, the son of Don Juan's deaf elder brother who had renounced his claims to the throne in 1933. Carlos Hugo, meanwhile, moved rapidly from the right to the left of the political spectrum in an attempt to secure the support of the democratic opposition – a move that appalled many of the traditional supporters of his cause. In December 1968 he made a speech openly attacking Juan Carlos and five days later the police gave him and his wife twenty-four hours to leave the country.

With the Falangists and the Carlists both now clutching at straws, the succession was Juan Carlos's for the asking. In January 1969 he asked. 'I am ready,' he told the official news agency, 'to serve Spain in whatever post or responsibility may be of most use to her.' The Prince's remarks took his father completely by surprise, but there was nothing he could do to stop the giddy progress of events. On 12 July Franco called Juan Carlos to see him and in the course of a forty-five-minute conversation told him he intended naming him as his successor. Ten days later Franco announced his choice to the *Cortes* which endorsed it by 491 votes to nineteen with nine abstentions. To drive home the point that Juan Carlos's title to the throne derived from his being Franco's protégé rather than Alfonso XIII's grandson, he was henceforth to be known as Prince of Spain, not as Prince of Asturias, the title traditionally accorded to the heir to the throne. The next day Juan Carlos swore his oath of loyalty to Franco and to the *Movimiento Nacional*. Don Juan, who had let it be known that he was at sea in his yacht, put in that afternoon at a little village on the Portuguese coast so that he could watch the proceedings on television in a fishermen's bar. His only comment when his son had finished speaking was 'Nicely read, Juanito, nicely read.' Back in Estoril, he disbanded his Privy Council and issued a statement bluntly pointing out that 'I have not been consulted and the freely expressed opinion of the Spanish people has not been sought.' From then on he maintained increasingly friendly contacts with some of the leading figures in the democratic opposition, including some who had once been openly Republican. Then in June 1975 he made a speech at a dinner in Barcelona lambasting Franco and his regime and was banned from re-entering the country.

As for Juan Carlos, his problems did not end with his being named successor. Neither the Carlists nor the Falangists were prepared to give up their aspirations. Carlos Hugo decided that his cause would best be served by forming a political party which espoused left-wing socialism and workers' control. The most extreme traditional Carlists subsequently rallied to his younger brother, Sixto Enrique.* A more serious threat to Juan Carlos emerged when, in 1972, Alfonso de Borbón-Dampierre married Franco's eldest granddaughter, María del Carmen Martínez Bordíu. As a consequence several members of Franco's family – in particular his wife, Doña Carmen – threw their weight behind the conspiracy hatched by Alfonso's Falangist champions to put him on the throne of Spain. Doña Carmen tried to have their marriage declared a Royal Wedding and it was proposed that Alfonso should be addressed as 'Your Royal Highness'. Both ideas were scotched only by Juan Carlos's personal intervention. Franco's royalism had always been in part a reflection of his own kingly pretensions† and throughout the last years of his life there was some apprehension among Juan Carlos's supporters that if the *Caudillo* became senile he might change his mind and transfer the succession to Alfonso in order to make himself the founder of a dynasty. In fact, Franco remained as sharp as ever right up to his final illness.

Juan Carlos's astute conduct of affairs during the first year of his reign did much to heal the breach between him and his father. In early 1977, as it became clear that Suárez's government was heading towards the setting up of a fully fledged democracy, Don Juan decided to give his son the public endorsement he had thus far withheld. On 14 May at the Palacio de la Zarzuela he renounced his rights to the throne in a speech reiterating his faith in democracy. At the end of it he stood to attention, bowed deeply and declared, 'Majesty. Spain. Above all.' Don Juan will, I suspect, go down in history as one of the tragic figures of the twentieth century – the King who never was, a simple man who always said that his happiest years were spent as an ordinary naval officer, an indecisive man caught between his distaste for a parvenu dictator and his responsibility for the survival of his dynasty, he

* In 1976 when followers of Carlos Hugo made the Carlists' traditional annual pilgrimage to the top of Montejurra, a high hill near Pamplona, they were set upon by a band of armed right-wingers led by Sixto Enrique. One man died and several were wounded.

† Among other things, Franco felt empowered to hand out titles of nobility. Today more than thirty Spanish families owe their peerages to the munificence of the son of a naval supply officer. One of the aristocrats he created, Pedro Barrié de la Maza, head of the Galician hydroelectricity concern, Fuerzas Eléctricas del Noroeste Sociedad Anónima (FENOSA), was allowed to take his title from the name of his firm, becoming the Count of Fenosa.

nevertheless proved himself in the end to be wise enough and humble enough to recognize that, having lost a throne, he need not lose another son.

The same year also saw the beginning of the end of another, far more momentous, division within the Bourbon family. In October Carlos Hugo returned to Spain after nine years in exile and made it clear in his very first speech that he saw himself as the leader of a political party rather than the head of a rival dynasty. Five months later he and Juan Carlos met and in 1979 Carlos Hugo was granted Spanish citizenship. Since then, his party has virtually disappeared from the political scene.

If Franco had not made him his heir and he had stayed in the army instead, Juan Carlos would by now have taken over his first battalion. His character and lifestyle are very much what you would expect from a go-ahead young lieutenant-colonel. He drinks and smokes little – the occasional whisky and a cheroot now and again. He keeps fit with half an hour's jogging or exercises every morning and until the pressure of work became too onerous he used to get in an hour's squash every night, sometimes playing the former Wimbledon lawn tennis champion, Manuel Santana. Apart from sport – and the King is also keen on judo, skiing and sailing – his great passion in life is for technological gadgetry. His office has a videotelephone connected to the Moncloa Palace, the Prime Minister's official residence, and an adjoining room is stuffed full of audio and video equipment, cameras, lenses and his short-wave radio set. The King is an enthusiastic amateur radio operator and sometimes links up with another regal 'ham', Hussein of Jordan.

On big occasions Juan Carlos still looks a bit awkward sometimes and, although he is improving, he continues to have difficulty with speeches. It is in the slightly more informal atmosphere of audiences and receptions that the King is at his best. Outgoing and casual, he is blessed with a good sense of humour and a prodigious memory for names and faces.

Sofía, on the other hand, is the retiring daughter of a formidable mother. She dislikes personal publicity, never grants interviews and has given only one press conference, which was during the Royal Tour of the United States in 1976. Her enthusiasms, though, are well known. Appropriately enough for a Greek, one of them is archaeology. When she was younger she took part in several excavations and wrote two books on her discoveries in collaboration with her sister Irene. She also takes a keen interest in subjects as diverse as U F Os and the problems of the mentally and physically handicapped. But her consuming passion is classical music and especially Baroque music. She plays the piano and spends much of her free time listening to records and going to concerts.

She has done an enormous amount to promote the cause of Spanish performers and composers both inside and outside the country, and in recognition of her contribution the national chamber orchestra has been named after her.

She is reputed to be deeply religious but since she had to convert from Orthodoxy to Catholicism in order to be able to marry Juan Carlos she is presumably not too fussy about dogma. Above all, Queen Sofía gives the impression of wanting to live as ordinary a life as her circumstances will allow. She dresses simply, buying most of her clothes 'off the peg'. Several boutiques in Madrid and Palma proudly display letters from the Palace enclosing payment for items she has selected during the shopping expeditions she makes from time to time with her friends. Curiously, one of her great delights in life is washing and setting her own hair and she has said that if she had not been born a Royal she would have liked to have been a hairdresser. One suspects, though, that she would have been happier still in the environs of a university. She had in fact enrolled at the Universidad Autónoma in Madrid when Franco died, but had to pull out of her course shortly afterwards when the burden of her official duties made it impossible for her to continue.

In public, Sofía tends to remain very much in her husband's shadow. But there is one 'duty' which she herself created and which she always carries out alone. Back in the late seventies, there was a horrific accident involving a school bus. That afternoon, Sofía took it upon herself to commandeer a helicopter to fly up to the area where the accident had taken place to see if she could be of any help. Since then, Spain – for reasons I shall be examining in a later chapter – has been the scene of several such tragedies. In the majority of cases the Queen has been there to offer comfort to the victims and their relatives. And I do not mean that she makes a stately tour of the hospital ward several days later – she usually arrives within hours of the incident, long before the casualties have been cleaned up and passions have died down. I vividly recall a photograph of her with her arms around two grief-stricken, middle-aged working-class women, both resting their heads on her shoulder and sobbing their hearts out. It is difficult to imagine any member of the British Royal Family, for example, allowing his or her dignity to be compromised to that extent. Sofía's obvious humanity on these occasions has served to bring this retiring lady much closer to her subjects.

Nothing is known for certain abut her political attitudes, but her views on other subjects suggest a woman of liberal leanings. She objects to furs, is something of a vegetarian and in her views on women one can detect a trace of feminism. 'The role of a woman is to help her husband but without losing her independence,' she told the reporters at her one and only press conference. The schools she has chosen for her children are known for their progressive methods and one of the most telling anecdotes about her concerns the primary school which Prince Felipe attended. Some of the parents, who felt that the cost of meals was too high, decided to boycott them and send their children to school with packed lunches. Queen Sofía took their side and thereafter the heir to the throne turned up every morning with sandwiches in his satchel. There is a school of thought which believes that Sofía, whose gentle looks belie a will of iron, may have had as much of an impact on recent Spanish history as her husband. The young Princess, so the theory goes, was horrified by the hold that Franco and his wife exerted over Juan Carlos and set about making him into his own man, converting him to the view that no monarchy supported by the followers of a totalitarian regime could survive in the twentieth century. How much truth there is in this will not be known for many a long year, if at all. But it is noteworthy that the future King began his secret meetings with politicians and others shortly after marrying Sofía.

As a couple, their closest friends are Sofía's brother, ex-King Constantine and his wife, Anne-Marie, who often spend time at Marivent during the summer. Among reigning royalty, they are probably closest to the British Royal Family, to whom they are both related. For more than a decade, however, contacts between the two monarchies were limited by the continuing dispute over Gibraltar. It was not until 1985, when the Spanish government lifted the restrictions imposed on the Rock by Franco, that the way was cleared for a state visit to Britain by the King and Queen the following year.

The shared experiences of the transition have helped to forge generally good relations between the King and Spain's leading politicians. Felipe González, bound by his party's fervently Republican traditions, has had to proceed carefully in public although he and Juan Carlos get along well in private. The relationship between the King and Fraga, on the other hand, is complicated by all sorts of historical problems such as Fraga's association with some of the Falangists who were keen to oust Juan Carlos from the succession and the King's decision not to put Fraga up for the premiership in 1976.

The King keeps in touch politically through the numerous audiences he grants to people from all walks of life and through the meetings which he holds once a week with the Prime Minister. But one of the ironies of today's Spain is that the Constitution, which would probably never have seen the light of day but for the King's efforts, drastically reduced the very considerable powers he inherited from Franco. The activities assigned to him by the Constitution - the promulgation of laws and decrees, the calling of elections and referendums, the appointment of Prime Ministers and ministers, the accreditation of ambassadors, the signing of international treaties and the declaration of war and peace – all require the prior consent of either the government or the legislature. Nevertheless, as a Spanish journalist once perceptively observed, Juan Carlos is 'a King with few powers but great influence'. According to the Constitution, it is the sovereign's job to 'umpire and moderate the orderly working of the institutions' and he has already shown that he is prepared to interpret that role very broadly indeed when he feels that circumstances require it. In 1981, after the abortive coup, he called in the leaders of all the major parties and, in effect, ordered them not to take punitive measures against the armed forces as a whole.

This in turn was a reflection of the one unambiguous and unqualified function which the Constitution does assign him – Supreme Command of the Armed Forces. The officer corps' attitude towards the King is a curiously schizophrenic one in which distrust for his endorsement of progressive ideas is perpetually at odds with respect for his role as C-in-C and Head of State. It is significant that when Armada, Miláns del Bosch and the others were trying to persuade their fellow-officers to back their plot they had to pretend that they were carrying it out with the connivance of the King. For his part, the King is scrupulous about keeping up contacts with the military. He has continued the practice begun by Franco of holding military audiences once a week, and he sometimes makes impromptu calls to senior officers in the armed services, using the special telecommunications centre he has had installed at the palace. He is known to have lobbied the politicians on the military's behalf for more money with which to boost salaries and improve equipment. But he is also capable of delivering blunt warnings to the officer corps if and when necessary. On one occasion he described the conduct of certain officers as 'frankly degrading'. The job of Supreme Commander is one that the King enjoys and which he takes extremely seriously – as well he might since it is from the armed forces that the only serious threat to his rule has come.

CHAPTER FOUR

THE ARMY: FRIEND OR FOE?

Just as Americans all remember where they were when they heard the news of Kennedy's shooting, no Spaniard will ever forget what he or she was doing on the afternoon of Monday, 23 February 1981 when a detachment of Civil Guards led by the elaborately moustachioed Antonio Tejero burst into Congress, interrupting a broadcast debate on the appointment of the new Prime Minister. The millions of people listening to the proceedings on the radio heard, first, a series of confused shouts and then a sustained burst of gunfire. The intention was to force the assembled deputies on to the floor, but to everyone listening it sounded as if a madman had wiped out the entire political class of Spain.

How many army units were meant to have risen against the government during the hours that followed will probably never be known. In the event only the Motorized Division under Lieutenant-General Miláns del Bosch, based near Valencia, actually took to the streets. Cristina Soler Crespo, a resident of Valencia, scribbled down what she saw and heard as it happened. Her account, published some days later by the Madrid newspaper *El País*, evokes something of the terror and uncomprehending outrage of that night.

> As I write these lines at 2 o'clock on a cold February morning, I can see a few metres from my window on the third floor of the Gran Vía in Valencia a tank – a huge, terrifying, green tank – parked calibrating its guns . . . aiming at thousands of windows, behind whose net curtains one can glimpse the terrified faces, the terrified eyes of peaceful citizens, of families with children, of old people who have seen these scenes before and are reliving the deaf, dumb, impotent panic of those who don't understand . . . Lorries full of soldiers arrive. Army jeeps and police cars occupy every corner along the wide avenue and the birds take to the air, as startled as the humans. Now

> the lights in the garden that runs down the centre have been put out and the scene takes on the appearance of a nightmare. I can see that the three young men in the nearest tank are no more than twenty years old. Their gun is now definitely aimed at the PSOE office with its red flag opposite my window. The people at the windows above it draw their curtains and put out the lights.

The events of 23–4 February made real something that the majority of Spaniards had dreaded ever since Franco's death. With a fine sense of euphemism, Spaniards refer to the armed forces as the *poderes fácticos* (the *de facto* powers) as distinct from the *de jure* powers like the monarchy, the government, the judiciary and the administration. Throughout the transition, the threat of military intervention distorted almost every aspect of Spanish life, conditioning the way that politicians approached a range of issues and, in particular, regional devolution, making them much more wary than they would otherwise have been. Since then, the Socialists have done much to bring the army under tighter control, but while the threat of another coup has receded to an extent that was unimaginable only a few years ago, it was not disappeared altogether, and this is reflected in the treatment accorded the officer corps by the rest of society. There is still a special Armed Forces Day. Senior military appointments are given considerable prominence in the media, and the speeches which generals and admirals traditionally deliver on taking up their jobs are picked over by pundits for clues as to their political inclinations.

The origins of the army's enthusiasm for meddling in the affairs of state have been traced as far back as the eighteenth century when senior officers were called upon to play an unusually prominent role in the administration. But it was the Napoleonic invasion in 1808 which created the pre-conditions for the persistent military intervention that became the hallmark of Spanish politics during the last century. One of the paradoxes of the War of Independence which followed the invasion was that while the middle-class administrators and officers who filled the vacuum left by the King and his court were busy fighting the invaders, they adopted many of the ideas that the French were bent on propagating.Of these the most basic was that the monarch should be subject to the constraints of a written constitution. Fernando VII, who was put back on the throne in 1814, refused, however, to acknowledge that times had changed and the result was that his reign was punctuated at frequent intervals by uprisings led by officers who had served in the War of Independence seeking to impose a constitution. The upheavals under Fernando gave the world two new words. One, which was coined to describe the opponents of absolute monarchy, was *liberal.** The other, first used by Major Rafael de Riego to describe his declaration of a rebellion against the Crown in 1820, was *pronunciamiento*. At first, *pronunciamiento* was used to describe only the initial call to arms, but it subsequently came to mean the uprising in its entirety. As the British historian Raymond Carr wrote, the *pronunciamientos* – of which there were forty-four between 1808 and 1936 – soon evolved a distinctive pattern. 'First came the preliminary soundings (the *trabajos*) and the winning over of officers and sergeants by a small activist group in touch with civilian conspirators, then the *compromisos* by which accomplices were bound to action; finally, the chosen leaders set off the last stage by the cry – the *grito*.' It was the formality of these often bloodless rebellions together with the earnestness and flamboyance of the participants which led foreigners to liken them to comic opera.

Fernando died in 1833 at a time when his heir, Isabel, was not yet three years old and Spain came to be ruled by that least authoritative form of government – a Regency, exercised in this case by Fernando's widow, María Cristina. Her shaky authority was still further undermined by the dynastic wrangle that had led Fernando's brother Carlos to declare war on the government and recruit to his cause all those who had a vested interest in the perpetuation of absolutism. The Carlist war made María Cristina exceptionally dependent on her army, so that when her two leading generals demanded that she agree to a constitution she was in no position to refuse. Theoretically, Spain was well-suited to a two-party parliamentary democracy. From the very beginning, the *liberales* had been split into two groups which now came to be known as the Moderates and the Progressives. Unfortunately, however, Spain's economic backwardness and political inexperience were such that the idea of one party voluntarily surrendering power to another by means of fair elections never really took root and the politicians soon got into the habit of getting the army to oust the government instead.

In a society where it was demonstrably impossible to assess public opinion through the ballot box the generals and colonels undertook to act as the interpreters of the will of the people. Throughout Isabel's reign, power usually changed hands by means of *pronunciamientos* by officers allied to one or other *liberal* camp – men like Espartero, O'Donnell and the indomitable Ramón María Narváez who, when asked by his deathbed confessor to forgive his enemies, is

* Although the word has since come to denote someone to the left of the centre of the political spectrum, it is important to understand that the nineteenth-century Spanish *liberal* would be considered a conservative in the twentieth century. To distinguish them from modern liberals I shall continue to use italics whenever I refer to the original Spanish variety.

said to have refused on the grounds that 'I have killed them all'.

Perhaps inevitably it was a *pronunciamiento* – led by an alliance of Progressive generals and admirals – which finally robbed Isabel of her throne in 1868. Unfortunately for the Progressives, however, their idea of importing a more amenable ruler from abroad did not work and the initiative passed outside the *liberal* camp to those who did not want a monarchy of any kind, constitutional or absolute. The politicians who ruled Spain during the short-lived First Republic were not only anti-monarchist, but anti-militarist. They espoused several ideas which the officer corps abhorred. In particular, a significant number of them favoured turning Spain into a federal state. In this respect they had something in common with the Carlists whose dream of putting the clock back to the eighteenth century included restoring traditional local rights and privileges. To the officer corps, whose principal task had been the suppression of Carlism, the devolution of power in any form was anathema and it was altogether appropriate that the Republic should have been overthrown by a general seeking to forestall the introduction of federalism.*

The experience of the First Republic persuaded the *liberales* that they had to make a two-party system work and the restoration of the monarchy in 1874 ushered in a period of contrived democracy in which the opposing *liberal* factions, rechristened Conservatives and Liberals, swopped power by means of rigged elections in an effort to keep the Republicans and other radicals at bay. Almost incidentally, this system succeeded in putting an end to the *pronunciamientos*. Its failing was that the only section of society whose interests were represented were the upper and middle classes. As parts of Spain industrialized over the next fifty years, an ever larger and stronger urban working class was left without a voice in parliament. It frequently therefore took its grievances on to the streets and successive governments had to call on the army to restore order.

The same period also saw a string of humiliating defeats overseas. It started with a forlorn struggle to hold on to Cuba which ended abruptly in 1898 when the United States declared war on Spain, wiped out her fleet and deprived her not only of Cuba but also of Puerto Rico and the Philippines. Six years later Spain received compensation of a kind when she secured two small chunks of Morocco. But almost immediately she was faced with resistance in the northern sector. From 1909 until 1925 she had to contend with a full-scale war there, waged by

* General Pavia's coup which brought down the First Republic in 1873 almost certainly provided the inspiration for Tejero's intervention. Like Pavia, Tejero led his men into the *Cortes* and ordered them to fire in the air.

the tribes of the Rif mountains,* which, although it was eventually won by the Spanish, was blighted by a succession of disasters for them. In the worst of these, caused by the defeat at Annual in 1921, they lost 15,000 lives and 5,000 square kilometres of territory in a matter of days. Like the leaders of many a defeated army before and since, Spain's officers sought to explain their lack of success in terms of the alleged incompetence or indifference of the politicians 'back home'. In the process, they became excessively sensitive to criticism. After the 1905 local elections, for example, the victorious party in Catalonia held a massive banquet that inspired the humorous weekly *Cu-Cut* to publish a cartoon showing a soldier asking a civilian about a group of people he saw gathered in front of a door.

'The victory banquet,' the civilian explained.

'Victory! Ah, then they must be civilians,' said the officer.

This cartoon so enraged the military that to appease them the *Cortes* passed a law that was to bedevil relations between the armed forces and the rest of society up until only a few years ago – the *Ley de Jurisdicciones*, according to which any offence against the army or its members could be tried by a court martial.

By 1923 when General Primo de Rivera seized power and set up a dictatorship, the Spanish army officer had begun to play the roles of both policeman and judge. And whether he was serving in the hills of Morocco or behind a desk in Madrid it was obvious that the distance between him and his fellow-citizens was growing. This posed a special problem for a body of men accustomed to regard themselves as instruments of the collective will and they began to evolve the curious belief that, even though they might not reflect the circumstantial preferences of the electorate, they none the less embodied the eternal values of the fatherland. And the fatherland, according to this theory, was infinitely more important than the sum of its inhabitants. A distinction was beginning to be drawn between Spain and the Spanish which in 1936 would serve to justify a war against the majority of Spaniards as a war in

* The Moroccan War saw the creation of what was to become the most renowned unit in the Spanish army – the Legion, founded in 1920 by Lieutenant-Colonel José Millán Astray. Like the French Legion, upon which it was modelled, the Spanish Legion was meant to have been composed of foreigners and was originally called the *Tercio de Extranjeros*. In fact, foreigners never accounted for more than a minority. But the Legionnaires with their distinctive quick march, exotic mascots and tasselled forage caps soon become a formidable combat force with a strong *esprit de corps*. Their most distinctive characteristic was – and is – an attitude towards death that borders on the affectionate and which perhaps owes something to the Moslem tradition of enthusiastic martyrdom that so inspired their earliest enemies. Millán Astray dubbed them *los novios de la muerte* (the fiancés of death).

defence of Spain. Even so, it required a prolonged bout of near-anarchy under the Second Republic to create the conditions for a successful uprising.

What is so striking about the army's role during the century that elapsed between Isabel's accession and the outbreak of the civil war is not that its political outlook changed so much, but that it changed so little. At first sight, it appears that an officer class fervent in its defence of liberalism during the nineteenth century was somehow transformed into a potent force for reaction in the twentieth. But that is more than anything the result of confusion over the changing meaning of the word 'liberal'. What in fact happened was that as the centre of gravity of political life moved steadily leftwards, as it did throughout Europe during this period, the officer corps stoutly continued to occupy the same area of the political spectrum, clinging to a view of politics which may have seemed radical by comparison with the absolutism of Fernando VII, but which was beginning to look somewhat conservative by the time of the First Republic and positively reactionary by the time of the Second Republic.

Having said that, it is important to stress that the area of the political spectrum occupied by the officer corps was always quite a broad one. When, as occurred under Isabel, the focus of political life fell more or less in the middle of it, its members could appear severely divided. Events during the First Republic served to make the views of the officer class somewhat more uniform than they had been, but they continued to vary significantly as the 1936 uprising showed. By no means every officer joined the revolt and a sizeable minority – including the majority of senior officers – stuck by the Republic.

What really changed things was the outcome of the civil war. The 3,000 officers who had remained loyal to the Republic and survived the war were removed from the army and about 10,000 young men who had joined the Nationalists as *alfereces provisionales* (temporary subalterns) and been put into the field after a brief training course were allowed to stay in. As a result, the officer corps became considerably more homogeneous and reactionary and this process continued as, with the passage of time, an increasingly large proportion of the officer class came to be made up of post-civil-war recruits – young men who had actively chosen to serve a dictatorship and were more inclined to define themselves simply as 'Francoists' than as supporters of a particular 'family' within the regime. Indeed, the army became rather more authoritarian even than the *Caudillo* himself. In 1956, 1969 and again in 1970 groups of senior officers, alarmed by the level of violent opposition to the regime, demanded and secured from Franco the introduction of measures more draconian than those he had himself contemplated.

Another effect of the changes which followed the civil war was to increase the size of the officer corps, thereby reviving a problem that had plagued every government for more than a century. The problem had arisen with the War of Independence which saw the recruitment of a large number of officers who were allowed to remain in the army afterwards. Throughout the nineteenth century there were usually about 10,000 of them – an acceptable enough figure in wartime when the army swelled to around 100,000, but a grotesque one in peacetime when there were less than half that number of men to command. In addition, politically inspired promotions ensured that the officer corps was absurdly top-heavy. The number of generals during this period rarely fell below 500 and the ratio of generals to subordinates was usually somewhere between 1:100 and 1:200. It seemed that the problem had at last been solved with the measures that were introduced under the Second Republic. But between 1936, when the normal officer-training programme was interrupted by the war, and 1946, when it resumed, the army's net intake of officers was – as we have seen – about 7,000. Before the civil war, the rate of commissions had been around 225 a year. So in ten years the army absorbed more than thirty years' worth of new entrants.

Laws were passed in 1953 and 1958 under which officers who wished to retire early were offered generous gratuities and pensions, but by that time the civil war veterans were about thirty-five and forty respectively and they were understandably reluctant to embark on a new career in 'civvy street'. Moreover, the intake of the re-constituted *Academia General Militar* at Saragossa – small at first – was incomprehensibly allowed to grow as the years passed until in 1955 well over 300 new officers were commissioned. Franco's way of reducing the ratio of officers to men was to keep a far larger number of men under arms than was needed. Immediately after the civil war, the army's strength was cut by about two thirds (from a million men or sixty-one divisions, to about 340,000 or twenty-two divisions). By 1975 the number had fallen to 220,000, of whom more than 24,000 were officers. But this was still far more than was needed for Spain's defence and it was also out of all proportion to the size of the other armed services. In 1975 the strength of the navy was 46,600 and that of the air force was 35,700.

In the years following the end of the civil war the army, navy and air force ministries together accounted for about a third of government spending. All three services were well armed and equipped and the pay of regular officers and NCOs compared favourably with that of other Spaniards during the forties. But once the threat of an Allied invasion had passed, Franco realized that there was no real need to invest heavily in the armed forces and he calculated, correctly, that he enjoyed sufficient prestige among his fellow-officers not to have to buy them off. From then on, defence spending as a proportion of total government expenditure fell steadily. Pay did not keep pace with the rise in the standard of living of the rest of society – especially during the *años de desarrollo* – and since the hours that Spanish army officers worked were not exactly demanding many took to doing another job in their spare time. Some worked as executives. Those from the more technical branches often held teaching posts in schools and universities.

Nevertheless, there were so many officers that paying them even a modest salary used up a large share of the defence budget. This in turn meant that proportionately less cash was available for buying and maintaining arms and equipment. 'Spanish officers,' wrote Juan Antonio Ansaldo, a distinguished Nationalist flier who became one of Franco's bitterest critics, 'suffer in silence like poor lads in front of a shop window on Christmas Eve.' In 1953, Franco concluded an agreement with the United States whereby the Americans were allowed to set up bases in Spain. Part of the price that the Americans paid was to give, loan or sell Spain outdated equipment at favourable prices. The air force got the best deal, acquiring their first jet fighters. But the army and navy remained woefully ill-equipped right up until Franco's death. The navy's flagship, the *Dédalo*, was a wooden-decked American helicopter-carrier which had been launched in 1941. Some squadrons of the army's 'crack' Armoured Division contained as many as three different kinds of tank, each requiring different spares, fuel and ammunition.

In 1970 the Director of the Army Staff College was dismissed for a speech in which he drew attention to the bad pay and poor equipment. But he was an exception. For the most part, Spain's officers did indeed 'suffer in silence' and perhaps the most important reason was that life in Franco's army, even if it was not very rewarding either financially or professionally, was nevertheless exceptionally secure. The whole of the first class to pass out of the reconstituted *Academia General Militar* became generals and although a degree of selectivity had to be imposed on their successors there was no selection of any kind until they reached the rank of colonel. Promotion up to the rank of colonel was dependent solely on length of service. Before any of the officers who had graduated from Saragossa in, say, 1960 could be promoted to a particular rank, *all* the officers who passed out in 1959 had to have reached that rank. An officer's ability was reflected in the commands he was given, but there again his ability was assessed on the basis of the class list or *escalafón* drawn up at the end of each officer-training course. On the day that he left Saragossa, therefore, an officer not only knew what rank he would hold thirty years later, but he also had a good idea of what sort of job he would be doing. Ironically, Franco himself was an outstanding example of the shortcomings of the *escalafón* system. After passing out 251st in a class of 312, he rose faster than any officer before or since by dint of sheer bravery and skill in the field. Promoted to brigadier-general at the age of thirty-three, he is believed to have been the youngest general in Europe since Napoleon.

But then the last thing that Franco seems to have wanted was to turn the army into an efficient fighting machine. The Institutional Law of the State, passed in 1967, which was the nearest thing that the dictatorship had to a constitution, made the armed forces responsible for guaranteeing 'the unity and independence of the country, the integrity of her territory, national security and the defence of the institutional system'. In other words, the armed forces were charged with protecting the regime from its internal as well as its external enemies. In practice, though, they were not called upon to do either to any great extent. The only fighting that the army had to do overseas was against Spain's colonial subjects in North Africa and there was precious little of that. The *Caudillo* was nothing if not a realist and for all his talk of reviving Spain's empire he realized that the tide was turning against colonialism. One after another, Spain's colonial possessions were relinquished at the first whiff of trouble. Spanish Northern Morocco went in 1956. Spanish Southern Morocco went in 1958 along with Ifni, a territorial enclave opposite the Canary Islands which had been ceded to Spain in 1868. Río Muni and Fernando Po jointly gained their independence as Equatorial Guinea in 1968. Back home, Franco re-instituted the division of the country into captaincies-general, each commanded by a lieutenant-general with significant civil as well as military powers. But unlike many of his predecessors he did not use the army on the streets to break up demonstrations.

The lack of any clear role for the army was reflected in its eccentric deployment. Leaving aside the Legion which remained in Africa until the last year of Franco's rule, the Spanish army was divided into two categories – the line regiments, or *Fuerzas de la Defensa Operativa de Territorio* (DOT) and the crack armoured and mobile units or *Fuerzas de Intervención Inmediata* (FII). The DOT were spread more or less evenly among the eleven captaincies-general (nine mainland military regions and two 'unified commands' in the Balearic and Canary Islands), whereas the FII were deployed selectively. Although neither could exactly be described as imminent, the only real dangers facing Spain stem, first, from the likelihood that Warsaw Pact forces, if they conquered the rest of Europe, would cross the Pyrenees and attack Iberia and, secondly, from the designs of the North African powers on her possessions there (latterly reduced to the two enclaves of Ceuta and Melilla). The conventional way of countering these threats would be to concentrate the armoured forces along the River Ebro, with perhaps one division deep inside the country as a reserve, and deploy most of the mobile units in the south and east of the country. Instead, Franco chose to station the three Armoured Divisions outside Madrid, Seville and Valencia respectively, put the Parachute Brigade at Alcalá de Henares a few miles from the capital, station the Airtransportable Brigade in Corunna and send the Cavalry Brigade to Salamanca. Over the years, I have asked several foreign military attachés in Madrid whether they could make any sense of it and I have never found one who could.

If there was a consistent aim in Franco's policy towards his armed forces, it was to encourage them into spheres of activity that in other countries would be regarded as pre-eminently civilian. Officers were prominent in politics, for example – not only did each of the three services have a minister of its own drawn from among its serving officers, but the *Caudillo* often appointed generals, admirals and air marshals to head ministries quite unconnected with defence. Of the 114 ministers who served in his cabinets, thirty-two were military men and eleven of them were given non-defence portfolios. The military also played an important role in the economy. From quite an early stage – long before *pluriempleo* was common in society as a whole – Franco followed a policy of using officers as executives in companies owned by the *Instituto Nacional de Industria* (INI). The navy and air force were given extensive control over merchant shipping and civil aviation, so that port administration and air traffic control, for example, both came under the control of the armed services. Most of the officers in the two paramilitary police forces were drawn from the armed forces as were most of the members of the intelligence services. In addition, officers were often called upon to try terrorist suspects at court martials. All this inevitably created an impression among officers that their job had as much to do with controlling society as with protecting it from its enemies.

Franco's rule also saw the officer class become something approaching a caste. There was – and is – a high rate of intermarriage among the families of officers and more than half the cadets at Saragossa at any one time are the sons of regular soldiers. A wholly disproportionate number come from Madrid or the provinces which house a military academy. Basques and Catalans account for only a tiny fraction of the intake, but this probably has a lot to do with the fact that the Basque and Catalan provinces are highly industrialized and until recently it was easier to get a good job there.

More seriously, the officer corps developed a view of life that was utterly at variance with that of the rest of the population. Shortly after Franco's death the authorities at the *Academia General Militar* conducted a survey of the cadets' attitudes and beliefs. The survey suffers from serious defects (there were only four responses available to each question, for example). But the results are nevertheless intriguing. At a time when young people were deserting the Church in droves, more than 40 per cent of the future officers of the Spanish army, asked what they found least agreeable about society, replied 'irreligiousness'. When asked 'What is the most valuable factor for the efficiency of an army?', less than 6 per cent chose 'the quality of its equipment and the technical proficiency of its regular soldiers'. The most popular reply was 'the patriotism of its members'. Indeed, the preferred options were consistently those which included a reference to patriotism or the fatherland. This is not surprising since throughout their course Spanish army cadets are subjected to a process akin to brainwashing. By the end of it the symbols of patriotism – the flag, the words '*España*' and '*Patria*' – act as 'triggers' for a touchy pride. The King has had to warn the armed forces on more than one occasion about the dangers of ritualistically invoking words without considering what they actually mean.

By the time Juan Carlos ascended the throne the army officer corps consisted of a minute progressive fringe whose members either belonged to or sympathized with the illegal *Unión Militar Democrática* (UMD), which was broken up shortly before Franco's death, a rather larger but still small group of dedicated Falangists and Carlists at the other extreme and, in between, the vast majority who simply regarded themselves as Francoists and were content to accept as their ruler and C-in-C anyone whom Franco selected. However, they regarded Juan Carlos as King by virtue of the oath he had sworn in 1969 rather than by virtue of his Bourbon blood. The question that soon emerged was whether the armed forces would regard the introduction of democracy as a betrayal of that oath. If they did, it would, in their eyes, negate the legitimacy of the government appointed by the King and give them a pretext for intervening. A month after his first government took power, Suárez held a meeting with Spain's most senior officers at which he set out his plans and asked for their support. The outcome was a florid communiqué, the gist of which was that the armed forces would put up with the government's reforms provided they were approved by the *Cortes* (which at that time was still filled with Franco's supporters). During the meeting, however, it appears that Suárez gave the impression that he would consult the leaders of the armed forces before legalizing the Communist Party. When, the following year, Suárez was prompted by events and – many believe – by the King to legalize the PCE, the reaction within the officer corps was one of outrage. Only one of the three armed service ministers actually handed in his resignation, but the damage done to Suárez and the government's standing in the eyes of the military was immense. Thereafter, there was always a mutinous undercurrent bubbling away just below the surface of army life.

The Centrists responded by virtually abnegating responsibility for discipline within the armed forces. In the five years between 1977 and 1982, there were several occasions on which officers were punished by the military authorities for expressing support for the Constitution while others who openly abused it were let off. The 1981 coup was itself a consequence of the UCD's timidity. Both Tejero and Miláns del Bosch had been caught plotting against the government and yet were allowed to continue in positions of responsibility. In 1976 Miláns del Bosch – without asking permission – had put his troops on the alert after a demonstration by the paramilitary police. In 1977 he had left his post – again without seeking authorization – to attend a meeting with other senior officers at the town of Játiva in Valencia. A year later Tejero was arrested for his involvement in a plot to kidnap the King and the Prime Minister which the press dubbed *Operación Galaxia* in honour of the café where it was hatched.

Yet far from persuading the government to alter tack, the attempted coup made the Centrists under Calvo Sotelo even more craven in their approach. The army was allowed to patrol the Franco-Spanish border in the Basque country in a forlorn attempt to stop ETA bringing in arms. One of the founders of the neo-Fascist review *Fuerza Nueva* was appointed Chairman of the Joint Chiefs of Staff Committee and the government accepted without demur the appointment as Captain-General of Saragossa of an officer who had been military governor in Valencia on the night the tanks were put on the streets. The Socialists' approach had been altogether tougher. Soon after coming to power, they summarily dismissed a lieutenant-general for remarks he made in a magazine interview, and that has been the pattern ever since – officers who dare to question the Constitution are dealt with swiftly and ruthlessly. It is a policy which has earned the young men in González's cabinet more respect from the military than the Centrists ever enjoyed. But it does lay them open to the criticism that officers are being judged on political as well as professional criteria.

Although the way in which the UCD and the PSOE have treated the armed forces has been very different, there has nevertheless been a good deal of continuity in their reform programmes. Indeed, most of the reforms carried through in the years since Franco's death took root in the mind of one man – Lieutenant-General Manuel Gutiérrez Mellado. With his pinched face, closely cropped moustache and heavy-rimmed spectacles, 'Guti' as he was nicknamed looked the very image of a Francoist general. Indeed, he had spent most of his adult life in the service of the *Caudillo* – first as an undercover agent for the Nationalist side in the Republican zone during the civil war and later as a talented staff officer and unit commander. But his views were not those of a Francoist. 'The army,' he declared in a speech shortly after Franco's death, 'is there not to command but to serve.' He was once asked by a news agency interviewer if he was a liberal and one can, I think, discern the depth of his feelings in the reply he gave. 'I don't mind being called a liberal,' he replied, 'if that means that I admit to not being utterly right all of the time, that I am ready to discuss things with whoever wishes to discuss things, that I prefer there should be no more fratricidal wars, that I want Spain to belong to all Spaniards, that I regard it as suicidal to want to start all over again from scratch, throwing overboard all that has been gained up to now, and that I think one has to look to new and brighter horizons, not restricting oneself with transient ideas and institutions that have been outdated by the reality of a young, restless, vibrant Spain which aspires to a better and juster world.'

Barely a month after Suárez took office, Lieutenant-General Santiago y Díaz de Mendívil, the Deputy Prime Minister with responsibility for Defence, resigned in protest at the government's plans for the legalization of trade unions and Suárez asked Gutiérrez Mellado, who by that time was Chief of the General Staff, to take over. The general threw himself into the job with Herculean gusto. Working with only a modest staff, sleeping as little as three hours a night, he drafted a string of decrees that reformed the pay system, laid down the limits of political activity in the armed forces and abolished their jurisdiction over terrorist offences.

Most important of all, he transformed the armed forces' command structure so that it began to resemble that of a democratic Western nation. Under Franco, each of the three services had its general staff headed by a Chief of Staff. But the Chief of Staff was not in any sense the commander of his particular service. Indeed, the question of who was in charge of what from there on upwards was a bit confused, except that the chain of command led ultimately to the Prime Minister (who, until the last years of his life, was Franco). Following one route the chain of command passed through the *Alto Estado Mayor*, a joint staff body usually commanded by an army general, which came under the direct control of the Prime Minister's office. Following another route it passed through the ministers in charge of the three armed service ministries who were responsible to the Prime Minister in their capacity as members of the cabinet. The most important point was that the armed forces' most senior representatives – the head of the *Alto Estado Mayor* on the one hand and the three armed forces ministers on the other – all had direct, routine access to the Head of Government. The armed forces did not come under the control of the government – they were part of it.

Gutiérrez Mellado rendered superfluous the armed service ministers by making the Chiefs of Staff the commanders of their respective services and then did the same to the head of the *Alto Estado Mayor* by transferring his powers to a newly created Joint Chiefs of Staff Committee, the *Junta de Jefes del Estado Mayor* (JUJEM), comprising the three service chiefs and a chairman. By early 1977 the lines of command were quite clear. They led from the three services to the JUJEM, from the JUJEM to Gutiérrez Mellado and from him to Suárez. The armed forces had been put firmly under the thumb of the government and the way was open for the abolition of the three armed forces ministries and their replacement by a single Defence Ministry immediately after the general election of June 1977.

Gutiérrez Mellado became the first boss of the new ministry, but his eventual aim was to work himself out of a job by preparing the way for the appointment of a civilian Defence Minister (although, since the general had reached retiring age and gone into the reserve shortly before the 1977 election, he was himself technically a civilian – a point stressed by the ultra-right-wing press who habitually referred to him as *Señor* Gutiérrez Mellado). After the 1979 elections direct control of the armed forces was handed – for the first time in forty years – to someone who was not, nor ever had been, an officer – Agustín Rodríguez Sahagún. Even so, Gutiérrez Mellado retained a seat in the cabinet as First Deputy Prime Minister with responsibility for security and defence. It was not until 1981 when Suárez threw in the towel that Gutiérrez Mellado also withdrew from the government, thus enabling Calvo Sotelo to form a cabinet devoid of military ministers.

But by that time Gutiérrez Mellado had initiated a host of other reforms. One which came to fruition while he was still in office was a revision of the *Reales Ordenanzas*, the standing orders for all three services which were drafted under Carlos III in the eighteenth century and which had never been altered since. The new, eminently modern, *Reales Ordenanzas* came into effect at the beginning of 1979. The same period also saw the introduction – albeit belatedly and under pressure from the Socialists and Communists, who made it a condition of their signing the Moncloa Pacts – of a law on military justice. The new act, which took effect in 1980, limited the jurisdiction of courts martial to the purely military sphere and set up committees to draft new codes of military justice and service discipline. By 1982 both committees had finished their work but neither of the two new codes nor the individual *Reales Ordenanzas* for each of the three armed forces – which had also taken shape by then – were put into effect during Calvo Sotelo's government. Indeed, the period following the coup saw the freezing of a whole series of laws drawn up on Gutiérrez Mellado's orders dealing with deployment, mobilization, training, military service and the defence industries.

Only two military reform bills got through the *Cortes* during Calvo Sotelo's premiership. However, they were both measures of cardinal importance. One gave the military authorities the power to remove officers from the active list for 'physical, psychological or professional incompetence' and changed the arrangements for retirement in such a way that the lower an officer's rank the sooner he was forced to retire. It also created a new category – the active reserve – into which officers who were made to retire earlier than they had expected could be put. The other made promotion dependent in part on merit by stipulating that officers had to go through selection processes before being made up to major and brigadier. The combined effect of these two laws, which came into force in 1981, was to allow the authorities to reduce the number of officers on the active list by removing the least talented among them – the longer it took an officer to get over the hurdles created by the second law the more likely it was that he would reach the age of retirement set for his rank by the first. Not surprisingly, these two laws were deeply resented by those officers who had come to regard the army as a meal ticket for life. Their fears were played on by the ultra-right-wing press and the campaign against the officers responsible for drafting the laws reached such a pitch that one of them – General Marcelo Aramendi – shot himself.

Nevertheless, the 1981 laws fell a long way short of what was logically required – to match the number of officers in each rank to the number of posts of corresponding importance. Although the annual intake of cadets had fallen steadily since Franco's death from a peak of more than 400 to just over 200, by the time the Socialists came to power there were still 21,800 officers – one for every eleven other ranks – of whom no less than 300 were generals. The Spanish army's officer corps was not only very large, but also very old. The average age for a general was sixty-two, that of a colonel fifty-eight and that of a captain thirty-eight.

González's choice as Defence Minister was the bearded and bespectacled former Mayor of Barcelona, Narcís Serra, who took almost a year before resuming – albeit with substantial modifications – the reform programme embarked upon by Gutiérrez Mellado. The centrepiece of his strategy is a massive reduction in the army's establishment, which the Socialists want to see cut by 30 per cent to about 160,000 by the year 2000. As a first step Serra had ordered an immediate reduction in the rate of conscription. Some 20,000 fewer recruits were called to join the army during 1984 than in previous years. To regularize the situation he has also laid before parliament a law on military service which cuts the number of months a conscript spends in the service from between fifteen and eighteen to between twelve and fifteen. The same law puts paid to two glaring anomalies. Firstly, it changes the age at which conscripts are expected to begin their military service (the *mili*) from twenty-one to nineteen so that they can now start immediately after finishing school. Secondly, it paves the way for the incorporation of women into the army by allowing them to volunteer for military service. A separate bill has been introduced to make conscientious objection, which Franco refused to sanction,* grounds for exemption.

But the real test facing the Socialists is whether they will be able to cut the number of regular officers and NCOs. Serra's plan is to siphon off more than 5,000 officers (some 23 per cent) and just under 1,000 NCOs (about 6 per cent) over a period of six years. It hardly needs to be stressed in view of all that has been written in this chapter that pensioning off the best part of a quarter of the officer corps in an army as volatile as Spain's is an operation fraught with hazard. It is no exaggeration to say that it is a gamble upon the outcome of which the survival of democracy in Spain will depend. To sugar the pill, Serra coupled a bill making the cuts with another on pay. Apart from simplifying the range of allowances for which Spanish officers can qualify and making their earnings accord more with their actual duties and less with their notional qualifications, the bill aims to put the pay of officers in the armed forces on a par with that of officials in the civil service with similar responsibilities.

It is not at all clear whether increased pay will have much or any impact on attitudes in an officer corps so deeply imbued with asceticism. But Serra can at least count on a growing appreciation among the more sophisticated and intelligent officers that a reduction in manning levels is essential if Spain is to have an army that can hold its own in the modern world. In 1979 staff officers began preparing their own blueprint for the future which they called the *Plan de Modernización del Ejército de Tierra* (META). Their conclusions were that the entire DOT should be abolished, that the number of divisions should be cut from twenty-five to about fifteen, and the number of military regions reduced from nine to six.

This is substantially the programme which the Socialist government ordered into effect when it approved the so-called *Plan Estratégico Conjunto* (PEC). The PEC also initiated a redeployment of the army. Although it was given the go-ahead several months before the referendum which confirmed Spain's membership of NATO in March

* One poor soul – a Catalan Jehovah's Witness – spent eleven years in a military jail before the *Caudillo* pardoned him in 1970.

1986, the PEC was drawn up on the assumption that she would remain within the alliance. In the event of an attack by the forces of the Warsaw Pact, therefore, Spain would be committed to sending forces into the rest of Europe long before the invaders reached the Pyrenees, so positioning troops solely for the purpose of countering an invasion from that direction was felt to be pointless except in the case of the army's two mountain divisions. A more relevant consideration was judged to be the threat to Spain's North African enclaves, especially since they fall outside NATO's sphere of operations. The biggest of the other three divisions will therefore be the Motorized Division whose three brigades will be spread across Andalusia. The Armoured and Mechanized Divisions, each consisting of two brigades and destined for a NATO support role, will continue to have their headquarters in Madrid and Valencia respectively, but with the politically significant difference that the Armoured Division, some of whose officers played a leading role in the abortive coup, is to have one of its brigades moved – for no obvious strategic reason – to Estremadura.

The Parachute Brigade at Alcalá de Henares and the Legion will form the general reserve. Today, even though a sizeable number of Legionnaires are still volunteers (including foreigners), who join up in the knowledge that no questions will be asked, the majority are conscripts. Nevertheless, the Legion remains the roughest, toughest outfit in the Spanish army and it is also reputedly the most reactionary. The PSOE originally argued that it had lost its purpose with the decolonization of the Spanish Sahara in 1976 and should be disbanded. One of its *tercios* or regiments was in fact disbanded shortly after the withdrawal. Of the remaining three, two were posted to Ceuta and Melilla and the third was sent to Fuerteventura, where some of its soldiers have been involved in some pretty ugly incidents, notably the hijacking by three Legion deserters of an Iberia plane. In 1980 the Legion's headquarters staff was moved from Leganés on the outskirts of Madrid to Ronda in Andalusia where – to everyone's surprise and delight – they have got on extremely well with the locals. There is now talk of moving more Legionnaires into the area.

One of the most curious aspects of the Socialists' defence programme is the emphasis they have put on promoting Spain's arms industries. She has long been an important exporter of arms, but traditionally her output has been confined to munitions and explosives, small arms and small- to medium-sized vehicles, boats and aircraft. In recent years, however, Spanish arms producers have embarked on several much more ambitious projects such as the construction of a new aircraft carrier for the fleet, which is to be called the *Príncipe de Asturias*, and the manufacture of high technology weapons such as rockets and missiles.

The Socialists have given their full backing to all these projects on the grounds that they would like to see Spain's armed forces become less dependent on foreign suppliers and especially – one suspects – the Americans. Ironically, González's premiership will witness the biggest arms payments ever made by Spain to the United States as the air force takes delivery of the seventy McDonnell Douglas F-18As ordered when the UCD was in power. The Socialists, who were initially keen on the European Tornado, ordered a re-evaluation of the deal but came to the conclusion that McDonnell Douglas's terms could not be bettered.

Spain's delicate relations with the United States also lay at the root of the row over her membership of the Atlantic Alliance. The Centrists, who were keen for Spain to join NATO because they regarded it as a way of consolidating democracy, considered the issue so sensitive that they did everything they could to avoid discussing it, and it was with a minimum of debate that Spain slid into NATO in 1982. The surreptitiousness with which this momentous decision was taken and implemented infuriated the left, and Felipe González came to power promising to hold a referendum on the issue. Less than a week after taking up the job, his Foreign Minister announced that Spain was freezing her integration with NATO's military structure. But it was soon made clear to the Spaniards by the other Western nations that they could not expect to enjoy the benefits of belonging to the Western 'club' unless they were prepared to accept some of the responsibilities. González eventually came out openly in favour of continued membership of NATO and succeeded in imposing his view on his party.

Suspicion of the United States is strong in Spain, on the right as well as the left. Right-wingers, and especially those in the armed services, cannot forget that it was against the US that Spain last fought – and lost – a war, although they appreciate the assistance which the Americans provided the dictatorship. Left-wingers, who have absorbed a resentment of 'Yankee imperialism' from their Latin American counterparts, take violent exception to the agreement whereby Franco was given diplomatic recognition by Washington in return for permission to install US bases in Spain. The Socialist government argued that, far from increasing Spain's dependence on the United States, belonging to NATO would make her less dependent. In 1985 ministers let it be known that they intended to negotiate a reduction of the US presence on Spanish soil.

González's victory in the referendum was won at the cost of immense disillusion among many of his supporters, in particular the young. The reaction of the armed forces is more difficult to gauge. The attitude of the military towards NATO is further complicated by the fear that the pitiful inadequacy of much of Spain's military equipment will make her soldiers, sailors and airmen objects of ridicule within the alliance. Defence spending still accounts for little more than 2 per cent of Spain's Gross Domestic Product. Leaving aside Luxembourg, the only country in the European Community with a lower proportion is the Republic of Ireland. Having said that, there is a significant variation in approach from service to service. The navy and air force have always been keener on entry than the army because they realize that membership will highlight Spain's real defence priorities and force the government to divert resources away from the army and towards them. However, if González moves too quickly in this respect, it could increase the level of discontent in a service which already feels it is having to put up with a lot – and one which has shown on numerous occasions in the past that its patience is severely limited.

CHAPTER FIVE

Boosting the Power of the State

The armed forces' propensity to intervene in politics is, as we have seen, a reflection of the instability of the monarchy. But it also owes a good deal to the traditional weakness of the administration in Spain. At first glance, weak government would appear to be the last thing Spain suffered from, having been ruled by dictators for most of this century. But although the regimes of Primo de Rivera and Franco may have been strong in the negative sense that they were capable of preventing people from doing this and that, the fact remains that they were weak in the positive sense of being able to encourage them to do things. The police may have been brutal, the army repressive, but the government's capacity to intervene and to regulate, to shape the pattern of society and the workings of the economy has always been severely limited. The contrast was particularly marked under Franco.

The avowed aim of the Nationalists when they came to power was to impose a New Order that would affect every facet of private as well as public life. In November 1936, a mere four months after the outbreak of the civil war with battles raging along two fronts, the government issued a decree unconnected with rationing that stipulated the number and content of the courses to be eaten at meal times. 'Henceforth,' it solemnly declared, 'both in restaurants and at home the egg dish will consist of a single egg.' All such attempts at social engineering soon ran into the sands and within a few years of Franco's victory they were abandoned. In fact, towards the end of his rule one of the most striking things about Spain was the virtual absence of petty restrictions. You could park three abreast or litter the streets without fear of anyone stopping you. It was not until 1982 that the government banned the sale of tobacco to children.

Attempts to mould the economy fared little better. Both the groups which gained a relative ascendancy during Franco's dictatorship were theoretically in favour of state intervention. They disagreed about the virtues of state *ownership* – the Falangists being largely for it and the technocrats largely against it – but neither was prepared to leave the operation of the economy to market forces. Yet in spite of their enthusiasm for government control, neither faction succeeded in ensuring that the economy followed the route they had set out for it.

The most substantial embodiment of Falangist economic thinking was the *Instituto Nacional de Industria* (INI). Modelled on Mussolini's state holding company IRI, INI's original purpose was to ensure state control over vital sectors of the economy and identify the fields in which private initiative had proved insufficient or where monopolies were in danger of developing and step in to take the appropriate action. There is no question but that INI became a major force. Its tentacles crept into almost every sector of the economy and by the time Franco died it owned the state airline, Iberia, and was responsible for turning out half the cars, ships, aluminium and coal produced in Spain. But the remarkable thing about INI was that it never fulfilled any of the objectives for which it was created. It failed to make its weight in an industry as essential for the nation's survival as defence technology. It inhibited rather than stimulated free enterprise and it did more to create monopolies of its own than to break them up. What is more, the companies it took over had a habit of becoming unprofitable soon afterwards.

The technocrats' aim was not to buy into the economy but to guide it from on high with a succession of plans, modelled on those initiated in France under the Fourth Republic. Within weeks of the cabinet reshuffle that brought them to power in 1957, a decree was issued creating a new Office of Economic Co-ordination and Planning. Five years later, a full-scale Planning Commissariat was set up under Professor Laureano López Rodó. Over the next decade he masterminded the introduction of three development plans whose proposals were meant to be binding on the public sector, although not on the private sector. Time and time again, there was a yawning gap between what the plans said would happen and what in fact did happen. In some areas, the state's contribution to investment was less than half what it was supposed to be.

The fact that two powerful groups, both committed to state intervention, first the Falangists and then the technocrats, should each fail so utterly to realize their objectives requires an explanation. It is tempting to put the whole thing down to the anarchic Spanish temperament. But there was also a sound practical reason, which was that the Falangists and the technocrats alike were saddled with the same inefficient civil service and the same inadequate financial resources as their predecessors going back at least until the beginning of the last century. Spanish governments have traditionally been incapable of reforming their bureaucracy or of raising enough tax and they have paid a heavy price for these shortcomings in their inability to influence events. Since Franco's death, determined efforts have been made – although with mixed results – to improve the performance of the government's employees and boost the size of its coffers. It is those efforts which form the subject of this chapter.

The problems associated with the bureaucracy go back to the days of the *pronunciamientos* when changes of government were frequently accompanied by a full-scale reshuffle of the civil service in which the hangers-on loyal to one faction would be replaced by the hangers-on loyal to another. In an effort to protect themselves against politically motivated appointments, dismissals and promotions, groups of specialists within particular ministries – principally lawyers and engineers at first – formed themselves into corps (*cuerpos*), admittance to which was usually conditional on the holding of a particular academic or professional qualification. With time, the *cuerpos* acquired an important say in the hiring and firing of their members and often controlled promotion too. The refusal of successive governments in this century to countenance trade unions in the civil service only consolidated the role of the *cuerpos* as the channel through which civil servants could put their demands to the minister in charge. Inflation and the absence of a pay-review body encouraged the *cuerpos* to drive a coach and horses through the hierarchy of office and scales of pay established by the government.

'Many corps,' Professor Kenneth Medhurst wrote, 'resolved the financial problems of their members by the simple expedient of abolishing the lower rungs of the career ladder and granting everybody "artificial promotions". The result was, for example, many officials with the rank and pay of departmental heads filling no more than clerical posts . . . But even these devices failed to resolve completely the problem of inadequate pay. The corps therefore used their influence to establish a multitude of sometimes spurious bonus and incentive schemes. Ultimately these were so commonplace that for most officials the basic salary became only a fraction of the net income.'* But in spite of all their efforts, the *cuerpos* were unable to ensure that civil service pay kept pace with inflation and during the thirties, long before *pluriempleo*

* Beneficial in the short term, these dodges have proved to be detrimental in the long term. Civil service pensions, which do not come within the Social Security system, are worked out as a proportion of officials' *basic salaries* and today the basic salary represents on average only about 40 per cent of a civil servant's total earnings. The meagreness of the pensions provided for state employees is one of the main grievances of the new generation of civil service trade unionists.

became a feature of Spanish society as a whole, this pernicious practice had taken root in the bureaucracy. The *cuerpos* benefited throughout from the lack of a proper legal framework. Right up until the 1960s the organization of the Spanish civil service rested on a provisional decree issued in 1852 and modified in 1918.

The *cuerpo* system has undoubtedly helped to create the idea – and the reality – of a non-political civil service in Spain. But this could have been achieved by other means and the system's disadvantages far outweigh its advantages. The number of officials in a department is frequently a function of the interests of the *cuerpo* rather than the needs of the administration. Promotion is invariably by seniority rather than by merit. Rivalry between *cuerpos* means there is very little co-ordination between departments and almost no mobility between ministries. This in turn leads to duplication of effort.

Under Franco little serious effort was put into reforming the civil service. This was partly because of the inherent conservatism of the regime and its leader, particularly where vested interests were concerned. But it also reflected the blurring under Franco of the distinction between the government (i.e. a policy-making body made up of politicians) and the administration (i.e. a policy-executing body made up of officials). Ministers under Franco were often drawn from the ranks of the bureaucracy and were themselves therefore members of a *cuerpo*. A law introduced in 1964 created a new hierarchy and reorganized, but did not abolish, the *cuerpos* while empowering the government to prevent the setting up of new ones. But the law was never fully put into effect and the overall situation became considerably worse.

Like a huge, untended creeper, Franco's bureaucracy sprouted myriad offshoots. Firstly, there were the *delegaciones provinciales*, each representing a particular ministry in a particular province. Together they made up a huge *administración periférica* which, by the early seventies, employed one in seven of the central government's employees. The *administración periférica* had all the disadvantages of dispersal and none of the advantages of devolution – its staff, although only intermittently in contact with head office, were first and last servants of the central government so all important decisions, and a lot of unimportant ones, had to be referred back to Madrid. Secondly, there were the quasi-autonomous agencies such as INI and a plethora of *Institutos, Comisiones* and *Servicios* set up by different ministries to look after special areas of interest, which became increasingly difficult to control both economically and politically. At the end of the sixties there were 1,600 of them and they accounted for about a third of government spending.

Being the arm of government under a dictatorship, the

Francoist civil service was effectively immune from criticism. There was nobody comparable with the Ombudsmen who operate in several European countries, nor – because of laws effectively forbidding pressure groups – could there be a body like Common Cause in the United States set up to press for better government. Left to their own devices, Spain's bureaucrats did what bureaucrats the world over will do in similar circumstances, which is to make their life as comfortable as possible. A discrepancy, that later became standardized, developed between their notional working hours, which were 8 a.m. to 3 p.m. and their real working hours, which were 9 a.m. to 2 p.m. It also became customary whenever there was only one day between a public holiday and the start or end of a weekend to join them up by means of an extra day off called a *puente* or bridge.

More seriously, there was a reversion to the practice whereby officials charged firms and individuals for their services or creamed off a share of the money handed over by the public to the state. A recent example was provided by engineers working for the Roads and Works Department of the provincial government of Madrid. In 1980 it was discovered that they were taking 1 per cent of the registration fees paid by contractors. The government's auditor calculated that during the previous five years more than 22 million pesetas had been divided up between some forty officials. In their defence the officials claimed that the practice was perfectly legitimate and cited a long list of precedents going back to 1877.

In Madrid it was – and no doubt still is – theoretically necessary to get official permission to wallpaper a room. Yet to obtain this or any similar permit you had to put in a morning's work. First, there was the queue for the application form. Then the queue to hand it in, only to find that the application was not valid unless presented with two other documents which could only be obtained from other departments which were almost always in a different part of town. Once you succeeded in getting them, and had queued again for your permit, it was time to discover that the permit did not take effect until stamped by the head of the department and that he had gone home for the day. The whole process was made infinitely more difficult by the opening hours of the *ventanillas* (the little grilles from behind which Spanish bureaucrats confront the public). Not only did the opening hours vary from department to department but they were always as short as possible – some areas of the administration were only open to the public between eleven and one every day. Anything of genuine importance could take weeks, months or even years. The inefficiency of the bureaucracy has given rise to a phenomenon which, so far as I know, is peculiar to Iberia and Latin America – *gestorías administrativas*. A *gestoría administrativa* is an agency for people who have more money than time. If you want a driving licence, say, you go to the *gestoría* with all the relevant papers and, for a fee, one of its employees will do the form-filling and foot-slogging for you.

The Spaniards' mistrust of officialdom goes so deep that it even nullifies the best-intentioned efforts to give the public a better deal. The cornerstone of Spanish land law, the 1956 *Ley del Suelo*, laid down a procedure whereby anyone who thought that a development contravened the planning regulations could appeal against it through the courts in the knowledge that at the end of the proceedings the state would pick up the bill. During the twenty years that followed the entry into force of the bill, Madrid, more perhaps than any other big city in Spain, was transformed by development. Housing estates and tower blocks were thrown up, some of the city's oldest and finest buildings were pulled down, parks were destroyed and picturesque boulevards with pavement cafés were turned into multi-lane one-way streets. Much of the development in Madrid took place before the paperwork required by law had been completed. Yet in all that time not a single *madrileño* exercised his right to call into question the changes that were taking place.

To an even greater extent than Franco's ministers, the members of Suárez's and Calvo Sotelo's cabinets were drawn from the bureaucratic élite and although they acknowledged that there was a need for change they were unable to come up with the radical reforms necessary. They pushed through a law that made it illegal for government employees to do extra jobs that might give rise to a conflict of interest. But it specifically excluded the two areas of government employment – health and education – where such conflicts of interest were most prevalent. The civil service which the UCD handed over to González was substantially the same as that which the Centrists had inherited from Franco. According to Javier Moscoso, the former public prosecutor who took over the cabinet portfolio which carries responsibility for the civil service, it contained 290 *cuerpos* and not even his own aides could supply him with a precise figure for the number of people who worked in it. A breakdown published in 1981 put the total at just over 1,200,000. Approximately 500,000 worked for the central government, 200,000 worked for local government and 180,000 were employed in quasi-autonomous agencies. The remainder worked for the health and social services, the police and the courts. One of the difficulties of arriving at an exact total was that, in addition to the numerous bureaucrats working for the civil service in the morning and for private firms in the afternoon, there were many doing – or being paid for doing – more than one job within the administration itself. An internal survey carried out shortly after the

Socialists came to power revealed that there were some senior officials supposedly doing three official jobs and some who had never even been seen in the office where they were meant to be working.

Moscoso's arrival was nothing if not dramatic. Within weeks of his arrival he issued a circular which the press dubbed the '*reforma de los relojes*' (the 'reform of the clocks') that shortened the Christmas and Easter vacations and ordered civil servants to work the number of hours for which they were paid – forty-eight hours for senior officials and thirty-seven and a half hours for junior officials. The new minister also sent out instructions that the *ventanillas* should be pulled down and that every government department should be open to the public from nine until two, that information desks should be set up to guide people to the right queue, that all the official forms and stamps needed for the processing of a particular document should be available within the same building and that members of the public should not be called on to locate and produce documents already in the possession of another government department.

Since then, however, the Spanish civil service's legendary capacity for resisting change has begun to re-assert itself. The government has had to grant officials an extra six days off every year in lieu of their lost Christmas and Easter holidays and the working week has been trimmed back so that although junior civil servants do now work a thirty-seven-and-a-half-hour week (usually eight to three every day and two and a half hours one afternoon), senior civil servants only do forty hours (working from eight to three and then returning for at least an hour and a half later on).

Historically, the state's inability to raise revenue was due to Spain's general disarray and poverty and, above all, to the fiscal exemptions which had been granted to various regions during the country's lengthy and difficult unification. Under Franco, however, none of these factors held good. With the single exception of the Navarrese, all Spaniards paid the same taxes and the country became more intensely supervised and more authentically prosperous than ever before. But one of the outstanding characteristics of Franco's regime was that with the exception of the odd working-class fascist all the *Caudillo*'s ministers came from middle-class backgrounds. They held to middle-class values and acted in middle-class interests and this was never more evident than in their taxation policy – or rather, the absence of one.

Apart from a limited reform in 1940, successive Ministers of Finance left untouched a system that had been in force since the end of the previous century. It was a system which above all favoured the well-to-do. In the first place, the proportion of the government's income raised by indirect taxes such as the duties on goods and services – which fall equally on all consumers regardless of their wealth or income – was always considerably greater than the share raised by direct taxes such as income tax – which by their nature fall more heavily on the rich than on the poor. Throughout the sixties the ratio of indirect to direct taxes was about two to one.

Of the indirect taxes, a comparatively high proportion came from charges on necessities like food and clothing and a relatively low share from duties on luxuries. Direct taxes fall into two categories – those levied on individuals and those levied on corporative profits. As far as income tax was concerned, an inordinately large amount derived from the charge on wages (which was usually deducted at source and was therefore difficult to evade) while only a small amount came from the separate 'personal income tax' that was paid by those who received high incomes or incomes from several sources (which was assessed and collected on an individual basis and was much easier to avoid). For those who could, the temptation to dodge taxes was overwhelming. There were very few tax inspectors and evasion was not even a criminal offence. The 'personal income tax' accounted for less than 1.5 per cent of total fiscal revenue. As for corporation tax, the situation was chaotic. Until shortly before the end of Franco's rule, each of the taxes to which a company might be liable was assessed by a different set of inspectors, so none of them could get a clear idea of the company's overall position. Double book-keeping was the norm rather than the exception and evasion became so widespread that for several years the authorities stopped trying to assess firms individually and worked out each firm's liability by the outlandish device of calculating the profits made by a particular industry in a particular region and then dividing the total by the number of firms. This led to a situation in which companies were unable to make even a guess at what their debt to the government might be because their liability depended in large part on the success or failure of their rivals.

Corporate tax evasion was one of the main reasons why the stock market continued to occupy a relatively unimportant role in the economy in spite of the boom. Firms dared not go public for fear of revealing too much about their true position, while potential shareholders were often deterred from buying equity because of the justified suspicion that the accounts of some quoted companies had been doctored. One of the incidental effects of this is the exceptional popularity of unit trusts in Spain – they offered a way of spreading the very high risk.

Apart from being grotesquely unjust, Franco's tax system ensured that the state remained as poor as ever, because the effect was to exploit that section of the community which had least to give. In 1975, when Franco died, fiscal receipts excluding Social Security contributions amounted to just under 20 per cent of the Gross Domestic Product. In the other nations of the 'West' – the member countries of the OECD – the average figure was 33 per cent.

The first step towards changing this situation was taken in 1977, a few months after the general election, when the then Finance Minister, Francisco Fernández-Ordóñez, steered through the *Cortes* an elementary tax reform law. It unified the system of income tax so that wage earners and non-wage earners were assessed according to the same rules and for the first time made evasion an offence. In the meantime, the Finance Ministry installed a battery of computers and recruited some 1,500 inspectors to deal with personal taxation. So that, from then on, no one would have an excuse for eluding their responsibilities, a team of advisers was provided by the government and anyone who had to fill in a return was entitled to call on their services. Among those who did so was the King who, in keeping with the egalitarian spirit of the new Spain, pays taxes like everyone else. An advertising campaign was launched around the slogan '*Ahora Hacienda somos todos. No nos engañemos.*' A literal translation would be 'Now we are all the Treasury, let's not deceive ourselves,' but it lacks the punch of the original.

The combination of carrot and stick worked up to a point. The number of Spaniards who submitted their returns by 1 August 1978, the deadline for declaring income received during 1977, was much higher than in previous years even though a number of them turned up on 31 July with blank forms on the principle that if the taxmen wanted the money then they would have to work for it. Of the total number of declarations about one in ten contained arithmetical errors (the vast majority of which were of course in favour of the taxpayer). More seriously, however, a sizeable number contained flagrant omissions. During the weeks and months that followed, Fernández-Ordóñez put into effect a plan, dubbed Operation Red File, aimed at flushing out the worst defaulters by using the records of other government departments to confirm the ownership of the shares, property or whatever else had been left off their returns.

The next step was to increase the number of people who had to fill in tax returns. In 1980, for the first time, anyone who owned or earned more than a certain amount or who, for example, owned a house worth more than a certain amount or a car of less than a certain age, employed more than one servant or had a seat on a board of directors had to fill in the hated form. Today, seven million of the country's eight million workers make out tax declarations. If you ever have to do business in Spain in the early summer you will find that wherever you go everyone from the receptionist to the boss is poring over their returns and swopping advice with their colleagues on how to fill them in.

The UCD's tax reforms have unquestionably made a difference to the Spanish way of life, but have they succeeded? Have they made the Spanish tax system more productive and more equitable? At first glance, the answer appears to be an unequivocal 'yes' on both counts. In the first place, the state has much more to spend. Fiscal receipts now represent 35 per cent of GDP, compared with an OECD average of about 45 per cent, so the gap between Spain and the rest of the West has narrowed during the years since Franco's death from 13 per cent to 10 per cent. In the second place, direct taxes have been contributing a progressively larger share of the total and in 1981 for the first time they provided more than indirect taxes. The reason for both these developments is that the revenue from income tax has gone up by leaps and bounds. But it has not, as you might expect, happened because of the tax reforms. It is because of a rise in the rates of taxation coupled with a phenomenon peculiar to periods of inflation which is known as 'fiscal drag' – what happens is that as salaries increase the people earning them move into ever higher tax brackets with progressively higher tax rates, so that the proportion of the taxpayers' incomes which the government takes away in tax goes up without the politicians having to lift a finger. The effects of 'fiscal drag' have been particularly pronounced in Spain because inflation has been even more severe there than in most other Western European nations.

Moreover, in spite of Fernández-Ordóñez's reforms, the weight of taxation continues to fall disproportionately on the working class. Firstly, the rate of taxation for the better off is still quite modest. A top executive earning, say, 6,600,000 pesetas a year would only pay 32.6 per cent and no one in Spain has to pay more than 45 per cent. Secondly, non-wage earners still contribute only a derisory proportion of total revenue (about a fifth). If one is to believe the tax returns, the average income of non-wage earners – that is, the entrepreneurs, landowners, and creative and professional people in Spanish society – is slightly less than that of wage earners – in other words those who work in offices and factories. This is patently a nonsense. At the root of the problem is the fact that, although it may no longer be as easy to defraud the taxman, the penalties if you are caught have been seen to be negligible. The judiciary has proved extremely reluctant to prosecute offenders and those cases which have been taken up have taken years to settle.

But the fact remains that – for whatever reason – the resources at the disposal of the state are now greater than they have ever been. The result is, as we shall see in the next few chapters, that the public sector is expanding steadily at the expense of the private sector in a number of fields. As this happens, Spain is gradually becoming more typically 'European' than 'American'. Up to now, it has been an anomaly in this respect.

The social changes which accompanied the 'economic miracle' created an immense new range of needs and demands – internal migration meant that flats had to be built in the cities to replace the houses that had been abandoned in the countryside, rising living standards stimulated a demand for better educational and medical facilities, and the weakening of family ties caused a vacuum that could only be filled by a comprehensive system of welfare payments and social services. But because the Francoist state's capacity for intervention was so severely curtailed by the inadequacy of its human and financial resources, it was quite unable to satisfy them. To the extent that it could, therefore, it offloaded responsibility on to private individuals and firms. This solution worked, but only up to a point. Ever since the end of the boom years, Spain – while rich in cash and possessions – has been poor in services and amenities.

According to the OECD, average disposable incomes in Spain are higher than in any Western country except Japan, yet – as we are about to see – low-cost housing, good schooling, health care and social services are all in much shorter supply than one would expect them to be.

CHAPTER SIX

Housing comes down to earth

Far and away the most urgent task was to find shelter for the millions of Spaniards who flooded towards the cities during the fifties and sixties. It has been calculated that one in seven of the population moved on a permanent basis from one part of Spain to another during those years and the majority set off without any guarantee of accommodation at the other end.

The governmment, whose experience of housing was limited to a relatively modest programme of reconstruction after the civil war, only became involved with the greatest of reluctance. It was not until 1957 in fact that Spain acquired a separate Housing Ministry and from the beginning it was clear that the new ministry would not have the resources to build and manage a massive stock of state-owned rented accommodation like the 'council houses' in Britain. In any case, the aim of the technocrats who dominated government thinking from 1957 onwards was to create an economically advanced but politically reactionary society in Spain and one of the keys to this was to encourage property ownership. There is nothing like having to meet monthly mortgage payments for deterring people from going on strike and, in a broader sense, property ownership gives people a stake in the prosperity and stability of the society in which they live. All but a very small proportion of the millions of houses and flats – free market and state subsidized alike – which were built during the *años de desarrollo* were offered for sale rather than rent. The rented sector's share of the total housing stock dropped from over half to under a quarter (in France and Italy, by comparison, 40 per cent of all properties are rented). But the transformation of Spain into a society of owner-occupiers, far from obstructing the advent of democracy, actually facilitated it because it did much to dilute that strain of radical extremism in Spanish politics which in the past had provoked a violent response from the forces of reaction.

The scheme under which all these new properties were brought on to the market was the *Plan Nacional de Vivienda* (National Housing Plan). Its aim was to ensure the construction between the beginning of 1961 and the end of 1976 of four million new dwellings. Now, it needs to be stressed that not all of this accommodation – nor even a substantial proportion – was to be built by the government. It was expected that a lot of it (about half as it turned out) would be provided by the private sector on its own terms. The rest was accounted for by subsidized housing – *Vivienda de Protección Oficial* (VPO). But only a relatively small proportion of VPO is 'state housing' in the sense that that term is understood in the rest of Europe. There are two kinds of subsidized housing under the Spanish system. Some of it – *VPO de Promoción Pública* – is indeed developed by the state (in the form of the local authorities or the central government's own housing agency, the *Instituto para la Promoción Pública*), but most of it – *VPO de Promoción Privada* – is developed by entrepreneurs in accordance with guidelines laid down by the government.

Moreover, what the government subsidizes is not the price of the house or flat, but merely the rate of interest at which the price is repaid. In the case of both publicly and privately developed state-subsidized housing, the buyers have to meet the real cost of construction, but – in order to do so – they are given access to loans at concessionary rates of interest and the state pays the difference between the rate charged to the buyer and the rate charged by the financial institution offering the loan, which is usually a savings bank. The rate charged to the buyer for publicly developed housing has always been pretty generous (5 per cent in recent years), but the rate for privately developed property has never been more than a few points below the market rate. What is more, whereas in the case of *VPO de Promoción Pública* the loans can be paid back over twenty-five years, in the case of *VPO de Promoción Privada* the money has to be repaid in only about ten to fifteen years. Yet the amount of VPO housing brought onto the market by private property developers has always been much greater than the amount provided by public bodies.

The target of four million dwellings set by the *Plan Nacional de Vivienda* was more than fulfilled. Acre by acre, the shanty towns gave way to the stark, multi-storey blocks which can be seen standing amid the wasteland on the outskirts of most Spanish cities. There are rarely any leisure facilities in the immediate vicinity and the apartments themselves are usually cramped and noisy. But they are a lot better than a leaky shack. To pay for them it was more often than not necessary to take in lodgers from among the ranks of those who had not yet been able to find or afford a place of their own. Francesc Candels, a Catalan author who wrote a bestselling book about Barcelona's immigrants, *Els Altres Catalanse*, estimated that by the mid-sixties one fifth of all the working-class families in the city were living in someone else's apartment. If it was simply a matter of a man on his own sleeping in the spare room or – in the case of one-bedroomed apartments – in the sitting room, it worked reasonably well. It also worked – although to a diminishing extent – with two, three or even four men on their own (and it was by no means uncommon during this period for a family with two or three children to be sharing a two-bedroomed flat in a tower block with several lodgers). It was when the men got together enough money to bring their families that the system usually broke down. Left alone all day, often with the children to look after, the wives would sooner or later start rowing and then the husbands would get sucked in to their often petty disputes. But as more blocks went up, even the horrors of lodging became less commonplace.

Because the scale of internal migration turned out to be even greater than expected, the fulfilment of the Plan did not solve the problem of homelessness altogether. After it had run its course, there were still some million and a half families without a home of their own, the worst affected regions being Andalusia, Estremadura, the Canary Islands and Madrid. Some still lived in shanty towns – there were 35,000 shacks outside Madrid alone – but most were living as lodgers, often with relatives – '*con la suegra*' ('with the mother-in-law'), as the saying went.

However, the real failing of the *Plan Nacional de Vivienda* was not that it failed to ensure enough housing, but that the housing subsidized by the government went to the wrong people. The problem was – and still is – that, because it relies on property developers to supply most of the housing it sponsors, the government has only a limited say in the type of accommodation produced under its auspices. And since there are bigger profits to be made from expensive accommodation than from cheap accommodation, there has always been a tendency for the property developers to go as far up market as the guidelines will allow. A senior official at the Housing Ministry during the Arias government is on record as saying that between 65 and 70 per cent of all VPO housing went to middle- and upper-class families. Incredibly, many of the high-rise blocks thrown up to accommodate the shanty town immigrants were put there by private enterprise without any kind of subsidy and the apartments in them were sold off on the open market at commercial rates.

The overriding concern of successive governments has been to find a way of diverting the cheapest accommodation towards the neediest sections of the population. The earliest attempt to do so was made under

Franco when a limit was put on the selling price of VPO accommodation. But the maximum was so high (576,000 pesetas – equivalent to about £24,000 or $31,000 at 1985 prices) that it was virtually meaningless. The next step was to limit the size of VPO apartments to 90 square metres, but there again that was well above the prevailing European average. The obvious thing to do would have been to introduce a means test. But in a society where there were no reliable tax returns and almost everybody was doing more than one job this was not practical. It was only after Fernández-Ordóñez's tax reforms that the UCD was able to make low income a criterion for access to VPO accommodation. In its Three Year Plan (1981–3), *Viviendas de Protección Oficial y de Promoción Pública* were restricted to those right at the bottom of the social pile. Since then, the Socialists, in their Four Year Plan (1984–7), have extended means testing to *Viviendas de Protección Oficial y de Promoción Privada*. Anyone can apply for them, but the rate of interest charged to buyers varies according to their income.

The Socialists have also introduced a series of measures designed to make it easier for families on low incomes to acquire their first home. A much larger share of *VPO de Promoción Pública* is to be offered for rental and buyers of *VPO de Promoción Privada* will not have to find such large down-payments, nor will they have to pay so much interest in the early years.

According to the latest survey, carried out in 1981, there are still about 230,000 Spaniards without a home of their own. Once other factors such as the growth in the population and the deterioration of the existing stock have been taken into account, the Socialists reckon that they will need to bring between 250,000 and 310,000 homes on to the market every year if homelessness is to be eliminated by the early nineties. In the Four Year Plan, it is envisaged that 80,000 of these new properties will be unsubsidized, 30,000 *VPO de Promoción Pública*, 120,000 *VPO de Promoción Privada* and that 20,000 initially – and more later – will be made up of formerly uninhabited properties renovated with the help of improvement grants – a mechanism hitherto unknown in Spain.

It is too early to say that the days of families living '*con la suegra*' are over. But one can say that the quantitative problems of Spanish housing – the problems posed by the massive migrations of the fifties and sixties – are within sight of a solution. Already the government has begun to turn its attention to the qualitative problems which are the legacy of those years. Within about fifteen years, Spain was transformed from a nation in which the overwhelming majority of people were cottage-dwellers into one in which more of the population lived in high-rise blocks than in any other country in Europe, East or West. In an effort to reverse this trend the Socialists are providing incentives to developers who produce low-level accommodation. The first fruits of this policy can be seen at Leganés, a giant working-class dormitory suburb outside Madrid, where – dwarfed by the surrounding tower blocks – you can see row upon row of little two-storey houses, each with a sloping roof topped off with a chimney. You could be on the outskirts of Birmingham or Amsterdam!

It was not only the working classes who moved into tower blocks during the *años de desarrollo*, as can be seen by anyone who visits an area like Pinar de Chamartín in Madrid. In the case of the middle classes, it was not so much a matter of necessity as of choice – they preferred to live high-rise with garages, a playground and a swimming pool than to live low-rise without those amenities. Today, the tide is turning in the middle classes too and it is more chic to live in what the Spanish call a *chalet*.

The shift in emphasis from high-rise to low-level has been accompanied by a change in attitude towards where to live. Whereas in Britain and America, the outskirts of the major cities are occupied largely by the middle classes, in Spain they are inhabited by the migrants of the fifties and sixties and their sons and daughters. The word '*suburbio*' has a pejorative connotation which sounds odd to Anglo-Saxon ears. If Spain follows the pattern set by the other industrialized nations (where the middle classes have progressively abandoned the 'inner cities') this is likely to change. But it is by no means clear that Spain will follow that pattern. Although the middle classes have undoubtedly become more aware of the benefits of life away from the noise and pollution of the city centre, there are two quintessentially Spanish considerations which limit their enthusiasm for living outside the city. The first is that commuting is extremely difficult for anyone working a split day and – in spite of the fact that very few modern urban Spaniards take a *siesta* – the split day is still the norm rather than the exception. The second is the Spaniards' compulsive sociability – their enthusiasm for going out in groups to cafés and restaurants, or simply wandering around the streets arm in arm with their partners. A lot of families who moved out of Madrid in the late seventies and early eighties to complexes like La Moraleja, north of Madrid, have since moved back into the centre out of sheer boredom.

CHAPTER SEVEN

A THIRST FOR LEARNING

One of the fondest memories I have of my time as a correspondent in Spain is of the dank night that I found myself in a bare, whitewashed storeroom in the shadow of the flyover that channels the traffic from Bilbao into Rekaldeberri. Rekaldeberri is one of the satellite towns that sprang up during the industrial revolution that transformed the Basque country at the end of the last century. Before the civil war it was known as 'Lenin's Nook' and until quite recently when they built the flyover, gangs of youths roamed the borders of the suburb mugging anyone entering or leaving it.

I had gone there to attend a meeting held to discuss the future of the 'People's University of Rekaldeberri'. 'University' was a more-than-somewhat grandiloquent title for what in essence was a scheme for twice-weekly night classes financed by a rag-and-bone operation – every week students toured the neighbourhood collecting jumble which they then sold off. But it was nevertheless a brave attempt to bring some learning into a community which sorely lacked it and obviously felt the need for it.

I subsequently heard that the experiment collapsed a few years later. But it had not been in vain. Some of the councillors elected when the left took control of many of the towns and cities in the local elections of 1979 had heard about the Rekaldeberri project and decided to imitate it. The first municipally sponsored People's University was set up in San Sebastián de los Reyes near Madrid the following year and there are now more than twenty in various parts of Spain. Unlike Rekaldeberri where the curriculum mirrored that of a conventional seat of learning, the new generation of People's Universities tend to concentrate on imparting the basic skills, starting with reading and writing, that many working-class Spaniards have never had the chance to acquire (an estimated 11 per cent of Spaniards over the age of fourteen are illiterate).

The spread of People's Universities is largely a consequence of officialdom's lamentable failure until quite recently to meet the demand for elementary adult education, although under the Socialists considerable progress has since been made in this respect. There are now more than 3,000 teachers employed in adult education. The majority come under the Education Ministry's *Servicio de Educación Permanente de Adultos*. The rest are employed by one of the two educational radio projects, *Radio ECCA* and the *Universidad Nacional de Educación de Distancia*.

But the People's University movement also underlines something which I, as someone from a country where intellectual achievement is widely regarded with suspicion, find both curious and refreshing – the reverence for education which is to be found at every level in Spanish society. One can only hazard a guess at the reasons for it, but it perhaps has something to do with the Spaniards' traditional disdain for manual labour. '*Inculto*' and '*maleducado*' are grave insults in Spain and if ever you happen to be in a working-class bar when an argument breaks out it is odds on that sooner or later you will hear someone tell his adversary that '*Usted no tiene cultura ni educación*' ('You have neither culture nor education'). The newspapers and magazines are stuffed with advertisements for correspondence courses and night classes. And it is, I think, revealing that one of the largest travel agencies in Madrid should be called the *Puente Cultural* or Cultural Bridge.

During the Second Republic the Spaniards' enthusiasm for learning took shape in travelling libraries and in the *ateneos libertarios* and *casas del pueblo* which were the Anarchist and Socialist equivalents respectively of the *casinos* set up by the middle and upper clases at which members could read the newspapers and discuss the affairs of the day. More recently, when prosperity came to Spain during the *años de desarrollo*, it was education that received the largest share of the newfound wealth. Between 1962 and 1976 the share of the budget given to education more than doubled, whereas the proportion spent on health and social services rose by just over half and the share allocated to housing actually fell.

The cornerstone of the modern Spanish school system is the 1970 *Ley General de Educación*, often referred to as the *Ley Villar Palasí* after the then Minister of Education, a multilingual lawyer and academic, José Luis Villar Palasí. The 1970 Act made it compulsory for children to attend school from the ages of six to fourteen. This compulsory schooling, called *Educación General Básica* (EGB), is meant to be available free. It is divided into three 'cycles' and once they have completed all three, those pupils who have achieved a certain minimum standard qualify for the diploma of a *graduado escolar*. After their EGB, Spanish schoolchildren face a choice between two sharply differentiated courses. One is the *Bachillerato Unificado Polivalente*, which consists of another three years of academic study. Those who succeed in passing their *bachillerato* can then go on to do a further one-year course, the *Curso de Orientación Universitaria*, which is intended to prepare them for the university entrance exams. Those who do not opt for the BUP take what is called *Formación Professional* (FP). This is divided into two two-year phases. The first, which is now obligatory for everyone who does not do the BUP, provides a general introduction to, say, clerical work, hairdressing, electronics or whatever, while the second offers a specialized vocational training.

The main criticism of this structure is that the choice between academic and practical studies is foisted upon children too early and an experiment is now underway in some thirty schools where the pupils are being kept together doing the same subjects until the age of sixteen. But as much as anything the problem lies in the irreversibility of the choice between BUP and FP. It is not possible for anyone who opts for *Formación Professional* to go to university, so there is a natural temptation for pupils to play safe by going for the *Bachillerato* even if they are more cut out for vocational training. Having said that, it was probably inevitable that in a country where manual labour is so thoroughly despised, any course devoted specifically to practical learning would acquire a poor image in the eyes of the public. At one time almost twice as many children chose to do BUP as FP, but the balance has shifted during the 1980s as a result of increased government investment in training and the recession, which has made the acquisition of a skill as important as the gaining of academic qualifications. The ratio is now nearer three to two.

A third of all Spanish schoolchildren are educated at private schools. Slightly less than half of them go to schools owned by the religious orders. The rest attend schools run for profit by secular proprietors. By and large, the religious orders offer a good education. There are a few excellent lay private schools but a lot of them are shoestring enterprises run from an apartment, usually badly equipped and as often as not staffed by the Head's relatives. Broadly speaking, the state schools rank mid-way between the two sorts of fee-paying schools in terms of quality, so private schooling as a whole is not associated with the creation of an élite in the same way that it is in some other European countries, notably Britain.

Although Villar Palasí's law provided for the introduction of continuous assessment, this aspect of it has never been fully implemented. In the majority of schools, pupils are subject to five *evaluaciones* every year, but they also have to sit exams at the end of each cycle. Those who fail to get the necessary marks have to stay in the same class for a further year unless they can pass another exam in the autumn – a practice which has given rise to the highly profitable business undertaken by many private schools of giving one- or two-month 'recovery courses' during the summer. In 1982 the government launched a novel scheme intended to provide the same service free of charge. The local radio stations in Madrid and on the Costa del Sol undertook to put out forty hours of educational broadcasting, the press in both Madrid and Málaga agreed to carry complementary texts, and a team of teachers and inspectors was assembled in the two cities to supply on-the-spot assistance.

It is impossible to draw exact parallels with the failure rates in other countries because standards vary, but the fact remains that Spain has one of the highest failure rates among countries with a comparable education system. Much of it has to do with the standard of teaching, which is nowhere near as high as it ought to be, largely because of a woefully inadequate teacher-training system and the poor rates of pay for teachers. Under the UCD, the high failure rate was regarded with considerable anxiety and in 1981, after three years' work by a team of psychologists, teachers, academics and Ministry officials, the government introduced its *Programas Renovados*, a revised curriculum for the EGB, which – in addition to updating the system by, for example, introducing the study of the Constitution – set out a list of things that every teacher was supposed to teach and every pupil was expected to learn. The *Programas Renovados* have, however, been criticized by educationalists for perpetuating the very emphasis on teaching – and learning – by rote which they claim is one reason for the high failure rate. The Socialists have taken an altogether more relaxed view of the situation, going as far as to abolish homework for all six- to fourteen-year-olds. But they have also significantly increased teachers' pay. The failure rate is now one in four compared with one in three when they came to power.

It has been clear for some time that certain pupils are failing at an early stage in their schooling to assimilate enough basic skills and knowledge to enable them to get by as the subject matter becomes more demanding. Paradoxically, this is a reflection of the ample provision of nursery schooling in Spain. The late sixties and early seventies saw an upsurge of enthusiasm for nursery education with first the private and then the public sector racing to fulfil the demand. Today some 90 per cent of Spanish children go to school for at least one year before they start their EGB. For some parents, nursery education represents an opportunity to give their children a better start in life than they have had. But for others it is simply an inexpensive and socially acceptable way of getting the children out of the way during the day – a lot of so-called nursery schools in Spain are more nurseries than schools. Even so, it is obvious that those who have had some sort of education, however rudimentary, have a head start over those who have had none.

Although the EGB curriculum does not actually depart from the premise that every child has been to nursery school, a lot of teachers now work on that assumption. The effect is to create a disadvantaged minority right at the start which, since almost half the nursery schools are still fee-paying, tends to be composed of children from poor backgrounds. These children, known as *los de la cartilla* (those of the primer) because they are still learning the alphabet when the others have moved on to more advanced exercises, often never catch up and there is a widespread feeling within Spain that nursery schooling, now that it is all but universal, should – like basic education – be made free for everyone who wants it.

Perhaps the oddest aspect of the 1970 Act was that it made basic schooling compulsory at a time when there were still not enough places to go round. During the *años de desarrollo* the government had initiated a crash programme of school construction, but it had not yet caught up with the demand for new places created by the movement of population from the countryside to the towns, increased prosperity (and expectations), and by the 'baby boom' which, from the late forties onwards, affected not just Spain but the whole of Europe. As late as 1977 when the UCD took power there was a sizeable gap between the number of children between the ages of six and fourteen and the number of places for them, so that the beginning of each school year saw harrowing scenes as children and parents were turned away from schools that had either not been completed or had reached saturation point. Nevertheless, the gap was gradually being closed.

The problem for the UCD was that at that time some 40 per cent of the places were being provided by fee-paying private schools. This was a far larger percentage than was required by those families who actually wanted to pay for their children's education. A lot of parents who had to pay would rather have sent their children to state schools. The authorities could claim that there were now enough – or almost enough – places to go round. But the places on offer were not, as Villar Palasí's law required, freely available. In Madrid, for example, there were considerably more places than children, but no less than 60 per cent of them had to be paid for. The Centrists' answer to the problem was to enlarge on a solution that had already been tried out by their Francoist predecessors, which was to give money to the private schools to enable them to provide their services free. In the years immediately preceding the Socialists' arrival in government the increase in that part of the education budget devoted to private schooling was eight times the increase for the system as a whole. By the time the Centrists left office, only a handful of EGB schools were not receiving state aid.

The Socialists inherited a situation in which the government was paying the piper, but was unable to call the tune. It was meeting the costs of the private schools, yet it could not, for example, insist that they give preference to children from near by. Because of the unplanned way in which schools have been built and pupils enrolled, children often have to travel long distances to get to school when there are schools in the vicinity filled with children from other parts of the city. When the Socialists came to power there were children in Madrid, where the situation is particularly dire, who were spending five hours a day travelling from one side of the city to the other on the buses which the government provides specifically for this purpose – 2,000 of them in the capital alone.

The *Ley Orgánica del Derecho a la Educación*, or LODE as it is known, which was passed in 1984, made a government subsidy conditional on the private school in question accepting the same criteria for admission as those laid down for state schools. It stipulated that every school should have a governing body, called the *Consejo Escolar*, with the power to hire and fire the Head and his staff. The *Consejos* are to be made up of the Head, three representatives named by the proprietor, four teachers, four parents, two pupils and one member of the school's non-teaching staff. The LODE also decrees that teachers' salaries are to be paid directly by the government, rather than – as before – distributed from out of a lump sum at the proprietor's discretion.

Not surprisingly, the LODE was regarded by much of the middle class as a threat to the educational advantages of which their children had seemed assured. With the backing of a large part of the Church, they set out to block it. No single piece of legislation laid before Parliament during the Socialists' first term of office caused as much controversy as the LODE. Demonstrations brought hundreds of thousands of parents on to the streets. More than half the government's total allocation of parliamentary time was taken up debating the numerous amendments to the bill tabled by the opposition, and it was not until after an unsuccessful appeal to the Constitutional Court that it finally came into effect. The government's determination to see it on to the statute book more or less intact was a measure of its conviction that only a radical measure of the kind represented by the LODE could open the way for a more egalitarian, and perhaps more secular, Spain.

As with secondary education, the Spanish university system makes a clear distinction between the 'academic' and the 'practical'. Students can choose between the five- or six-year courses in traditional disciplines which are offered by the conventional *Facultades* and *Colegios* and the three-year courses, given at the so-called *Escuelas Universitarias* which train nurses, teachers, opticians and the like. In both cases, the student can expect to emerge with a degree or *licencia*, but the degrees offered by the *Escuelas* inevitably have a lower status than those given by the *Facultades* and *Colegios*.

The Church's presence in the universities is not as great as in the schools. Of the thirty-three universities in Spain, only four are run by the Church (three by the Jesuits and one by Opus Dei). Together they account for only about 3 per cent of the student population. One of them, however – the Opus Dei university in Navarre – is extremely fashionable with conservative upper-middle-class Spaniards and therefore exercises a far greater influence than its size would suggest. Of the state-run universities, by far the biggest are the Complutense in Madrid, which has more than 90,000 undergraduates, and the Central in Barcelona, which has almost 70,000. One Spanish student in every five attends one or other of these two. But in spite of their immense size, the Complutense and the Central tend to be regarded as the best.

Under Franco the universities were a prime focus of discontent. The earliest troubles were in 1956. They broke out again in 1962 and became endemic thereafter. From 1968 until 1973 the police were in permanent occupation. But the demonstrations staged by the students tended to obscure the fact that the universities in Spain were essentially right-wing, middle-class institutions. The majority of professors were conservatives who won their chairs through the good offices of other conservatives. The scarcity of grants meant that all but a handful of undergraduates came from well-to-do families. One of the most striking changes under the Socialists has been the increase in both the number and size of university grants. One in seven students now gets a grant compared with only one in ten when the Socialists came to power. The average value of a grant is twice what it was then.

The growth of the university system during the *años de desarrollo* was even more rapid than that of the schools system. Between 1960 and 1972 the number of students rose from 77,000 to 241,000 and the government had every intention that it should carry on growing. Villar Palasí's Act entitled anyone who passed the *bachillerato* to a place at college. Four years later, once the full implications of this undertaking had become apparent, another law had to be passed reintroducing university entrance exams. Even so, Spain today has some 500,000 undergraduates studying in *Facultades* and *Colegios* and a further 190,000 in the *Escuelas* which is more, frankly, than a country of her level of economic development requires, especially in a recession. Ever since the mid-seventies graduate unemployment has been a serious problem.

The universities have not only had to absorb vast numbers of students, they have also had to take on huge numbers of lecturers to teach them. And since the normal method was far too slow, a way was found of offering them contracts. By 1982, these untenured lecturers – called PNNs – accounted for more than three quarters of the total. The Socialist government has set up a selection process so that the best of them can be taken on the staff by October 1987, when their existing contracts will expire. By the end of the Socialists' first government, the proportion of PNNs had been cut to half the total, but there appeared to be little chance of the problem being resolved altogether in time for the deadline.

The law which set up the selection procedure for PNNs – the Socialists' *Ley de Reforma Universitaria* – gave the whole higher education system a much-needed shake-up. It made the universities independent of the government, which they had not been under Franco, and contained a series of measures designed to put them more in touch with the rest of society by, for example, creating in each university a new body responsible for financial and administrative matters which includes not only academics but also businessmen, trade unionists, local town councillors and so on.

Things may not yet be as they should in Spanish education, but there are clear signs that they are getting better. For one thing, the politicians and officials responsible for education can take heart from the thought that for the first time since the civil war demographic factors are on their side. The 'baby boom' ended in Spain – as in the rest of Europe – in the early sixties. But whereas elsewhere in Europe the birth rate then dropped, in Spain, where contraception was still illegal, it stayed about the same right up until the year before Franco's death. There then followed a slow decline. But since 1977, with contraception readily available and the recession taking its toll of jobs and incomes, the fall has been dramatic. Today the Spanish birth rate is dropping at a faster rate than that of any country in Europe. Spain's education system has been through its baptism of fire. From now on things can only get better. Unfortunately, the same cannot be said of the welfare system in Spain.

CHAPTER EIGHT

WELFARE STATE?

If you go any Tuesday morning to the street that runs behind the Medinaceli Church in Madrid, you will find a line of several hundred people that stretches down the block and around the corner. At about nine o'clock, a friar appears from inside the church carrying a bag full of coins and makes his way along the queue, doling out 50-peseta pieces. Many of the recipients are the sort of sad cases who can be found collecting charity the world over. But some – a substantial minority in fact – are simply men and women who have fallen through one of the many gaps in the Spanish welfare system.

Of all of them, the one that has looked the biggest since the onset of the recession affects the unemployed. Young people who have never worked at all, who account for almost half the jobless, are not entitled to any benefits at all. The assumption – a very Mediterranean one – is that they will live at home, supported by their parents. Depending on how long they have been making contributions, workers are entitled to claim really quite generous unemployment benefit (70 per cent of their previous salary) for up to twenty-four months. It is when they lose their entitlement to unemployment pay that the problems begin. Those who can then prove that they have 'family responsibilities' qualify for a severely reduced allowance. But those who cannot, lose all entitlement to benefits, and since there is nothing in Spain comparable to Supplementary Benefit in the UK or Supplemental Security Income in the US, they then have to get by as best they can, doing odd jobs here and there, living off friends and relatives – and taking handouts from charitable institutions like the one run by the friars at the Medinaceli Church. The reaction of the Centrists to the onset of the recession was hastily to tighten up the regulations to protect the state's coffers. The result was that by 1984 only a quarter of the jobless were entitled to draw unemployment pay – a flagrantly iniquitous and potentially explosive situation in a country which by then had the highest unemployment rate in Europe. The Socialists have since introduced legislation which, it was hoped, would get the figure down to less than 60 per cent by the end of 1986.

Unemployment benefit does not in fact come within the scope of Spain's main welfare system – the *Seguridad Social*. The *Seguridad Social* was set up in 1966 to replace the various services provided by the *sindicatos*, insurance companies, mutual aid associations and the state-run *Instituto Nacional de Previsión*, which was founded shortly after the turn of the century. It is not the only welfare system in Spain – there are separate systems for members of the civil service and the armed forces and a variety of other bodies like the *Fondo Nacional de Asistencia Social* (FONAS) which provides old age pensions for those who do not qualify under any of the other schemes – but it is certainly the biggest. The *Seguridad Social* covers well over 80 per cent of the population and offers a complete range of welfare provision – cash benefits, medical care and social services. Cash benefits are administered by the *Instituto Nacional de Seguridad Social* (INSS). The *Instituto Nacional de Salud*, known as INSALUD, is responsible for medical care and the *Instituto Nacional de Servicios Sociales*, known as INSERSO, is responsible for social services.

In recent years the share of the *Seguridad Social*'s spending which has been met by the state has grown steadily while the proportion proffered by employers and employees has declined. In the early seventies the state's offering was a mere 5 per cent. Ten years later it exceeded 20 per cent. But this is still quite low by the standards of the rest of Western Europe. The German and British governments, for example, pay around 30 and 40 per cent respectively. In Spain just under two thirds of the total is paid out in cash benefits. Of these, the lion's share is accounted for by pensions (old age pensions and the pensions paid out to widows, orphans and to the disabled). Rather less than a third is spent on health and social services. The rest – 3 to 4 per cent – is accounted for by administrative costs.

The principal defect of the *Seguridad Social* is that, in common with its French counterpart, each year's outgoings have to come out of that year's income. This to some extent explains why it has been so susceptible to the pressures exerted on both the revenue and expenditure sides of the balance sheet in recent years. As the recession took effect, the first thing that many companies did, in an effort to cut costs, was to suspend their Social Security contributions – something that they are able to do in Spain without fear of being penalized. At the same time, the system has had to cope with an upsurge in the demand for cash benefits, especially pensions. This is partly because a lot of people who have lost their jobs and whose entitlement to unemployment benefit has run out have succeeded in wangling disability pensions to which they are not really entitled. But the main reason is that, in common with other Western countries, Spain has more and more old people and is therefore having to pay out more and more in the way of old age pensions. The problem is particularly acute in Spain's case because it is in this area that cash benefits are most generous. Generous is hardly the word. Old age pensions in Spain vary according to how much the pensioner earned when in work and, calculated as a proportion of former earnings, Spanish pensions are the highest in Europe after Sweden's. What is more, until recently there was no limit to the amount that could be paid. In 1983 the government stepped in to curb the highest pensions, but even then the limit that was set – 187,000 pesetas (about £850 or $1100) a month was not exactly stingy.

By 1983 the decline in the number of companies paying money into the system, coupled with the rise in the number of claimants drawing money out of it, had brought about a situation in which, for every beneficiary, there were only 2.3 contributors (compared with an average of five in the rest of Western Europe). In recent years Spanish officials have talked seriously about the possibility that the system may go bankrupt. The state urgently needs some way of laying part of the responsibility for social insurance on to the private sector. In contrast to the situation in housing and education, where private enterprise has always played an unusually prominent role, in this area the private sector's involvement is minimal. There are, for example, no pension funds in Spain. A bill that would have given them legal standing was drawn up as far back as 1978, but has never managed to win enough parliamentary time to get on to the statute books – a prime example of how much-needed social and economic legislation in Spain has been deferred while the politicians grappled with strictly 'political' issues like the Constitution.

The provision of health care and social services is notoriously uneven. First and foremost, there is a massive imbalance between the resources allotted to the two areas. Health care accounts for about twenty-five times as much of the *Seguridad Social*'s budget as social services.

There are less than 2,500 social workers in the whole of Spain and the homes provided for the elderly and the mentally and physically handicapped by the *Seguridad Social* are few and far between.

As far as medical attention is concerned, the shortcomings are vividly illustrated by the fact that although the ratio of doctors to inhabitants is well up to Western European standards, Spain has still not succeeded in eradicating preventable diseases such as TB, tetanus, diphtheria and typhoid and even harbours odd cases of leprosy and trachoma, afflictions more in keeping with the Third World. At the root of the problem is the fact that the *Seguridad Social*'s resources are woefully badly distributed and administered. In the late seventies, the magazine *Cambio 16* found a hospital in Asturias that had been open for two years without admitting a single patient. Another, near Seville, was so overloaded that no one had time to clean up patients after operations, with the result that the incidence of post-operative infection was very nearly 100 per cent. By and large the worst-served areas are the workers' suburbs. At the time of *Cambio 16*'s survey, Vallecas, near Madrid, with a population of 700,000, had no hospital at all and only three GPs' practices where the doctors were found to be dealing with patients at the rate of one a minute. While the majority of small practices lack the staff and resources to keep proper medical records, some of the bigger hospitals have mainframe computers that are barely used.

In July 1978 the whole system was seen to be out of control when the government announced that the money for that year had already been spent. The resulting cutbacks were so severe that in some hospitals the amount of food given to patients was reduced. Inefficiency is compounded by the widespread practice among Spanish doctors of working in several places and putting in fewer hours than they should in each. In 1981 an *ad hoc* committee of unemployed doctors in Madrid got hold of the staff lists and rotas of several hospitals and practices in the capital and, by comparing them, succeeded in proving what everyone had long suspected – that doctors meant to be on twenty-four-hour stand-by in hospitals were in fact working elsewhere at the time. For its part, the medical establishment accuses the administration of having deliberately fostered *pluriempleo* in order to have to pay doctors less money for each job or shift. So far the administration has managed to sabotage every effort to make *pluriempleo* illegal. The combination of administrative disorder and vested interest which characterizes Spain's state health service has put paid to a whole series of attempts at reform. In 1978 two important and detailed decrees were issued regulating hospital organization and the pharmaceutical industry. Neither was ever implemented. In 1980 a bill was passed by the *Cortes* which, in line with modern medical thinking, aimed at shifting the emphasis within the health service from curative to preventative medicine and set out plans for rationalizing and democratizing the system. It was never put into effect. Plans for a family-planning programme and for campaigns against diabetes and tuberculosis also sank without trace.

So did a planned revision of the food regulations, which expired in 1982. But then that would have been slightly ironic given that – probably as a result of inadequate food inspection – Spain was by that time in the throes of what has been called the worst public health disaster of modern times. The still unexplained 'toxic syndrome', which was originally thought to have been spread by rape seed oil intended for industrial use that had been treated and sold by door-to-door salesmen as olive oil, first made its appearance in 1981. Over the next three years it claimed well over 300 lives. In its advanced stages, the victims of 'toxic syndrome' aged rapidly. They became emaciated and paralysed and their skin turned brittle and scaly. It was perhaps the grisliest tragedy Spain has seen in recent years. But it was by no means the only one.

CHAPTER NINE

Coming to terms with progress

In recent years Spain has been the scene of a quite extraordinary number of man-made disasters. In 1977 583 people died in the world's worst aviation disaster when two Jumbo jets collided on the runway at Los Rodeos airport on Tenerife. The following year 215 holidaymakers perished when a tanker loaded with a highly inflammable chemical exploded as it was passing the Los Alfaques camp site near Tarragona. A few months later a train hit a school bus on a level crossing at Muñoz in Salamanca killing thirty and injuring sixty. In 1979 another school bus left the road and plunged into the River Orbigo in Zamora causing the deaths of forty-five children, their four teachers and the driver. The summer of that year also saw two horrific blazes – a hotel fire and a forest fire – in Gerona which between them cost ninety-nine lives. In 1980 forty-eight children and three adults were killed in a gas explosion at a school at Ortuella in the Basque country.

By Spanish standards the next couple of years were relatively free of disaster. But within a period of thirty days at the end of 1983 which the press dubbed 'Madrid's Black Month', a plane crashed in the mountains outside the city, two more collided on the runway at Madrid airport and a fire trapped a crowd of young people in a disco. The combined death toll was almost 400.

Now, some of these disasters could have occurred anywhere at any time. But there comes a point at which sheer bad luck ceases to be an adequate explanation. For one thing, these were not isolated incidents. The accident at Muñoz, for example, was only the worst among dozens of fatal rail accidents in recent years. Between 1973, when the annual casualty totals began to mount, and 1983 almost 300 people died on Spain's railways – far more than in any other Western European country. In the worst year – 1980 – no less than seventy-eight passengers and employees lost their lives.

Part of the problem, I think, lies with the Spanish temperament. No one who has spent time among the Spaniards can fail to be impressed by their contempt for danger. Spain, after all, has given the world both bull-running and bull-fighting. The festival of San Fermín in Pamplona, which combines both, is the best known of Spain's suicidal revels, but it is certainly not the only one. During the *nit del foc* in Valencia, for example, gangs of youths fight pitched battles with fireworks and the local authorities regard it as a success if only about thirty people are injured.

The driver of the bus which was sliced in two at Muñoz later admitted that he had seen the train coming but decided to try to get over the level crossing before the train reached it.

It would be unfair, though, to put it all down to Spanish impetuousness. Another reason for these ghastly tragedies is the cocktail of high technology and low standards of both professional competence and business morality which is a legacy of Spain's rapid economic growth.

The principal cause of the Los Alfaques camp site tragedy was that the tanker, which had been incorrectly welded together in the first place, was overloaded – partly because its nominal capacity was bigger than its real capacity and partly because the loading was not properly metered. After the gas explosion at Ortuella, the mayor of a town near Madrid ordered a survey of the gas installations at the schools in his area. Every single one of them was found to be defective in some way.

But perhaps the most important reason of all has been the government's unwillingness or inability until very recently to regulate the increasingly sophisticated and complex society which has emerged from the *años de desarrollo*. Nowhere is this more evident than in the field of public health. That well-known complaint of the foreign holidaymaker, 'Spanish tummy', is not just the result of the change in climate and diet. Shortly before the start of the 'toxic syndrome', the local authorities in Madrid inspected more than 3,000 restaurants, bars and hotels in the capital. They found that 35 per cent of the wine, 41 per cent of the spirits, and 75 per cent of the milk and ice was unfit for human consumption. Those succulent *gambas* and tasty *jamones* you see invitingly displayed in Spanish bars are almost certain to have been treated at some stage with boric acid to ward off flies, even though its use has been banned since 1965. *Sangría*, especially that which is served up on the holiday *costas*, is often made with 'moonshine' liquor. DES, the first hormone to be identified as a carcinogen, is still used in Spain for fattening livestock, and chloropicrin, which was the basis of one of the gases used during the First World War, is sometimes employed in the production of cheap wine.

Although containers and additives are analysed in advance by the government's chemists, food and drink itself – with the exception of certain bottled drinks and dietary products – does not have to undergo any sort of check before being put on sale. Contrary to what many Spaniards themselves believe, the numbers printed on packets and wrappers next to a government stamp do not mean that the product concerned has been endorsed by, or even registered with, the authorities. They are simply the numbers given by the government to the factory where the product was manufactured. It has been calculated that in the whole of Spain there are fewer than 1,000 people working full-time to check the quality of the food and drink in the 225,000 places where it is manufactured, distributed, sold and consumed.

Until recently the authorities' failure to hold the ring was equally patent in environmental matters. That is no longer true, although more of an impact has been made in the towns than in the countryside and the credit for what has been achieved is due largely to local rather than central government.

By the mid-seventies, Madrid rivalled Athens as Europe's most polluted capital. The River Manzanares, which runs through Madrid, and the River Járama, which skirts it, were quite literally open sewers into which the city's raw waste was poured so that it could be carried down to the Tagus and out to sea off the Portuguese coast.

The air was so polluted that the evening papers used to carry pollution charts sprinkled with symbols indicating the atmospheric conditions in different parts of the city that day. As you approached Madrid across the *meseta* a huge, dingy cloud could be seen hanging over the city at most times of the year. The worst period was between November and January when the heavy use of heating oil and the prevalence of high-pressure systems combined to increase the risk of a temperature inversion.* Madrid never suffered a killer smog like the one which struck London in 1952, but there were times when, standing in the Plaza de Cibeles, one could only just make out the outline of the huge arch in the Plaza de Alcalá less than a quarter of a mile away.

The atmospheric pollution in Madrid was not, as you might expect, the fault of industry. Hardly any of the industry in and around the capital is heavy industry and most of it is situated on the eastern

---

* A temperature inversion reverses the normal situation in which the air over a city is cooler than the air at ground level. It is a phenomenon that occurs frequently at night in temperate regions, but is usually corrected by the arrival of the day. It is when it persists that the problems begin. Smoke and fumes are trapped close to the ground and act as nuclei for the formation of smog. The smog then prevents sunlight from reaching the city so that the temperature at ground level stays low and a pattern is set which can remain fixed for several days.

fringes, so the prevailing winds blow what fumes there are away from the city. The problem was that Madrid – in common with other cities which expanded rapidly during the boom years – was built upwards rather than outwards. The population density is high and not only are there a lot of people to the square mile, but there are also lots of cars, homes and offices all packed into a relatively small area. The main pollutants in Madrid are, in ascending order of importance, carbon monoxide (which comes from oil-fired central heating systems and petrol-driven vehicles), sulphur dioxide (which originates principally from central heating systems) and the tiny fragments of ash that scientists call 'suspended particles' and which a layman would call smoke which, in Madrid, derive mainly from the traffic. Among the most prolific sources of suspended particles are diesel vehicles, especially badly maintained ones. In 1975 the *average* level of suspended particles in the Spanish capital reached 217 microgrammes per cubic metre. By comparison, the level recommended by the government is eighty. It was then that the local authorities started to act. They set up two vehicle control centres and formed an Ecological Patrol within the Municipal Police with powers to fine the owners of vehicles emitting too much exhaust and, if they failed to make the necessary repairs, impound their cars, lorries, buses or whatever. With their green cars and green accessories (including green holsters for their guns), the members of the Ecological Patrol cut bizarre if not comic figures. But they have certainly made an impact. By 1977 the average level of suspended particles had slumped to seventy-one and it continues to fall by a few points every year.

A similarly dramatic transformation has been brought about in the rivers. In 1981 the left-wing administration which had taken over the city council two years earlier embarked on a 32,000-million-peseta scheme to install seven water treatment plants and by the end of 1984 all the residual water reaching the Manzanares and the Járama was pre-purified.

Headed by the much-loved and respected *viejo profesor*, Enrique Tierno Galván, whose death in 1986 led to one of the most impressive funerals Madrid has seen, the city administration also succeeded in turning Madrid into an altogether much greener city. On paper the Spanish capital has always had a higher percentage of green space than any capital in Europe. But this is because the vast Casa del Campo, which is actually outside the city, comes within its administrative boundaries. There are not many parks in the rest of the city and what few there are are in the generally more prosperous centre and north. This did not matter so much when Madrid was a city of tree-lined boulevards, many with gardens running down the centre. But the *años de desarrollo* saw most of these splendid avenues converted into multi-lane, one-way streets. The left-wing council's most important initiative – as much for its symbolic as for its practical value – has been the inauguration of an annual 'tree festival' during which some 18–20,000 saplings are planted by volunteers. Already it has made an enormous difference to the bleak expanses of the M30, Madrid's ring road. Work has also begun on a number of new parks in the poorer south of the city (one of which is to be laid out on the site of a huge rubbish dump) and on laying gardens along either side of the newly purified Manzanares. There is even talk of restoring some of the streets in the centre to their former glory. But that would require a drastic reduction in the volume of traffic and may remain no more than a dream.

Another pollution blackspot has always been Bilbao. By contrast with Madrid it is industry rather than heating or traffic which is the cause of the atmospheric pollution. One of the most dramatic incidents was in 1980 when the city was covered for several days in a thick cloud of chemicals, including DDT, which turned out to have blown off an unauthorized tip 500 yards from the province's main hospital. Industry is also to blame for the state of the River Nervion which runs through Bilbao. According to a survey carried out in 1977, 385 factories poured their effluent in it and as it passed through the city it contained only 5 per cent of oxygen, compared with the 60 per cent which is needed if fish are to survive. In those days, it was so polluted that it could change colour in front of your eyes as one load of chemicals followed another downstream. Atmospheric pollution remains a serious problem, but in 1981 the city council launched an ambitious 23,000-million-peseta scheme to clean up the Nervion and it is hoped that by the mid-1990s it will be possible to swim in it.

Although considerable progress has been made in the big cities like Madrid and Bilbao, pollution is still severe in many of the smaller industrial centres. Perhaps the worst of all is Avilés in Asturias. Since the beginning of the sixties Avilés has grown from a town of 25,000 to a city of 200,000 as migrants have flocked from other parts of the country to work in the giant state-owned chemical complex there. About once a week on average the levels of airborne pollution exceed the maximum levels laid down by law and in the five years between 1975 and 1980, the lung cancer rate went up by 141 per cent.

So far as the countryside is concerned, the main subject of controversy is the role of the *Instituto para la Conservación de la Naturaleza* (ICONA), a body answerable to the Ministry of Agriculture which is responsible, among other things, for the management of Spain's nine National Parks. A lot of what goes on in them is the subject of intense criticism by environmentalists. In the Covadonga National Park in the north of Spain, beech woods have been cut down, iron and manganese mines have been sunk and a hotel has been allowed to open. In the Teide National Park on Tenerife, pumice is still being mined from the sides of the Montaña Blanca, a spectacular 3,000-year-old volcano, in spite of the fact that the mining company's licence, which was granted before the area was given government protection, expired in 1977 – nobody, it seems, told the Ministry of Industry about the environmental issues at stake and the company's application for a renewal went through on the nod. Right up until the early eighties, moreover, ICONA was allowing shooting parties to blast away at the infinitely precarious eco-system in the Doñana National Park. But then the Doñana is a case apart and by no means the sole responsibility of ICONA.

A 39,000 square kilometre stretch of dunes and marshes south of Seville, the Doñana is the biggest nature reserve in Europe outside Russia. It is the home of such rare animals as the Iberian mongoose, the Mediterranean lynx and the world's fourth rarest bird, the Imperial eagle. Only fifty pairs now survive, all of which nest in southern and central Spain. Of these, about a quarter breed in the Doñana. ICONA has undoubtedly made mistakes in the Doñana (its well-intentioned policy of rooting out the alien eucalyptus trees that had been planted in the early years of Franco's dictatorship led to the destruction of several Imperial eagle nests). But the main problem is that ICONA is not really in a position to control what happens in the Doñana. The trouble is that the National Park, although immense, does not cover the whole eco-system of which it is part. Except where it meets the Guadalquivir, the Doñana does not extend to its natural limits. To seaward, it is cut off by a strip of land a kilometre deep running along the coast, while inland it takes in only part of the marshes known as Las Marismas. Yet what happens in the areas outside ICONA's control often has a direct bearing on conditions within the National Park.

The first threat arose in the seventies from a plan to build a main road from Huelva to Cádiz along the coast. That project was soon seen off. But a scheme to construct a massive *urbanización*, providing holiday apartments for some 70,000 people, did get underway. In fact, it managed to creep more than four kilometres along the coast before it was stopped. Its multi-storey buildings and the noise and the light generated by the people who stay in them are bound to affect the millions of migratory birds which flock to the area. But an arguably even greater threat is posed by what is happening on the other side of the National Park where the government's agricultural development agency, IRYDA, is busy draining the marshes.

Wildlife in Spain is generally in a fairly precarious situation. Ignorance and poverty both play a role. Although it was long ago proved to be a fallacy, the belief is widespread that birds of prey reduce the stock of game and every year thousands of owls, hawks and kestrels nominally protected by the law are slaughtered by gamekeepers before the start of each season. Despite the help they give to farmers by eating pests and the laws protecting them, which go back to the turn of the century, millions upon millions of insectivores are trapped and netted every year – sparrows and others in Navarre and Aragón (most of which end up as *tapas*, the hors d'oeuvres which are displayed on the counter in Spanish bars) and thrushes in Jaén (which are sold to France where they are transformed into *pâté de alouette*). Those responsible are mainly peasant farmers and landless labourers and their families and by and large the authorities do not have the heart to clamp down on an activity that helps them alleviate their poverty. But to give an idea of the scale of the slaughter, it is estimated that more than thirteen million are killed in Jaén alone between October and March. Spain is also one of the few countries which continues whaling. The entire industry is in the hands of a single family, the Massós, who run two factories – at Cangas de Morrazo near Vigo and at Caneliñas near Corunna – and a fleet of three ships (two others were sunk by saboteurs in 1979). Some 60 per cent of the Massós's catch goes to Japan.

The consumer and environment movements in Spain are both still finding their feet. The government-financed *Instituto Nacional del Consumo* has stayed more or less inert since its foundation in 1977 and the initiative as far as consumerism is concerned has remained firmly in the hands of private bodies – the *Federación de Amas de Casa y Consumidores*, the *Federación Española de Consumidores* and the *Organización de Consumidores y Usuarios* whose guiding spirit, Antonio García Pablos, was once in charge of consumer affairs at the Ministry of Trade. He resigned to set up OCU in 1975 saying that 'what the public needs protecting against most of all is the government itself'. He subsequently mounted an energetic campaign against the state telephone monopoly's refusal to itemize bills or publish tariffs. But neither OCU nor either of the other groups has so far addressed itself to the outstanding consumer issue in Spain which is the low standard of food inspection.

The first environmental group to be set up in Spain was the *Asociación para la Defensa de la Naturaleza* (ADENA), a branch of the World Wildlife Fund which was headed in its early days by Spain's 'TV naturalist', the late Félix Rodríguez de la Fuente. ADENA has undoubtedly done much to educate people about the plight of wildlife, but it has always been pretty restrained in its criticism of the government. The first genuine pressure group in the environmental field was the *Asociación Española para la Ordenación del Territorio y el Medio Ambiente* (AEORMA), which was set up in 1970. Four years later it produced a radical declaration of principles – the Benidorm Manifesto – which has provided a point of reference for Spain's environmentalists ever since. AEORMA collapsed in characteristically Spanish fashion in 1976 when its general secretary, who had been voted out of office, refused to leave. But by that time its place at the head of the environmental movement was being taken by another group, the *Asociación de Estudio para la Defensa de la Naturaleza* (AEPDEN), founded at the end of the previous year. It was AEPDEN which mounted the first really aggressive campaign – against the building of an *urbanización* in the Gredos Hills, an area of great natural beauty a few miles outside Madrid which is home for some of Spain's Imperial eagles. There was a time in the mid-seventies when it was impossible to travel in or around Madrid without seeing 'Save Gredos' graffiti.

Partly because the rise of the ecological movement in Spain coincided with a growing enthusiasm for regional autonomy it has always suffered from excessive fragmentation. No one knows how many local groups were founded during the seventies to deal with specific issues like the building of a dam or the destruction of a forest, but the total certainly ran into three figures.

In 1978 AEPDEN was accepted as a full member of the International Federation of the Friends of the Earth. But this did not stop some of the regional groups joining it later. The following year a Spanish *Federación de Amigos de la Tierra* (FAT) was formed to bring AEPDEN and the other groups together into a single organization and it was in this somewhat 'cart before horse' manner that Spain finally acquired an authentically national movement. Since then FAT, and the recently created Spanish arm of Greenpeace, have shown themselves capable of mounting effective campaigns. In 1985, following a conference at Cardedeu in Catalonia, a Green Party was formed which made its debut on the hustings at the following year's general elections.

CHAPTER TEN

Law and order, crime and punishment

Every so often after some unfortunate tourist is mugged, raped or even murdered in a Spanish resort, articles appear in the press which give the impression that the crime rate has soared since Franco's death to the point where Benidorm and Lloret are little better than New York. One of the worst scares was in the autumn of 1984 when no fewer than four British holidaymakers were set upon and either killed or wounded within the space of a month. Such incidents are particularly horrific when the victims are meant to be enjoying themselves on holiday. But are they representative? Has the crime rate gone up and, if so, by how much? Who, if anyone, is to blame? And is Spain today more dangerous or more secure than other European countries?

Recent years have indeed seen an increase in the crime rate, but a relatively modest one. Between 1974 and 1982 the number of offences reported to the police in Spain went up from about 217,000 to about 368,000, the annual increase in most years being between 5 and 10 per cent. Moreover, it is clear that part of the rise is due to the fact that – because of increased confidence in the police – there is a greater willingness on the part of the public to report crime. The problem, from the point of view of Spain's image abroad, is that a disproportionate share of the increased crime is being committed on the *costas* where women holidaymakers carrying shoulder bags are ideal prey for the *tirón* or bag snatch, which – if carried out by a pillion rider or car passenger travelling at speed – can inflict really quite nasty injuries. By 1978 Torremolinos, where there were thirty to forty *tirones* a day, had enough crime to attract the services of a full-time bounty hunter – a gypsy and former legionnaire called Manuel.

It is never easy to say what makes crime rates rise. In the case of Spain it would have been surprising if the disappearance of the dictatorship and the lifting of so many restrictions within such a short time had not had some effect. But if you look at a graph based on the crime figures, you will see that the line begins its ascent in the year *before* Franco's demise, and this suggests that it had less to do with political factors than with the social and economic pressures that built up during the *años de desarrollo* which, by coincidence, ended at almost the same time as the dictatorship. One of those pressures was the emergence of a class new to Spain – the disaffected urban young. Sons and daughters of the migrants who arrived in the cities during the fifties and sixties, they were beginning to come of age at about the time that the recession reduced the number of jobs and cut the value of wages. By contrast with their parents, they tend to measure their wellbeing not by the standards of the impoverished Spanish countryside but by comparison with the glamorous lifestyles they see depicted on television and in films. When they find their own circumstances to be lacking, they sometimes set out to change them by the most direct possible route. But compared with disaffected British and American youths, who tend to go in for mugging and burglary, Spain's alienated youngsters are a good deal more ambitious – their favourite crime is armed robbery. It is in this area that crime figures have shown genuinely alarming increases. Between 1974 and 1978, for example, the number of armed robberies went up by 1,000 per cent.

The film director Carlos Saura became fascinated by these alienated, frustrated youngsters and in 1980 he spent some time mixing with them in a suburb of Madrid. Out of his experiences grew a film, *Deprisa, Deprisa*, in which he used as his actors some of the young people he had met there. The following year *Deprisa, Deprisa* won the Golden Bear at the Berlin Film Festival, but within a few months two of its young stars had been arrested for holding up banks.

Another factor which has helped to push up crime rates is Spain's growing drug problem. Because of her proximity to North Africa and her links with Latin America, drugs are not difficult to come by. According to a survey by the army's drugs control unit (and the fact that the army feel the need for one is significant in itself), 60 per cent of conscripts have experimented with drugs by the time they enlist at the end of their teens. Even that could be an underestimate. The popularity of pot-smoking has increased significantly as a result of unemployment and it is difficult to find a young Spaniard of either sex nowadays who has not at some time smoked a *porro* (joint) of *chocolate* (marijuana). But the real problem is the spread of hard drugs. This did start at almost exactly the moment of Franco's death – perhaps reflecting a perception among traffickers that democratic Spain looked a 'good bet'. The sudden onset and rapid growth of the problem can be gauged by the number of robberies at chemists' shops. In 1974 not a single pharmacy was broken into anywhere in Spain. Five years later the figure was 1,900. By that time, Spain had 80,000 heroin addicts and 60,000 cocaine addicts. Although it now has some of the most sophisticated drug detection equipment in the world, Madrid's Barajas airport remains an important point of entry for drugs destined not only for Spain but for the rest of Europe. According to Interpol, 60 per cent of all Peruvian and Bolivian cocaine comes in through Barajas. One courier arrested recently had the drugs trapped in his intestines. He had to be operated on to get them out.

But, even with the current drug problem, the amount of crime committed in Spain is still much, much lower than in most of the rest of Europe. The 368,000 offences reported to the police during 1982 represented about 970 crimes per 100,000 inhabitants. In Britain that year there were 3,708,000 crimes – a rate of 6,655 offences per 100,000 inhabitants, or about seven times the Spanish rate.* As Spain's way of life and standard of living come more and more to resemble those of other Western countries, it is very likely that her crime rate will also edge closer and closer to theirs. But for the moment the Spaniards are not a particularly delinquent nation. The organized crime in Spain, such as it is, is mostly in the hands of foreigners – the prostitution of Barcelona, for example, is run almost wholly by French, Corsican and Latin American racketeers.

In spite of this, the ratio of police to inhabitants is comparable to that of other more populous and more criminal countries. Altogether, there are some 150,000 police officers in Spain which is roughly the same number as in Britain. That means that whereas for every police officer in Spain there are approximately 250 inhabitants, in Britain there are some 400. And in Britain the police have to contend with vastly more crime.

The urban areas of Spain are patrolled by three different sorts of force. Firstly, there are the *Policía Municipal* who are to be found in every town with a population of more than 5,000. Then, in towns with more than 20,000 inhabitants and in a few highly industrialized centres with a smaller population, there are the uniformed *Policía Nacional* (formerly *Policía Armada*) and the plainclothes *Cuerpo Superior* (formerly *Cuerpo General*) *de Policía*, soon to be formed into a single force in which the uniformed police will come under the command of the plainclothes police rather than, as before, officers on secondment from one of the armed forces.

---

* The true disparity is even greater because in Britain's case I have only counted the more serious crimes (those defined in England and Wales as 'notifiable offences', in Northern Ireland as 'indictable offences' and in Scotland as 'crimes') whereas the Spanish total is for '*delitos communes*', a broader category.

The *Policía Municipal* are recruited and administered locally. They are paid for by the town and city council concerned and their job is essentially to uphold the local by-laws. There are between 25,000 and 30,000 *Policía Municipal*. Most of them carry guns (in many cases reluctantly) but they have never really been regarded as a repressive force, even under Franco. In Madrid the left-wing council has raised their status and enlarged their role considerably. 'When we took over, they were a sort of a Sancho Panza's army,' confided one councillor. 'We have done our best to change that.' Discipline has been tightened up and in 1980 a training school was established for the first time. Under Franco the Madrid *Policía Municipal* was basically one big traffic department with a few specialist units tagged on to it. But in recent years, and especially since the left took over, officers have been siphoned away from traffic duty to become what are called *policías de barrio* (neighbourhood policemen). When the Socialists' plans are fully implemented, each of the 123 zones in the city will have two patrolmen from the *Policía Municipal* and the force itself will consist primarily of *policías de barrio*, supplemented by various specialist units, one of which will deal with traffic. In the early years of the transition, there was a lot of speculation about whether the *Policía Municipal* might not form the cornerstone of a new national policing policy. But, although their importance has increased in several cities such as Madrid, any thought of making them into police of the future has been made redundant by the encouraging progress made with Spain's urban paramilitary police.

The *Policía Armada* – literally the 'armed police' – were perhaps the most hated body of men in Spain during the Franco era. Whether nursing their submachine pistols at the entrance to public buildings or cruising the streets in their white shooting brakes, the *grises* (greys) as they were called after the colour of their uniforms were the visible symbols of repression. In 1978, in an effort to change their image, the government renamed them the *Policía Nacional* and kitted them out in brown and beige. To a foreigner, the new battle-dress-style uniform looks rather more intimidating than the old one. But the change seems to have served its purpose. Spaniards do not now think of the *Policía Nacional* in the same way that they thought of the *Policía Armada*. One of the reasons why they do not is that the change of name and uniform was matched by a much more profound change in outlook and attitude under the commander who took over shortly afterwards. Between 1979 and 1982 the *Policía Nacional* was the responsibility of one of those decisive figures of the transition who are virtually unknown outside Spain – Lieutenant-General José Antonio Sáenz de Santa María, a burly moustachioed soldier whose tough professionalism went hand in hand with a genuine commitment to democracy. In 1981, when Tejero occupied the *Cortes*, Sáenz de Santa María sided unhesitatingly with the government and ordered his *Policía Nacional* to encircle the building. People have not forgotten that. To the average Spaniard today, the *Policía Nacional* is the force which, when the chips were down, took the side of democracy.

Their image improved still further a few months later when the close-quarters battle unit of the *Policía Nacional*, the *Grupo Especial de Operaciones* (GEO), which had been formed to deal with terrorist sieges and the like, stormed the Banco Central in Barcelona and released more than a hundred hostages unharmed in one of the most spectacular and successful operations of its kind. Men of the same unit later freed the father of the singer Julio Iglesias after he had been kidnapped by criminals.

There are some 50,000 uniformed members of the new joint force and 10,000 plainclothes officers. Trainees for the plainclothes branch, who need to have the qualifications for university entrance, undergo a rigorous three-year course at a special school in Avila. Within the plainclothes branch, there is a sharp division (by no means peculiar to Spain) between the *policías de brigada* who belong to the various specialist squads and branches, most of which are based in Madrid, and the *policías de comisaría* who work in the local stations, traditionally locked in an unceasing and unequal battle against mountains of paperwork. The first are paid more than the second and whenever the authorities want to show their displeasure with a member of a *brigada* they dispatch him to a *comisaría*.

Not being subject to military discipline, the officers of the *Cuerpo Superior* are entitled to join a trade union and not long after the first general election the then Interior Minister, Rodolfo Martín Villa – one of the more conservative figures in the UCD who had been head of Franco's official student union – surprised the *Cuerpo*'s officers by suggesting that they might do well to have a trade union of their own. Ironically, the *Asociación* (later *Sindicato*) *Profesional de Policía*, founded in 1978, was organized by officers who had served in Franco's secret police, the *Brigada de Investigación Social** and particularly by the then Director-General of Police, José Sainz. Ironically? Well, perhaps suspiciously would be a better word. It has always been suspected that the exercise was conceived in the belief that a police trade union was inevitable and in the hope of preventing the left gaining influence over an

* I have had to use the term 'secret police' because it is the only one in English which conveys the sense of a squad dedicated solely to tracking down dissidents and stamping out opposition, but there was never anything secret about the BIS.

institution that occupies a crucial position within the state. If that was the aim, then its instigators succeeded – or rather they need hardly have bothered since the balance of political opinion within the *Cuerpo Superior* has always been to the right of centre, as it is in most police forces.

On the other hand, if the plan was to create a trade union that could be manipulated by the government, then it seriously misfired because the SPP has never ceased to be a thorn in the flesh of both right- and left-wing administrations. The trouble began in 1979 after two police officers were murdered in the Basque country and the SPP issued a now-famous statement implicitly criticizing democracy and declaring that its members were 'sick and tired' ('*dolorosamente hartos*' were the exact words) of the loss of life among the police. The statement prompted some of the more progressive officers in the SPP, drawn almost exclusively from the *comisarías*, to leave and form their own group, the *Unión Sindical de Policías*, which is broadly sympathetic to the PSOE. The following year the Interior Minister closed down the SPP's offices in Madrid and Barcelona and suspended four of its leaders from duty after one of them was reported as suggesting that the government should hold a referendum in the Basque country to see if the population wanted the police to stay.

Since the Socialists came to power, there has been something of a *rapprochement* between the SPP, which now has about 5,400 members, and the much smaller USP, which has around 900. But this has led to the creation of a third union composed entirely of senior officers called the *Sindicato de Comisarios*. In 1983 the SPP and the USP jointly organized a one-day go-slow and a demonstration by some 3,000 officers in front of police headquarters in the Puerta del Sol. More than any other section of society, the plainclothes detectives – and particularly those in the more 'political' units such as the anti-terrorist squad – are notorious for their addiction to intrigue. In addition to the problems posed by the unions, both the Centrists and the Socialists have had to deal with a persistent air of conspiracy hanging around police headquarters. There is evidence that plainclothes officers tapped the telephones of ministers and destroyed embarrassing files. Ever since the PSOE's victory the upper reaches of the service have been racked by sackings and purges.

The *Policía Armada* and the *Cuerpo General*, as they were until very recently, were both Francoist creations. They were set up in 1941 with the help of advisers from Nazi Germany to replace two forces created in the 1870s – the *Cuerpo de Seguridad* and the *Cuerpo de Vigilancia* – which, in the words of the law that abolished them, had become 'imbued with apoliticism'. By contrast, the *Guardia Civil* – which patrols the countryside, the highways and the frontiers and provides Spain with her customs officers – can trace its history back to 1844 when it was set up by the government to combat banditry.

There are more than 60,000 *Guardia Civil* scattered across the country in 3,500 *puestos* or stations. The uniformed officers in their distinctive patent leather tricorns patrol the immense, sparsely populated expanses of rural Spain in cars and jeeps, on motorbikes and even sometimes on horses and donkeys. But although their job is to get to know as much as possible about the local population, they and their families tend to live a life apart from the rest of the community. They rarely come from the region where they are posted, their quarters are often just outside the town or village for which they are responsible, and they and their families often do not mix socially with the locals. The force also has some plainclothes detectives, most of whom work in the field of anti-terrorist intelligence.

Richard Ford, the English writer who was living in Spain at the time the *Guardia Civil* was founded, remarked on how efficient the new force was. But he added that 'They have been quite as much employed . . . for political purposes rather than those of pure police, having been used to keep down the expression of indignant public opinion, and, instead of catching thieves, in upholding those first-rate criminals, foreign and domestic, who are now robbing poor Spain of her gold and liberties.' He was not the last commentator to see in the force an instrument for the oppression of the poor by the rich.

Supporters of the *Guardia Civil* argue that it has merely stood by authority, whatever its political complexion, and they point out that when the civil war divided Spain into two camps, its members gave their loyalty to whichever faction had come out on top in that part of the country. That is true, although it overlooks the fact that in several areas the *Guardia Civil* was instrumental in ensuring that the uprising succeeded rather than in defending the legitimately elected authorities. As with the army the *Guardia Civil* became ideologically more homogeneous and more reactionary under Franco's influence. But it was always much more popular with the average Spaniard than the *Policía Armada*. The courtesy and efficiency of the *Guardia Civil* highway patrols, who not only enforce the speed limits but also help motorists in distress, enhanced the force's reputation still further. Yet of all Spain's police forces it is the *Guardia Civil* which has had most difficulty coming to terms with democracy. As late as 1980 *Guardia Civil* units received a telex from headquarters – apparently sanctioned at the highest level – stipulating that on all official premises there ought to be, in pride of place, the portrait of 'HM the King and, in a fully visible place, the portrait of Generalísimo Franco'. Tejero's part in the abortive coup was unfortunate in this respect because it provided the most reactionary elements within the service with a hero and martyr.

The reason why the *Guardia Civil* has proved more resistant to change than the police is that it is far closer to the army both sentimentally and organizationally. In spite of its name the *Guardia Civil* is and always has been an essentially military body. Its members are subject to military discipline and qualify for military decorations. Those of its officers who do not come up through the ranks are graduates of the *Academia General Militar*.* Under Franco, moreover, the *Guardia Civil* was responsible to the Ministry of Defence, whereas the *Policía Armada* and the *Cuerpo General* came under the Ministry of Interior – a division of authority that made it virtually impossible to co-ordinate the policing of the country. During the early years of the transition there was a lot of talk about having to 'civilianize' the *Guardia Civil* among politicians who did not perhaps fully appreciate how fiercely proud the force was of its military status. A formula was eventually worked out whereby the *Guardia Civil* was made responsible to the Ministry of Interior in time of peace and to the Ministry of Defence in time of war. But by that time the ultra-right had a heyday exploiting the force's apprehension. A lot of the misgivings about democracy within the *Guardia Civil* stem from that period.

In 1983 the Socialist government put the *Guardia Civil* under the command of General Sáenz de Santa María in the hope that he would be able to bring about the same sort of transformation that he wrought in the *Policía Nacional*.

Leaving aside the *Policía Municipal*, the other three forces – jointly known as the *Policía Gubernativa* – earned a fearsome reputation for toughness under Franco which they have still not shrugged off. It would be nice to be able to report that they no longer deserve it. Nice, but not truthful. Some progress has undoubtedly been made. The riot squads do not wade into demonstrations with quite the same abandon as they did under Franco and you do now see people approach the police in the street to ask the time or the way, which would have been unthinkable only a few years ago. But scarcely a week goes by without some innocent Spaniard getting shot after failing to notice a roadblock or getting into an argument with an off-duty policeman in a bar and it is extremely unusual for those responsible to be brought to book. According to Amnesty International the torture and ill-treatment of detainees is 'persistent'. Most of the complaints are lodged by people detained under the anti-terrorist legislation, which was first introduced as an 'emergency' measure in 1977 and which allows the police to hold anyone suspected of

* Both sorts of officer trainees then undergo a course at the *Guardia Civil*'s own training school.

a wide range of offences for up to ten days. But the rules governing detention under the anti-terrorist laws ought not to be seen in isolation. They are merely one aspect of a system in which the odds are weighted against the defendant from the moment of arrest to the point of sentencing.

Even in normal cases, the police have seventy-two hours before they have to bring the person they have arrested before a court. It was in an attempt to limit abuses during this period that the Socialists introduced a law providing a limited right of *habeas corpus*. This allows suspects to appeal to the courts if they believe that they have been illegally or illicitly arrested, if the period of their detention exceeds the time allowed by law or if they have been mistreated. The Socialists have also passed legislation giving suspects an automatic right to legal assistance, although suspects detained under the anti-terrorist laws – who, it was feared, might have used sympathetic lawyers to pass messages to their colleagues – must accept a duty lawyer.

As far as the period between committal and trial is concerned, there appears to be an alarming discrepancy between what should happen and what does happen. In theory, everyone shuld have a lawyer, whether hired by the defendant or appointed by the state. But in a survey carried out among 500 remand prisoners at Carabanchel gaol in Madrid in 1977, 67 per cent of those who replied were not aware of having any sort of legal representation. Some 90 per cent said that they had never seen the instructing magistrate and that their statement when charged had been taken by a court official. Although 341 of them had written to the courts, only thirty-four had received a reply.

Under Spanish law, the trial is divided into two phases – a written stage and an oral stage. The Constitution states unequivocally that 'the procedure shall be predominantly oral'. But despite this the majority of cases are still dealt with mainly on paper. An Act passed in 1980 which allowed the courts to dispense with the initial, written phase in cases where the defendant had been caught red-handed has proved to be a failure, largely because there are very few cases in which guilt is that obvious. The Socialists now propose to introduce a new classification according to the seriousness of the offence – the courts will be able to forgo the written stage in minor cases but not in major ones.

Although it continues to suffer from immense defects, the legal system has benefited from two reforms of great importance during the post-Franco years. The first was the freeing of the judiciary from the influence of the government with the creation of a *Consejo General del Poder Judicial*. This body, which was invented by the authors of the Constitution and inaugurated bythe UCD in 1980, is a panel of twenty-one senior figures from the legal profession chosen by parliament. Its main task is to appoint the judges and maintain ethical standards within the legal profession. Similar bodies exist in both France and Italy but neither has the clout of its Spanish counterpart.

The other major legal reform has been – or will be – the overhaul of criminal law embarked upon by the Socialists. A totally new code of laws is unlikely to emerge for several years yet. So far, a draft version has been prepared which envisages the introduction of several progressive concepts such as weekend imprisonment. But the Socialists have already carried out a substantial partial reform, affecting about a sixth of all the articles in the penal code. Much of it was concerned with adapting the penal code to the Constitution and updating the jurisprudential underpinnings of the system. But it also introduced suspended sentencing, imposed stiff penalties for failure to comply with the food and drink regulations, made pollution of the environment a crime, and created a clear distinction between 'hard' and 'soft' drugs for the purpose of sentencing growers, manufacturers and traffickers. Finally, and most controversially, it re-affirmed a little-known peculiarity of Spanish law which is that the possession of a small quantity of soft drugs for personal use is not an offence. In fact, the police in Barcelona recently had to return to its owners some cannabis seized during a raid on a bar.

The Socialists have also begun to tackle another fundamental problem of the legal system, which is its dire lack of funds. Under the UCD, the amount allocated to running the courts and prisons never accounted for more than 2 per cent of the budget, which is less than half the average in the EEC. The lack of cash has meant that the system was and is incapable of dealing with the increasingly heavy load put on it by rising crime rates. There are *Juzgados de Guardia* (the courts where it is decided which courts should handle which cases), dealing with 600 cases a day and the average delay in bringing a case to trial is about eighteen months for minor offences and between two and four years for serious offences.

Of the remand prisoners who took part in the survey mentioned earlier only 10 per cent had spent less than six months in Carabanchel. The majority – 59 per cent – had been there for between six months and two years, 21 per cent had been inside for between two and four years and the remaining 10 per cent had been in gaol awaiting trial for even longer. It is difficult to know how much weight to give this story, but when a newspaper reporter visited Carabanchel in 1981, he recorded that he was buttonholed by a South American who told him that he had been there for fifteen years without ever being brought before a court because his file had been lost.

Delay generates corruption, and specifically what Spaniards call the *corrupción de las astillas* – the bribery of court administrators by lawyers in an effort to speed up their clients' cases. It is sufficiently commonplace for the Plaza de Castilla, the site of the main law court in Madrid, to be known as the Plaza de las Astillas.

One of the paradoxes of recent years has been that the proportion of defendants remanded in custody rather than on bail was greater in the new, free Spain than under the dictatorship. The nineteenth-century *Ley de Enjuiciamiento Criminal*, which remained in force throughout Franco's dictatorship, allowed judges to grant bail to anyone not accused of an offence for which the penalty was six years or more in prison. In most cases they did. But in response to concern about the increase in crime and, in particular, the suspicion that criminals caught by the police and bailed by the courts were responsible for much of it, a law was passed in 1980 under which bail was only available to those accused of crimes for which the penalty was six *months* or more. By the time that the UCD left office more than half the inmates of Spain's gaols were still awaiting trial.

The Socialists came to power determined to make bail once again the norm rather than the exception and ensure that theoretically innocent remand prisoners did not have to spend unduly lengthy periods in gaol. Soon after their victory at the polls, they passed a law which restored the situation provided for by the *Ley de Enjuiciamiento Criminal* and stipulated that no one should remain in custody for longer than three years awaiting trial for serious offences or eighteen months in gaol awaiting trial on minor charges.

The trouble was that, because of the delays in the system, huge numbers of prisoners on remand – guilty and innocent alike – qualified for release on the day that the law came into effect and were promptly let out. The results were catastrophic. During 1983 the number of crimes reported to the police soared by a third. The biggest increase was in armed robberies which went up by a staggering 60 per cent. Amid the public outcry that ensued, the government hastily raised the detention limits to four years and two years respectively. The Socialists are hoping that greater investment in the administration of justice will gradually solve the problem by ensuring that people are brought to trial more speedily.

The delays facing remand prisoners were among the grievances which provoked the string of fifty or so riots that rocked the Spanish penal system between 1976 and 1978 and which left three inmates dead and numerous others injured. Daniel Pont Martín, the man who founded the organization behind the riots, the *Coordinadora de Presos en Lucha* (Association of Prisoners in Struggle) (COPEL), had to wait five years before he was brought to trial. When he did eventually get to court, he and his two fellow defendants caused a sensation by pulling out knives, cutting the arteries in their arms and – with blood spurting from their wounds – launching themselves at the judge shouting, '*Fascist!*' But whatever the ostensible grievances of the prisoners, the underlying cause of the unrest in the gaols was the succession of amnesties granted after Franco's death – first, a general one for common prisoners and then a series of partial ones for political prisoners. It was only the passing of the Constitution, which categorically forbids any further general pardons, that finally dashed the common prisoners' hopes.

The constitutional ban on amnesties put paid to the riots, but it created another problem in the process. Franco, who declared numerous amnesties, used them to reduce the prison population whenever it looked like getting too big. The blocking of this safety valve has led to enormous pressures building up within the prison system and to cope with them the government has been forced to expand it. A large part of the extra resources made available to the Ministry of Justice have therefore had to be diverted into an ambitious prison construction programme.

But what are the conditions like in Spanish gaols? It is not easy to come to an overall conclusion. Contrary to what one might expect, Spaniards themselves tend to be more critical of the system than foreigners. In 1978 a Senate commission submitted a report that gave the impression that the inmates lived little better than animals. Yet only a year before, the International Red Cross had found the facilities 'satisfactory in the majority of cases' and described Yeserias, the Madrid women's prison, as 'a model for the rest of the world'. There are undoubtedly gaols which leave a good deal to be desired. Recently, for example, the Governor of the Model Prison in Valencia was found to be punishing prisoners by confining them to so-called 'blind' or 'black' cells without light or ventilation. Yet there are several open prisons, some prisoners are allowed out for periods of between a day and a week and all prisoners are permitted sex with their wives or husbands, or even with their girlfriends and boyfriends, once every forty-five days. Although rehabilitation facilities are virtually non-existent the rate of recidivism is no worse than in Britain and considerably better than in the United States.

Perhaps one reason for the discrepancy between Spanish and foreign assessments is that Spaniards, with their passion for freedom, find the very idea of imprisonment so abhorrent that they would regard almost any penal system as an outrage. It is notable that during the last hundred years, in which time Spain has not exactly been at the forefront of social reform, it has produced two eminent penal reformers – Concepción Arenal and the Republican prisons director, Victoria Kent. Most of the measures these two women introduced have been superseded now, but their example and inspiration lives on and it would surprise me for one if, once they have overcome the problem of overcrowding, the Spaniards do not succeed in creating a first-class penal system.

CHAPTER ELEVEN

The media: Franco's spirit lives on

For a people whose recent history has been nothing if not eventful, the Spaniards are surprisingly unenthusiastic newspaper readers. The best-selling Spanish daily *El País* has an average circulation of just under 350,000 and only eight papers in the entire country sell in excess of 100,000 copies a day.* Less than one Spaniard in every ten buys a daily newspaper – and that includes those who read papers like *As, Marca, Sport, Dicen* and *Mundo Deportivo* which are devoted exclusively to sport. In fact, the only countries in Europe with a lower newspaper readership are Greece, Portugal and Albania.

To a large extent, of course, newspaper readership is an indication of a country's level of development. It is no coincidence that the countries just mentioned as having lower newspaper readerships are those which are also less developed economically. But the correlation is not exact. The British, for example, are not as well off as the French or the Germans yet they buy more newspapers than either. Some of the reasons why Spaniards buy so few papers are to be found within Spain itself, and in particular in the absence of a popular press.

Spanish journalists would say that *El Periódico* and *Diario 16* fit into that category because they have bigger headlines and more photographs than the other papers. But they are a long way from being popular papers in the sense that that term is understood in Britain, Germany and the States. Both give extensive coverage to 'serious' political and economic news and although they carry stories about, for

* These figures refer to the average circulation between Tuesday and Saturday. There are no Sunday newspapers as such – the morning newspapers which publish in the week also come out on Sunday – and Sunday sales are generally 50–100 per cent higher. So that the majority of journalists do not have to work on Sundays as well as on Saturdays, the press guilds in some cities organize skeleton staffs to produce a special Monday morning paper called the *Hoja del Lunes* (Monday Sheet).

instance, the private lives of the celebrities, they rarely lead with them. By comparison with popular papers in North America and Northern Europe the resources they devote to crime coverage and court reporting are paltry. In fact, *Diario 16* and *El Periódico* are precisely the sort of 'popular' papers that middle-class critics would like to see replace tabloids such as the *New York Daily News*, the *Sun* and *Bild Zeitung*. The only Spanish daily which ever came near to emulating them was *Diario Libre* which was set up in 1978 and once carried the memorable headline '*Maricas en el Ministerio de Cultura*' (Poofrahs in the Ministry of Culture). It failed to win a sizeable readership and collapsed after only a few months.

The demise of *Diario Libre* highlighted the fact that, in Spain, daily newspaper reading is overwhelmingly a middle-class habit. It was because *Diario Libre* did not appeal to the middle classes, whereas *El Periódico* and *Diario 16* did, that the first failed while the other two succeeded. But it also showed that Spanish journalists were incapable of coming up with a product that would appeal to the working class. And this is because the journalistic profession in Spain is virtually monopolized by middle-class intellectuals. Almost without exception, Spanish journalists are graduates of the 'Faculties of Information Science' which Franco created to ensure that aspiring journalists were thoroughly indoctrinated before they had a chance to exercise their chosen profession. And as has been pointed out in an earlier chapter, the overwhelming majority of the young people who go to university are from well-to-do families.

As in so many other areas of society, the changes in the Spanish newspaper industry have been gradual and partial. The years since Franco's death have seen the re-creation of a vernacular language daily press with the setting up of *Avui*, which is written entirely in Catalan and published in Barcelona, and two papers written partly in Basque, *Deia* and *Egin*, which represent the moderate and radical strains of Basque nationalism respectively. As for the Castilian language press, although there have been virtually no new newspapers set up in the provinces, Madrid and Barcelona have between them acquired three new general dailies – *Diario 16* in Madrid, *El Periódico* in Barcelona and *El País* which now publishes separate editions in both cities.

Of all the new papers, the most influential is unquestionably *El País*, founded in 1976. Its editor, Juan Luis Cebrián, who was only thirty-one at the time of his appointment, was given generous resources and was able to take his pick of Spain's ablest young journalists. From day one, the paper was required reading for anyone seriously interested in the nation's affairs. It has 'broken' several important stories such as the government auditors' report on RTVE mentioned later in this chapter. But perhaps an even greater contribution was made by *El País*'s leader writers who, day in day out during the transition, explained patiently and clearly how this, that and the other was done in a democracy. What made this so valuable was that although Suárez and his ministers were responsible for reintroducing the ballot box to Spain they had enormous difficulty understanding such concepts as collective responsibility, ministerial accountability, and where to draw the line between a permanent administration made up of officials and a transitory government made up of politicians. Since the UCD's demise and the Socialists' accession, *El País* has had to cope with a more difficult role, not only because Felipe González and his team have a much firmer grip on what democracy implies but also because what they are putting into practice is largely what *El País* has been proposing, and newspapers which support the government of the day are always at a disadvantage by comparison with those which oppose it. Nevertheless Cebrián and his team have acquired such an influential position both within and beyond Spain that their newspaper's future seems assured.

There are two main differences between the papers founded since the restoration of democracy and those which functioned under the dictatorship. The first is political. As one might expect, the latter tend to be to the right of the former. But the second is purely professional. Whereas the new newspapers have all hit the streets with a clean, clear, modern look, most of their older rivals have not seen fit to change a method of presentation which had begun to look dated long before the restoration of democracy. The big conservative morning papers – Barcelona's *La Vanguardia* and *ABC*, which comes out in Madrid and Seville – both still favour a wrap-around cover with prominently displayed photographs. The evening papers – *El Noticiero Universal* and *El Correo Catalán* in Barcelona and Madrid's *El Alcázar* – at least have normal front pages (although they only offer summaries of the main stories, the full details being inside). But they are dominated by thick coloured rules that do more to confuse the eye than attract it and there is usually a bewildering variety of type faces and rules, an excessive number of boxed stories and far too many straplines (the brief phrases, often underlined, above or below the headline).

In their different ways the lay-outs of the old Madrid and Barcelona papers all reflect a concept of presentation which was outdated by the infinitely greater visual resources of television. But they also reflect the mentality of journalists who, because of censorship, became accustomed to disguising the true meaning and relative importance of news.

Not surprisingly, the older papers have been losing ground steadily to their younger rivals. After a difficult start, the vernacular papers have now won a firm foothold in their respective catchment areas, each selling between 40,000 and 50,000 a day. The three new Castilian language papers in Madrid and Barcelona are all members of that select group with circulations of over 100,000. *El País*, which passed *ABC* in the late seventies to become the biggest-selling paper in the capital, overtook *La Vanguardia* in the early eighties to become the biggest-selling paper in the country. An exception to this general rule is the ultra right-wing *El Alcázar* whose circulation has soared from less than 15,000 in 1975 to almost 100,000. This may be due in part to the nostalgia for Francoism which has gripped a certain section of the middle classes ever since the dictator's departure. But it also owes something to the fact that *El Alcázar* carries a lot of articles on or by officers in the armed forces. Many people buy it to see if they can pick up hints of military intervention.

In the late seventies the Spanish newspaper industry entered a period of acute crisis as the result of a series of otherwise unconnected factors – the deepening of the economic recession, which cut into both advertising and circulation revenue, the advent of consensus politics, which dampened the public's interest in current affairs, and the vertiginous rise in paper prices, aggravated in Spain's case by customs restrictions which forced them to buy poor-quality, home-produced newsprint at a price higher than that which they would otherwise have had to pay on the international market. The crisis was particularly acute for the established newspapers which were already losing advertising and circulation to their new rivals.

Characteristically, they turned to the state for a solution to their problems. In 1978 a joint working party was set up to see how best the government could help them out. It would be unthinkable in the United States or indeed the majority of Western European countries, but the proprietors justified their action on the grounds that one of the reasons why the privately owned press was in such a mess was because of the unfair competition it faced from the state-run media. Not only did they, like some of their European counterparts, have to fight for advertising against a government-run radio and television network, but they also had to compete for both circulation and advertising with a chain of newspapers whose losses were automatically met by the state.

In 1936 Franco had decreed the expropriation of all those newspapers which belonged to parties, unions or individuals favourable to the Republic. Four years later, the papers concerned were handed over to the *Movimiento*. The premises of the great Madrid daily *El Sol* were used to produce the Falangists' newspaper *Arriba;* the Anarchists' paper, *Solidaridad Obrera*, became *Solidaridad Nacional*; and in the provinces a string of liberal and radical local papers were turned into mouthpieces for fascism. The state's interest in the media was later boosted still further by the creation of a Madrid evening newspaper, *Pueblo*, which was to serve as the organ of the *sindicatos*. Right up until the seventies, the majority of these newspapers paid their way. *Pueblo* was the biggest-selling daily in the country. But in the last years of Franco's life their circulations plummeted and from the point of view of the new, democratic government the newspapers they inherited from the *Movimiento* and the *sindicatos* were as much an economic liability as a political embarrassment. By 1977 the thirty-six newspapers in the chain were costing the government 640 million pesetas a year. *Arriba* alone accounted for half that sum. But enfeebled as they were, the state-owned newspapers were still capable of draining enough circulation from the privately owned press to distort the operation of a free market.

The press barons' appeal to the government met with a really quite generous response. As a way of compensating them for having to buy Spanish paper, the government agreed to refund the difference between the cost of domestic and foreign newsprint. But it also undertook to provide a subsidy of one peseta per copy sold and an unspecified amount to fund the introduction of new technology. From the point of view of a free press, this arrangement – which began in 1979 – was and is a perilous one. In particular, the government never set out the criteria whereby the new technology money would be allotted, and was therefore in a position to dole it out selectively. The Socialist government has promised to put the whole arrangement on a proper footing. But the bill they propose would also provide a further indirect subsidy in the form of specially reduced postal and telecommunication charges and whether either side – journalists or politicians – should be seeking to make the press a special case in a free society is open to question.

What the talks between the newspaper executives and government officials did not resolve was the problem posed by the state's own chain. Indeed, its capacity for mischief-making was highlighted in the year that the new subsidies came into force when *Informaciones*, Madrid's only 'quality' evening newspaper and a model of enlightenment and professionalism, went bust. It is very likely that but for the competition from a heavily-subsidized *Pueblo*, *Informaciones* would have survived.

That year, the government closed six of the biggest loss-makers in the state chain, including *Arriba*, and the following year it got rid of two more. But that still left another twenty-eight, excluding *Pueblo*, which, towards the end of the UCD's period in office, were costing the treasury a cool 2,876 million pesetas a year. One, *Suroeste*, had a circulation of only 1,645 in spite of being published in a city the size of Seville. In 1981 the *Cortes* approved a UCD bill to auction them off with the proviso that co-operatives formed by the employees would be allowed to bid. The bill was opposed by the Socialists on the grounds that the newspapers concerned had effectively been stolen from their rightful owners and that to privatize them would be to endorse an injustice. But by the time that they themselves came to power, they had little option but to carry out the spirit, if not the letter, of the UCD's policy. The new government immediately closed a further six papers and put all the rest – with the exception of *Pueblo* – up for sale in the early months of 1984. More often than not they went to local businessmen and institutions. Only one was acquired by an employees' co-operative. The soccer fans' paper, *Marca*, went – somewhat oddly – to a firm which has close links with Opus Dei. But only a few had to be closed and those printers and journalists who were deprived of a job as a result of the auction have all been given jobs in the civil service. As for *Pueblo*, it too was closed a short while later, in spite of protests from the Socialist trade union, which wanted to convert it into a modern trade union newspaper.

The sale or closure of the *Movimiento* and *sindicato* papers does not mean that the state has withdrawn entirely from the world of written journalism, since it still owns the bigger of Spain's two news agencies – EFE. Successive governments have been far too preoccupied with the problem of what to do about the state-owned newspapers to worry overmuch about EFE, but it is clear that at some time in the future someone is going to have to confront the anachronism of an ostensibly free press which gets much of its routine information and illustration from a body that is wholly owned and heavily subsidized by the government.

No one visiting Spain for the first time can fail to be impressed by the news-stands in the big cities – particularly the ones on the Gran Vía in Madrid and the Ramblas in Barcelona. Shut up at night to form mysterious steel boxes on the pavements, they open out in the morning like variegated tropical blooms. Every available space on the walls inside, on the counter and on the opened-out doors is taken up with the vividly coloured covers of every conceivable kind of magazine. Usually there are so many on sale that the owner of the stall has to set out trestles at the front and sides to accommodate them. There are news magazines and general and special interest magazines, including a good few published in the States and elsewhere in Europe. There are humorous magazines, educational magazines, 'adult' magazines (for gays and lesbians as well as for heterosexuals), literary and scientific reviews, part works, comics for children and comics for adults.

The news-stands are a tribute not only to the Spaniards' genius for display, but to the resilience of the Spanish magazine trade, for if there is any business that has gone through the wringer during the transition then it is this one. As in most countries, it survives by filling the gaps left by the newspaper industry. None of the Spanish newspapers, for example, has an equivalent of the social diaries or gossip columns that you find in the British and American papers. As a result Spain has a plethora of highly profitable glossy magazines devoted to the lives and loves of the famous. The pioneer was *¡Hola!*, founded in 1944. Since then it has been joined by others like *Pronto, Diez Minutos, Lecturas, Semana* and *Garbo*. These magazines – generically known as the *Prensa de Corazón* (Press of the Heart) – occupy six of the top ten places in the magazine sales table and sell more than two and three quarter million copies a week.

Sensing another gap in newspaper coverage, the magazines did their best to satisfy the clamour for uninhibited reporting of current affairs during the latter years of the dictatorship and the early years of the monarchy when the newspapers were unwilling or unable to do so. The first opposition current affairs magazine was the quaintly titled *Cuadernos para el Diálogo* (Notebooks for the Dialogue), which was founded by a group of Christian Democrats back in 1963. But *Cuadernos* was above all an intellectual publication with a penchant for the results of sociological investigations. The first real news magazine was *Cambio 16*, which hit the news-stands in 1972. Similar to *Time* or *Newsweek*, it rapidly achieved a high standard of professionalism and was followed in to the market by a host of other, similar weeklies. By 1977 there were fifteen of them selling a total of two million copies a week. But as *El País* and the other new newspapers began to assert themselves they started to wilt. *Cuadernos* was one of the first to go. Others followed in rapid succession. Today *Cambio 16* is the only survivor of those giddy days, although it has now been joined by a new, mildly sensationalist rival, *Tiempo*.

Cambio 16 was the product *par excellence* of the rather serious, impassioned atmosphere that prevailed in the years leading up to Franco's death. But the magazine which best reflects the more liberated spirit of the years that followed is *Interviú*. Founded in Barcelona soon after the end of the dictatorship, *Interviú* set out to provide its readers with the two things that they had been denied under Franco – uninhibited coverage of politics and pictures of naked women. It has done so in a way that has proved particularly appealing to the Spanish market. Instead of wrapping its reports in code and metaphor in the way that had been customary until then, *Interviú* went straight to the politicians themselves, asked them blunt, provocative questions and printed the answers word for word. Rather than rely on the professional, usually foreign, models who were beginning to make their appearance in other magazines, *Inter-*

viú approached Spanish actresses and singers with the beguiling proposition that by shedding their clothes they would be putting their democratic credentials beyond question. The message projected to the readers was – and is – that sexual and political liberation are one and the same thing. To anyone who did not live in Spain during the late seventies it is a peculiar concoction, and for the non-Spaniard it is made even more peculiar by the regular inclusion of full-colour photo-features on surgical operations, killings and accidents, often made up of pictures considered too explicit for use in the daily press. But it is nevertheless a highly successful formula. When it hit its peak in 1978 *Interviú* was selling almost 750,000 copies a week. Since then, its circulation has fallen off, as has that of most magazines in Spain, but it remains among the top ten.

Interviú acts as a unique bridge between current affairs journalism and what H. L. Mencken once called one-handed reading. By contrast with the news magazine market, the erotic magazine market has stood up well to the changes in fashion that have swept through Spain in the post-Franco era – further evidence perhaps of the way that magazines prosper in areas which the daily press neglects. Contrary to initial predictions, slick foreign products like *Playboy*, *Penthouse* and *Lui* have not swamped the domestic output. Spain's bestselling 'adult' magazine is none of these, but a quintessentially Iberian product called *Lib*, which is in effect the parish circular of Barcelona's clubland. The photo spreads are of well-known strippers and other 'artistes' and there are reports on nightlife in the major cities of Spain and elsewhere. In *Lib*, sex is not presented as an intimate activity but as something social, communal, Dionysian. In fact, you could almost see *Lib* as the erotic version of *¡Hola!*.

The biggest selling magazine in Spain, though, is neither *Lib* nor *¡Hola!*. Nor is it *Interviú* or *Cambio 16*. It is the weekly television review *Tele-Indiscreta*. Surprisingly perhaps, the Spanish are a nation of TV addicts. The viewing figures for Europe as a whole reveal a situation that is precisely the opposite of what you would expect. By and large the people who watch television least are those with a reputation for being withdrawn and who live in the colder, northern countries, whereas the people who watch television most are those who live in the warmer, southern nations and have a reputation for being gregarious. There is an exception to this general rule. Britain, a northerly country with a proverbially reserved population, has the highest viewing figures of all, but this may be because of the exceptionally high quality of British television's output. Leaving aside the British, the people who spend most time glued to their TV sets are the Spanish, followed by the Portuguese and the Italians. Almost every home in Spain has a television set – even those which lack other, more useful amenities. Andalusia, for example, is the hottest region in Europe yet there are more televisions there than refrigerators. The influence of television in Spanish society is further increased by the fact that Spaniards, as we have seen, take only a relatively small proportion of their information and opinion from written sources. It is no exaggeration to say that whoever controls television in Spain stands fair to control the mood and outlook of the nation and this explains why successive governments have taken such an intense interest in who controls it and what they use it for.

Televisión Española (TVE) was set up as a state monopoly in 1956. As with every sort of creative activity under Franco, the programmes it transmitted were subject to censorship. But TVE was subject to a unique double filter. First, the programming plans were scrutinized by 'advisory commissions' made up of judges, priests, officers in the armed forces and the like. Then, the finished product, whether made in Spain or bought from abroad, underwent what was euphemistically described as 'content evaluation'. Partly as a result, the censorship in television was much more stringent than in other areas – things that were permitted in films and on stage were not allowed on to the small screen.

In 1980 *El País* got hold of the reports of one of Franco's censors, a Dominican monk called Antonio Sánchez Vázquez who was responsible for scrutinizing material imported from abroad. These are the cuts he ordered in Billy Wilder's *The Lost Weekend*:

> 1) Kiss at the point of farewell.
> 2) When he steals the woman's handbag, eliminate the shots in which she and her companion behave with excessive affection (two or three times). At least, temper these shots.
> 3) Kiss and conversation while holding one another. Temper the kiss.
> 4) After the nurse says good night . . . one of the patients suffers *delirium tremens*. Allow it to start, cut quickly to when the doctors come in and he makes off with the doctor's coat.

But Fr Antonio was not just concerned with sex and violence. After seeing a French comedy film he wrote that 'Although the intention may be humorous, the Gestapo and their chief in Paris are held up to ridicule in their behaviour and references to the *Führer*.' Indeed, he seems to have had a remarkably sensitive set of political antennae for a priest. Mindful of Spain's position as a colonial power, he cut from a film called *Jaguar* a phrase about how the English exploited the Africans. Soon afterwards, relations with Britain entered one of their periodic crises over Gibraltar and the records show that Fr Antonio sent in another report suggesting that the phrase be reinserted. Perhaps his most memorable remark, though, accompanied a recommendation not to show a film called *The Morals of Mrs Pulska*. '"Strong" subject,' he wrote. 'Criticism of hypocrisy. I warn you this will cause a rumpus.'

The censors did not disappear with the ending of the dictatorship. Fr Antonio was one of four on the staff of TVE as late as 1980, although by that time their job was not so much to cut material as to find ways of toning it down – substituting 'dung' for 'shit' in subtitles, for instance. More importantly, the advent of democracy has not freed TVE from control by the government. In this respect it was particularly unfortunate that the first Prime Minister of a democratic Spain should have been a man who had held high office in RTVE, the state corporation which controls both state-run radio and television, under Franco. Suárez had been controller of the first television channel and subsequently Director-General. He was thus thoroughly imbued with the Francoist notion of television as an arm of government. It was only at the insistence of the Socialists and Communists that the 1977 Moncloa Pacts included a commitment to set up a governing body, responsible for guaranteeing RTVE's objectivity, scrutinizing its finances and – most important of all – drawing up a charter. Even then, the composition of this *Consejo Rector*, as it was called, was heavily weighted in favour of the ruling party. The charter which it drew up for RTVE, and which came into effect in 1979, created a new governing body called the *Consejo de Administración* made up of six members elected by the lower house of the *Cortes*. Its membership tends therefore to reflect the composition of Congress and Congress will always have more deputies supporting the government than opposing it. So far the *Consejo de Administración* has proved itself to be a pretty toothless watchdog. Although the charter says that the Director-General cannot be replaced except for manifest incompetence, the UCD managed to get through three of them in its last two years in office.

The arrival of the Socialists brought yet another new Director-General, a commercial lawyer called José María Calviño who had previously been the PSOE's representative on the *Consejo de Administración*. But it did not bring about any obvious change in attitude. A matter of weeks after Calviño's appointment an edition of the current affairs programme, *La Clave*, which was to have featured a rebel Socialist councillor, was abruptly cancelled. In 1985, Calviño incurred the wrath of Fraga by sanctioning an unashamedly one-sided report on his time as Minister of the Interior and then admitting in a radio interview that he would personally do all he could to prevent the opposition leader returning to power. Fraga's outrage soon came to be shared by other critics of the government – in the campaign leading up to the NATO referendum, the 'box' was overtly manipulated to bring the electorate around to the Socialists' new-found point of view. So far, however, the government has refused to dismiss Calviño, although it has agreed that future Director-Generals should be elected by Congress.

The earliest allegations came soon after the end of the dictatorship. In 1977 a group of workers set up an 'anti-corruption committee' and the following year *Cambio 16* published a lengthy report exposing some of the worst abuses – inflated salaries, people drawing two salaries for doing (or pretending to do) jobs in both radio and television, members of staff being paid on a freelance rate for work they did in RTVE's time, and so on. 'There are those who earn, literally, twice as much as the King,' remarked the authors of the report, who among other things unearthed the case of a gentleman who, while living and working in Brazil where he was the representative of a Spanish company, was earning 65,000 pesetas a week for 'co-ordinating' a programme which, as the magazine commented, he probably never even saw.

It was largely because of all this extravagance and graft that RTVE had become unable to pay for its expenditure with the revenue it received from advertising. It first had to ask the government for a subsidy in 1976 and the whole of the next year was spent in a state of acute financial crisis. It was clear that unless something were done to sort out the corporation's finances, RTVE would soon get into the habit of taking ever larger hand-outs from the state. In 1978 Suárez sent in the government's auditors to find out where the money was going. Unfortunately for the government the report they produced found its way to *El País*, which found enough material in it to fill seven articles.

Written with a wry sense of humour, the auditors' report revealed a degree of inefficiency and dishonesty that at times beggars belief. For a start, there were no proper accounts. 'There is an abundance, even an excess, of accounting data,' the authors of the report remarked, 'but one cannot speak of a genuine system of accounting. It is impossible to draw up a balance or calculate the income and outgoings . . .' They found, for example, that the box-office takings of the RTVE's symphony orchestra were being paid into a bank account opened by the administrator, who also used it to meet the orchestra's day-to-day expenses.

After nine months of investigation, the government's accountants confessed that they were unable to say for certain how many people worked for RTVE or how much property and equipment it owned. There were departments with far too many people, others with far too few. There were employees with job descriptions that meant nothing and others who were called one thing but did another – 'In RTVE, there are production assistants presenting programmes, reporters who direct, directors who present, commissionaires who film and even radio announcers who'll do their job in front of the cameras if they're paid a bonus, with which anything is possible.' RTVE employees were entitled to a seemingly endless list of extra payments by reason of the jobs they did, the position they held and so on. According to the report, thirteen members of the staff earned more than 1,000,000 pesetas a year in bonuses alone. That was without overtime. By the time the auditors arrived at Prado del Rey – RTVE's headquarters outside Madrid – the staff had managed to secure a five-day week of seven-hour days which had the effect of maximizing the amount of money that needed to be paid for out-of-hours working.

Huge numbers of books and records and large amounts of clothing and film were found to be missing. In fact, theft was so widespread that there was a special euphemism for stolen goods at RTVE. They were called *depósitos personales* (personal stores). Theft apart, the auditors noted that there seemed to be genuine confusion in people's minds over where to draw the line between what belonged to the corporation and what belonged to individuals. 'There are cases of directors and producers who regard their programmes as private property and, in extreme cases, flatly refuse to return them.' This could explain why so little archive material is shown on Spanish television. The government investigation also discovered that it was customary for performers to hang on to the clothes in which they appeared and that this had given rise to a tax dodge whereby artistes received a share – sometimes a large share – of their payment in clothing. 'To look at some contracts,' the authors of the report remarked, 'you'd think that RTVE hired its performers naked and then proceeded to dress them.'

Programme planning was so chaotic that programme makers had far too little time in which to prepare. Producers and directors often agreed to ideas without seeing a script and only got to look at one a few days before the programme concerned was due to be televised. The result was that they were virtually forced to accept whatever they were given.

El País's 'scoop' provoked a lengthy and indignant rebuttal from the then Director-General. But two years later an internal audit of RTVE's 'flagship' programme, a satellite link-up between Spain and the Spanish-speaking countries of Latin America called *300 Millones*, which was also leaked to *El País*, showed that waste and corruption were as prevalent as ever.

The effect of all this on the quality of the output can be gauged by RTVE's inability to sell its programmes abroad. The only idea originating in Spain to have had any impact on the European market is the quiz programme *Un, Dos, Tres*. Interestingly, 'light entertainment' does not enjoy the same immense popularity among Spaniards that it does with other viewing publics. The audience figures reflect that same thirst for learning of which I spoke earlier in the book. Documentaries are particularly popular – Jacques Cousteau's programmes have been high in the Top Ten for years now – and so are RTVE's two main current affairs programmes *Informe Semanal* on Channel One and *La Clave* on Channel Two. To an outsider, though, the most remarkable thing about Spanish television is that programmes frequently do not come on at the time for which they are announced. Sometimes they are half an hour late. Sometimes they are half an hour early. And on occasions, they do not come on at all because the production team has failed to get the programme together in time. It is to be hoped that the introduction of commercial television, which the Socialists have finally agreed to, will raise standards.

Radio in Spain, which is part state-run and part private, is professional and entertaining. The Spaniards are natural broadcasters. They are good speakers (as the Hispanicist Ian Gibson once said: 'When did you ever meet an inarticulate Spaniard?') and they realize instinctively that radio is at its best when it is spontaneous, flexible and just a little unstructured.

Until the civil war, the only stations in Spain were private ones. But in 1937 Franco created a state network, *Radio Nacional de España* (RNE). During the course of his rule he also allowed pressure groups within the regime such as the *Movimiento*, the *sindicatos* and the Church to set up networks of their own. By 1964 there were some 450 stations all competing for space on the medium wave (there are no long-wave stations in Spain). By a series of measures the government succeeded in getting the number down to less than 200 by the mid seventies. But this was still far higher than envisaged by the 1975 Geneva Conference which allotted only three medium-wave networks to each country. Spain was unable to meet the requirements of the Geneva Conference, but in 1978 it did manage to cut the number of medium-wave networks to four – RNE, whose first channel is broadcast on medium wave (the other two being on FM); *Radio Cadena Española* (RCE), which is made up of stations formerly owned by the *Movimiento* and the *sindicatos*; *Cadena de Ondas Populares Españolas* (COPE), which is owned by the Church and, finally, the largest of the commercial networks, SER. Stations not belonging to one of these four networks were either closed or transferred to FM. The four networks with a presence on the medium wave have since been joined by a Catalan radio station. All five broadcast on FM as well. The most popular by far is SER with a total average daily audience of more than six million.

Since 1978 the focus of interest has shifted from the medium wave to FM. In 1982 the government redistributed the franchises, allowing a number of new stations and networks on to the air. The result was to raise dramatically the status, quality and popularity of FM broadcasting. A number of leading radio personalities have been lured away from the medium wave and they in turn have persuaded an extra half million listeners to tune in to FM. Today more Spaniards listen to FM than to medium wave.

The possibilities which radio offers for communicating the news as it is happening or at least within a very short time of it happening went virtually unexploited under Franco for the obvious reason that the faster the news was processed the more difficult it was to censor. In any case, the commercial stations were only allowed to carry the news bulletins prepared by RNE. Since the ending of RNE's monopoly in 1977, the coverage has become altogether faster and better, as radio's performance during the abortive coup attempt showed. The radio correspondents in the *Cortes* press gallery kept up a running commentary until the moment that Tejero ordered his men to loose off their fusillade, and throughout the night that followed their colleagues back in the studios succeeded in conveying urgency and concern without appearing to panic. A lot of Spaniards feel that the broadcasters 'held their hand' during that anguished night and there is now an affection and admiration for the medium as a whole which it would be difficult to find in other countries.

CHAPTER TWELVE

The White Goddess's revenge

The scars left by the civil war healed at different rates according to where they were inflicted. The economy regained its pre-war level in 1954. Politics returned to their normal course in 1977. But the arts have still not recovered from the civil war and until quite recently there was a widespread feeling that they never would.

In 1936 Spain was what you might call a creative superpower. She had given the world three of its greatest contemporary painters – Picasso, Dali and Miró. She could lay claim to one of the finest established composers – Manuel de Falla – and to several of the more promising younger ones like the Catalan, Roberto Gerhardt, and the Valencian, Joaquín Rodrigo. Her fledgling film industry had already managed to produce a director of the calibre of Buñuel. In literature, the leading figures of the celebrated 'Generation of '98' – the philosophers Unamuno and Ortega y Gasset, the novelist Pío Baroja, the playwright Jacinto Benavente and the poets Valle-Inclán, Machado and Jiménez – were all still alive, able to advise and influence younger writers. But more importantly, a further generation, variously known as the 'Generation of '25' or the 'Generation of '27', was just entering maturity. Outside Spain, the best known of the writers who belonged to it is Federico García Lorca. But there were many others of equal if not greater stature – poets like Rafael Alberti, Vicente Aleixandre, Luis Cernuda, Gerardo Diego, Jorge Guillén and Pedro Salinas and novelists like Max Aub, Francisco Ayala and Rosa Chacel.

The vast majority of Spain's artists and intellectuals took the side of the Republic against the Nationalists. Some, like Lorca, were killed. Of those who survived, most fled into exile. Once the fiercest period of retribution was over, they faced a grim choice. Returning home offered an opportunity to re-establish contact with the cultural traditions of their homeland, but it also meant handing the regime a propaganda victory and resigning themselves to a lifetime of censorship. Staying abroad meant losing touch with their roots but it did guarantee them their creative integrity. Miró returned, but the majority opted to remain in exile. Seen as a set of individual personal decisions it was understandable. Seen as a development in the nation's cultural history it was catastrophic. Most of what the exiles wrote, painted, sculpted and filmed went completely unnoticed within Spain until the sixties when Fraga at the Ministry of Information and Tourism eased the restrictions on imported works. But by then, much of it was ten, fifteen, even twenty years old and of little or no use as a stimulus or inspiration.

The intellectuals' opposition to Franco meant that throughout his dictatorship he and his supporters harboured a deep suspicion towards all things intellectual. Culture *per se* became dangerous. 'At home, we didn't even listen to the radio,' the Catalan rock singer Pau Riba later recalled. 'Books were simply bound objects that you didn't touch.' What makes his reminiscence all the more remarkable is that Pau Riba does not come from a family of shop-keepers or factory workers, but from a line of eminent literary figures – his grandfather, for example, was the poet and philologist, Carles Riba.

The artists and intellectuals born in the twenties, thirties and forties had to make their way as best they could without guides or maps. In retrospect what is surprising about Franco's Spain is not that there was so little good music, art and literature but that there was so much. Probably the best-known creative work of the Franco era was Rodrigo's popular classic, the *Concierto de Aranjuez*. But the same period also saw the emergence of a number of outstanding painters like Tápies, Saura, Gordillo and Millares and at least one internationally renowned sculptor in Eduardo Chillida. Alternately duping and defying the censors, playwrights like Antonio Buero Vallejo and film-makers like Luis García Berlanga, Juan Bardem and Carlos Saura managed to create works of depth and integrity. The printed word became a medium of protest – a way of recording the shallowness and hypocrisy of Franco's Spain. The pioneers were the poet Damaso Alonso and the novelists Camilo José Cela and Miguel Delibes, who began to make an impact in the late forties. Then came an entire generation of writers committed to 'social realism' of which perhaps the most talented representative was Juan Goytisolo.

But by no stretch of the imagination could Franco's Spain have been described as a major force in world culture. Indeed, it was probably incapable of becoming one while only a very small proportion of the state's resources was devoted to cultural activities. The lack of encouragement and opportunity prompted many creative young Spaniards to seek their fortune elsewhere. The conductor Jesús López

Cobos, who became general director of the Berlin Opera, Josep María Flotats, star of the *Comédie Française*, Victor Ullate, principal male dancer in Maurice Bejart's 20th Century Ballet and his wife Carmen Rocha, prima ballerina of the Gulbenkian Ballet, are just a few examples of the cultural 'brain drain' of the Franco era.

The end of the dictatorship, the advent of democracy and the lifting of censorship created widespread expectation. Inside as well as outside Spain it was felt that a torrent of pent-up creativity was about to be released that would put Spain back into the artistic and intellectual vanguard. Spain according to this view was like an athlete, chained around and weighted down. What its proponents failed to grasp was that the weights and chains had been on for almost forty years and many of the athlete's muscles had long since turned to flab. The New Spanish Renaissance failed to materialize and the pundits shrugged their shoulders and turned away in despair. Some said that Spain would never recover from the civil war and the forty years of cultural abandonment which followed. Others predicted it would take fifty or a hundred years.

But behind their backs, and within only the last few years, things have begun to stir. The period immediately following Franco's death was one of tremendous disorientation and introspection. The regime which had provided so many creative Spaniards with a target on which to unleash their energies had been whisked away as if overnight. While the regime's supporters were complaining that '*Con Franco vivíamos mejor*' (We lived better with Franco), the novelist Manuel Vázquez Montalbán spoke for many of his fellow intellectuals when he remarked that '*Contra Franco vivíamos mejor*' (We lived better *against* Franco). At the same time, there were new freedoms to exploit and influences to absorb. Sex was no longer taboo and the temptation to describe or depict it proved irresistible to all but the most ascetic. Then there were the exiles who returned to Spain in considerable numbers and whose work, it was felt, had to be published or exhibited and then assessed before any further steps were taken. As for the public, a lot of Spaniards found that they were too worried about the fate of democracy to be over-concerned with the fate of the arts. This rather abnormal period ended in the early eighties. To some extent, it was simply that people had grown tired of sexploitation and had begun to decide what of the exiles' experience and output was worth re-incorporating. But it also had something to do with Tejero's abortive coup which, while it may have fulfilled people's worst fears, also dispelled them – like the cloudburst which comes at the end of a thundery day. All of a sudden, there is a feeling of excitement in the air that presages great things to come.

So far, the signs of recovery have been unevenly distributed. But it is noticeable that the recovery has been slowest and weakest in those art forms, such as the novel and the theatre, which were most exploited for political ends under Franco, and strongest and fastest in those such as art and cinema which, either by their nature or because of the rigour of the censorship applied to them, were of little or no use to the democratic opposition.

In *En Ciernes*, published the year after Franco's death, the Catalan novelist Juan Benet wrote that:

> Literature does not forgive. It evolves in a different way from society. It has its gods and cults and it likes nothing less than for its ritual offices to be used for purposes other than purely literary ones. The White Goddess is fairly spiteful and sooner or later she takes her revenge on those who claim to love or worship her but whose thoughts are in fact fixed on another deity.

By the time *En Ciernes* was published, a lot of Spain's better writers had come to the same conclusion as Benet. In fact, the earliest departure from 'social realism' had been made no less than fifteen years earlier with the publication of Luis Martín Santos's novel, *Tiempo de silencio*. It had the plot of a 'social' novel – it was the story of a feud set amid the poverty and squalor of the late forties – but it was primarily concerned with style and language. Martín Santos, who was killed in a car accident in 1964, was half a decade ahead of his contemporaries. It was not until 1966 that his fellow-writers began to desert the 'social' genre. In prose the transition was marked by the publication of Juan Goytisolo's *Señas de identidad*, in poetry by José Angel Valente's *El inocente* and Jaime Gil de Biedma's *Moralidades*.

As far as poetry was concerned the abandonment of 'social realism' heralded the appearance of a new generation of writers – the so-called *novísimos*, whose work was characterized by an adventurous admixture of antiquated and vernacular language, an interest in symbolism and a fascination with the media culture. Unrepentant social realists regarded them as decadent, reactionary *señoritos,** but the *novísimos* saw themselves as successors to the Generation of '27 and seem to have been regarded as such by the older poets – or at least by Aleixandre who wrote a prologue to one of their earliest anthologies. The *novísimos* were – and are – poets of considerable stature. Pere Gimferrer's *Arde el mar*, published in 1966, Guillermo Carnero's *El Sueño de Escipión* (1973), Antonio

---

* Although strictly speaking no more nor less than the masculine equivalent of *señorita*, *señorito* has acquired a distinctively pejorative connotation. It is used to denote a rich, idle young man – a playboy or a dilettante.

Collinas's *Sepulcro en Tarquinia* (1976) and Luis Antonio de Villena's *Hymnica* (1979) are regarded throughout the Hispanic world as major works.

As far as prose was concerned, no similar generation emerged to fill the gap left by 'social realism'. Of the prose writers who have reached maturity since 1966, only one – Juan Benet – has achieved universal critical acclaim and he now stands head and shoulders above his contemporaries.

It is not easy to explain why the novelists have lagged behind the poets in the years since 'social realism' went out of fashion, but one reason could be the success in recent years of South American novelists. Several Spanish authors were so impressed by their achievements that they were seduced into imitating them, with predictably disappointing results. Ironically, Spain's novelists enjoy hardly any reputation in South America whereas her poets have considerable standing.

The gap has not been closed since Franco's death. The youngest poets, most of whom for some reason come from predominantly rural areas like Castile, Valencia and Andalusia, have begun to reject the Baroque mannerisms of the *novísimos* while accepting their commitment to aesthetic purity. The singularities of these young poets have raised hopes, if not yet expectations, that a new generation may be about to emerge which will carry Spanish poetry forward into new terrain.

Those who work in and with prose are altogether more pessimistic. 'The great discovery we all expected has not materialized. We are paying the cultural debt of forty years of dictatorship,' lamented a friend who is editorial director of one of the big Barcelona publishing houses. Even so, there have been some encouraging developments, since the end of the seventies. Benet has embarked on a cycle of novels about the civil war which, it is hoped, will be the definitive literary work on Spain's fratricidal struggle. Gimferrer, the pioneer and theorist among the *novísimos*, has abandoned poetry for prose and the publication in 1983 of his first full-length novel, *Fortuny*, was the nearest thing in recent years to a literary sensation. The period since Franco's death has also seen the arrival on the scene of a wave of young women novelists, mostly from Catalonia, of whom the best known and most successful is Monserrat Roig. Then there is the extraordinary mission undertaken by the young writer, Julian Ríos.

In the early seventies Ríos – with the encouragement of the Mexican writer Octavio Paz – began a work which, in the words of one critic, aims 'to integrate the whole of universal literature, destroy and construct the literary language of its time and take up the most audacious and scandalous position in the vanguard in order to move ahead of it . . .'

Quite some task for an author who had published hardly anything before he embarked on it. Ríos intends that the as yet unnamed series will consist of five volumes plus an appendix. The first of them, *Larva*, which took him ten years to write, was published in 1984. It is an account of an orgy written primarily in Castilian which hops at intervals into a variety of other languages including Bengali. The notes which appear on the left-hand pages are a commentary on the text, which appears on the right-hand pages. As with Sterne, the writing is interspersed with diagrams. If Ríos's work succeeds it will provide the impetus which Spanish prose writing has been in need of for years. But while his fellow-writers are impressed by Ríos's dedication and ambition, many of them have deep misgivings about what he has so far produced. As one of them put it: 'What is the point of doing what Joyce did, only sixty years later and in Castilian?'

From the point of view of the publishers the most profitable development has been the growth of the Spanish crime novel. The earliest '*novela policiaca*' written in Castilian was Mario Lacruz's *El inocente*, published back in the fifties. But the genre did not acquire any real impetus until it was discovered and adopted by Manuel Vázquez Montalbán, who had been a minor figure among the *novísimos*. Vázquez Montalbán writes with skill and verve and he has created in Inspector Pepe Carvalho an engagingly human hero. Several other writers have now begun to follow in his footsteps. A Spanish Simenon or Christie is no longer unthinkable.

In the last century Richard Ford wrote that Spanish theatre suffered from 'the steady hostility of the clergy, who opposed the rival to their own religious spectacles and church melodramas . . . The clergy attacked the stage by denying burial to the actors when dead, who, when alive, were not allowed to call themselves *Don*.' The Church's hostility evaporated a long time ago. But traces of its legacy can still, I think, be discerned in the Spanish public's attitude to the theatre. It is not that they object to it, but by and large they do not value their dramatic heritage as highly, nor do they respect their actors and actresses as much, as in other countries.

Spain is frequently credited with possessing the richest theatrical tradition in the world after England. Yet the country which produced Lope de Vega, Tirso de Molina, Guillén de Castro, Calderón, Benavente and Guimerá did not have a repertory company dedicated solely to staging the classics until 1985 when the *Compañía Nacional de Teatro Clásico* came into being under the direction of the actor and producer Adolfo Marsillach. There are over thirty theatres in Madrid alone which, even allowing for the fact that a lot of them are quite small and rather shabby, is a healthy figure for a city of only three million. However, most of those theatres stay in business only because of the ludicrously low price of seats. And the reason why managements can keep down the cost of seats is that the actors and actresses are severely exploited. Until 1972 the majority of plays were put on twice a night (at seven and half past ten or eleven) for seven nights a week. By threatening to strike, the actors and actresses succeeded in securing a day off. But the practice of staging two performances a night is still widespread even though most theatres do not now put on two showings every night of the week.

The role of the state in the Spanish theatre is directed towards ensuring that a modicum of quality work is staged. There are two ways it does this. The first is by subsidizing commercial theatres which undertake to stage 'serious' works. The second is through the *Centro Dramático Nacional*, which was set up in 1978. The CDN, which is based at the Teatro María Guerrero in Madrid, is not a repertory company like, say, the National Theatre in Britain. It is a production centre headed by a director which vets original scripts and ideas for revivals and then puts on a season of quality productions, contracting different actors for each of them. The María Guerrero is used for staging mainstream plays, while experimental works are put on at another theatre run by the CDN, the Sala Olimpia. Shortly after coming to power, the Socialists took the adventurous step of appointing a thirty-year-old Catalan producer, Lluis Pasqual, to become director of the CDN. As a way of signalling his intention of broadening the CDN's appeal, Pasqual began his first season with a comedy which was staged, free of charge, beside the lake in Madrid's Retiro Park. Since then, he has put on recitals and concerts, arranged seminars on the productions being staged by the CDN and sent some of its productions on tour.

The basic structural problem of the Spanish theatre is that it is over-centralized. The vast majority of Spain's theatres are in Madrid and Barcelona. According to a survey by the Ministry of Culture published in 1978, more than 95 per cent of the people who live in towns and villages with a population of less than 10,000 have never been to a theatre.

There was a time when the provinces were packed with theatres but competition from radio, television and the cinema combined with government indifference put all but a handful of them out of business. In the long term, the Socialists plan to renovate some of the country's several hundred dilapidated provincial playhouses and set up a touring circuit of publicly owned venues. But, as a first step and as a way of rekindling a taste for drama in the provinces, the government has provided incentives for the impresarios of Madrid and Barcelona to take their productions on tour.

Under Franco, the theatre was employed for political ends

more even perhaps than literature had been. The censors seemed less concerned with what was put on the stage than with what was shown on the screen, maybe because the theatre had a smaller audience than either cinema or television. Authors were not free to write whatever they pleased, but provided they wrapped up their criticism in metaphors they stood a much better chance of seeing their work performed than the writers of critical screenplays or TV scripts. During the last years of the dictatorship, the theatre acquired an enthusiastic and sizeable following among those members of the middle class who were opposed to Franco's rule and the playwrights of the time were only too happy to provide them with plays criticizing the regime, albeit in a round-about fashion. The end of the dictatorship created a serious crisis. Once the system against which Spain's playwrights had directed their energies was removed, much of modern Spanish drama became irrelevant. With the exception of Antonio Buero Vallejo, virtually the entire theatrical canon of the Franco era has been put into cold storage. Adolfo Marsillach once remarked that 'We shall have to wait until the same authors write new works in which the little old lady in black is no longer Spain and the local bigwig isn't Franco.' But unfortunately those same authors have so far shown themselves to be incapable of adapting. Only a couple of playwrights whose works were being staged in Franco's Spain have had their plays performed with any frequency since the advent of democracy.

The problem for the impresarios, therefore, is that there is virtually nothing written in Spain during the past fifty years which is worth staging. One solution has been to replace political titillation with sexual titillation. The years immediately following Franco's death saw a succession of reviews and farces whose principal aim is to secure the exposure of as much human flesh as possible. Another response has been to retain the element of political criticism, but reverse its direction. Just as the theatre had been a platform for democratic ideas during the dictatorship, so it has become a platform for authoritarian ideas in a democracy. At the beginning of 1978 the Teatro Arlequín in Madrid put on a play called *Un cero a la izquierda* (*A Nought for the Left*), written and directed by the leader of a minor provincial repertory company, one Eloy Herrera. It was a runaway success. Written as a satire on those who had conveniently switched their allegiances from totalitarianism to democracy, *Un cero a la izquierda* was not of itself anti-democratic. But it provoked scenes that were undeniably anti-democratic. On more than one occasion the audience broke into the fascist anthem, *Cara al sol*, and there were regular '*¡Vivas!*' for Franco and '*¡Mueras!*' for his successors. Herrera's next work was unequivocally Francoist and it was not long before others were imitating him, notably Fernando Vizcaíno Casas, a lawyer-turned-author, who at about that time was having immense success with a novel, *Y al tercer año, resucitó*, which poured scorn on democracy while bathing the Franco era in affectionate nostalgia.

The most generalized response to the crisis has been to dig back into the past and revive plays written before the civil war. The last few years have seen the re-staging of works by Valle-Inclán, García Lorca, Muñoz Seca, Jardiel Poncela, Casona and Azaña. The one solution that has not been tried is to put on serious works by new authors. The blame for this cannot be laid entirely or even principally at the doors of the impresarios. In 1984 Lluis Pasqual told me that of the 500 plays sent to the CDN since he had taken over, he would not have considered staging more than about three. He had regretfully come to the conclusion that Spain was suffering from the same script crisis which for some reason is affecting all the Latin countries at the moment. In spite of this the 1983–4 season saw an unexpected increase in box-office takings and actors, producers and impresarios alike are keeping their fingers crossed that the theatre will draw some benefit from the revival which is now beginning to gather strength and pace in the other arts.

CHAPTER THIRTEEN

THE STATE OF THE ARTS

The symbol of Spain's renewed success in the arts is the slender golden statuette which a young Spanish film director, José Luis Garcí, collected from the Hollywood Motion Picture Academy in April 1983. Garcí's Oscar – for best foreign film – came as a complete surprise. He is regarded within Spain as a competent but not outstanding director and his film, *Volver a empezar*, had been a box-office flop in his native country. Spaniards found the subject matter – a romance between a returning exile and his childhood sweetheart – too sentimental for their taste. No doubt its popularity with the Hollywood jury owed something to its strongly American flavour – the principal character had spent much of his life in the United States and the theme tune was Cole Porter's 'Begin the Beguine'. *Volver a empezar* nevertheless demonstrated what sort of impression a Spanish director was capable of making on a foreign audience when he had the aid of a bit of common ground.

The post-Franco era has seen the emergence of several first-class young directors, among them Jaime Armiñan, Fernando Trueba, Manuel Gutiérrez Aragón and Pilar Miró whom the Socialists put in charge of cinematic affairs at the Ministry of Culture.* They have succeeded where, by and large, the playwrights and novelists have failed in capturing the atmosphere of the new Spain. They have made films about urban youth, like Trueba's *Opera prima*, about fascist violence, like Gutiérrez Aragón's *Camada negra*, and about some of the most dramatic events in Spain's recent history. More importantly, though, their attempts to transcend day-to-day issues and events have frequently

* Miró's appointment was supremely ironic because she had spent more than a year at the start of the eighties battling with the authorities to get permission for the showing of a film of hers, *El crimen de Cuenca*, which had upset the military.

met with success. Armiñan's *El nido* is perhaps the best example – a haunting, allegorical film about the power of love and the lure of the irrational.

Meanwhile, although Bardem has been out of fashion – and frequently out of work – for much of the period since Franco's death, both the other major figures of the Franco era, Berlanga and Saura, have continued to turn out films of substance and quality. Berlanga has devoted himself to a trilogy about the Spanish aristocracy – a hilarious but affectionate look at a disappearing class in which the leading part is played by an actor who is himself a Marquis. Saura's output has been more uneven – he has made truly awful films like *Dulces horas* but he has also made truly excellent ones like *Carmen*.

The cinematic successes of recent years have been achieved against a background of continuous conflict within the industry between, on the one hand, the producers and directors and, on the other, the cinema owners and managers. The nub of the issue is how many foreign films should be let in. Spain has long been an important market for films. Franco's rule turned one of the raciest countries in the world into one of the most tedious. Films offered people some of the glamour and excitement that was missing from their lives. At one time, Spain had more cinema seats per 1,000 head of population than any country in the world except the United States. Cinema-going became a firmly entrenched habit and in recent years cinema audiences have declined more slowly in Spain than in other parts of Europe.

But what really makes Spain such a gold mine for foreign distributors is the fact that the majority of foreign films released there are dubbed. An example of the effect of dubbing was provided recently by the British film *Chariots of Fire*. It was originally sent to Spain in a subtitled version and flopped. Then it won an Oscar. Re-released with voice-overs it was a box-office smash. The prevalence of dubbing is yet another legacy of Franco's rule – it was made compulsory in 1941 so as to give the censors total control over the content of imported films. During the dictatorship, the dubbing business grew into a major industry. Today there are many highly paid actors and actresses in Spain who do very little except dubbing and their voices – which are selected to resemble in tone and pitch those of the stars whose lines they speak – are inextricably linked in the public mind with those stars. As far as the Spanish cinemagoer is concerned, Robert Redford, Steve McQueen and Woody Allen all speak perfect Spanish and some would no doubt be upset to learn that 'Robert Redford' (Simón Ramírez) wears spectacles and that 'Steve McQueen' (Manolo Cano) is balding. Curiously Woody Allen's vocal 'double' (Miguel Angel Valdivieso) also looks just like him. Dubbing is no longer mandatory. In fact, distributors now have to obtain a permit from the government before they can dub a film. But it remains popular with the public.

Without protection it is almost certain that the introduction of compulsory dubbing would have put the Spanish film industry out of business. But Franco liked Spanish films – he even wrote the screenplay for one, called *Raza* (Race) – and he saw that they offered a way of propagating the regime's ideas. In 1955 the Spanish government was so firm in its insistence on protectionist measures that the American Motion Picture Export Association called a boycott of Spain which lasted three years. But in the end it was the MPEA which had to cave in, reluctantly accepting a stipulation that the number of foreign films distributed in Spain must not be more than four times the number of Spanish ones and a tax on the takings of dubbed films, the proceeds of which went into financing Spanish productions. By the end of the dictatorship, domestically directed and produced works accounted for almost 30 per cent of box-office receipts – a healthy figure by any standard.

In 1977, however, the decree which abolished censorship in the cinema and replaced it with a classification system also did away with the four-to-one distribution rule and replaced it with a much stricter condition that one day of Spanish films had to be shown for every two days of foreign films. This so-called *cuota de pantalla* or screen quota was intended to strengthen the industry, but it was enacted at a time when – for a variety of reasons including the chaotic state of the financial arrangements for domestic film production – Spain's film-makers were unable to rise to the challenge. The cinema owners and managers, who had to dredge up films from the Franco era to meet the demands of the decree, appealed to the courts and in 1979 the Supreme Court abolished the screen quota altogether.

The Supreme Court's decision brought the industry face to face with disaster. It was only saved by a law passed the following year which, while reintroducing the screen quota, fixed it at the more reasonable ratio of three days of foreign films to one day of Spanish. It also set up a complex system whereby the number of dubbing permits granted to a distribution company is dependent on the success of the Spanish films financed by that firm, the aim being to make it impossible for foreign distributors to get foreign films into Spain by financing the production of low-cost, low-quality Spanish films. So far, the system has worked well and in 1983 the Socialists tightened it up, reducing the maximum number of dubbing permits allotted for each Spanish production from five to four. The same measure also instituted a new system of state aid whereby the government can provide up to 50 per cent of the costs of production. In recent years, Spanish films have accounted for almost 30 per cent of the number distributed and over 20 per cent of the box office.

The Spaniards' talent for film-making may owe something to their visual sensitivity, attested to by a lengthy inventory of great artists stretching from Velázquez to Picasso. Painting and sculpture are *the* Spanish art forms and it is not surprising that, within a few years of the Spaniards' regaining their freedom, art should be reasserting its pre-eminence. The turning point was the 1979–80 season which began with a timely exhibition entitled *1980* organized by three Madrid critics as a way of demonstrating to the public the sort of work they believed would dominate the Spanish art world over the next decade. The same season also saw a renewal of interest in contemporary Spanish art in the United States, where the Guggenheim Museum staged an exhibition of work by young Spanish artists and *Art News* devoted an entire issue to contemporary Spain.

The effect of all this was to inspire a new sense of purpose and confidence which carried over into the following season. It began with another seminal show, *Madrid Distrito Federal*. The catalogue accompanying the exhibition, written by one of the critics who had selected the works for *1980* a year earlier, included a ringing declaration:

> There are cities which, at a given moment and because of a set of circumstances, manage to make themselves into the capital of a style, almost without intending to and sometimes almost without realizing it themselves. To say 'Paris 1905' or 'New York 1944' or 'Lisbon 1915' or 'London 1960' is to define, with the brevity of a *haiku*, successive, emphatic situations in art. It may be that one day it will also be enough to say 'Madrid 1980'.

It was an ambitious aspiration, but the authorities have done their best to fulfil it, by channelling a healthy proportion of their resources into contemporary rather than historical exhibitions.

On the other hand, all the critical confidence and official enthusiasm in the world will not make a blind bit of difference without the support of the public. For years, the Spaniards' attitude to modern art has been much the same blend of majority hostility and minority enthusiasm that is to be found in other Western nations. But at some point in the early eighties it underwent a profound change. It is impossible to say when exactly that change took place, but it is possible to pinpoint the moment when it began to manifest itself – February 1983 when the second government-sponsored International Festival of Contemporary Art, held in Madrid under the title of *Arco-83*, was almost overwhelmed by the number of people who packed in to see it. When I visited Madrid a year later, I was struck by an atmosphere that I had never encountered before – that of a city gripped by art fever. Everywhere I went – in cafés, bars and restaurants – there were posters advertising exhibitions and on all sides friends and acquaintances had a story to tell of how they had to queue for hours to get into this or that exhibition. As the Professor of History of Art at the Universidad Complutense, Antonio Bonet Correa, wrote at about that time:

> All of a sudden, the Spaniards – who for years knew nothing of the art world and were deprived of contemporary international art – have woken up to discover a new terrain. The habit of going to exhibitions in order to know about modern art has entered into the customs of those professional people who would wish to be considered as cultured.

What is so odd about this explosion of interest is that it has taken place in a country where for the moment the level of artistic promise is not, frankly, very high. The younger Spanish artists spent the seventies divided into opposing abstract and figurative camps and although by the end of the decade a truce had been called between the two groups neither had proved conclusively that it knew where it was going. Despite a good deal of bravado, there is also a good deal of confusion. Foreign influences are haughtily rejected one moment only to be slyly absorbed the next. The result is works which are muddled in approach yet defiant in execution. They are all too often heavy-handed and overblown. Yet it is difficult to believe that the current wave of enthusiasm will not carry Spain's young painters and sculptors on to better things in the near future.

For centuries now, music has been the Cinderella of the Spanish arts. In the sixteenth century the quality of the music composed in Spain was comparable to that of almost any other European nation. But the Counter-Reformation isolated Spain from the Protestant North of Europe just as Germany was taking over from Italy as the leading musical influence within Europe. The works of Bach, Handel, Haydn and Mozart reached Spain as but faint echoes. In the last century Spain was again opened up to foreign influence and through the achievements of, first, Albéniz, then Granados and, finally, Falla it was beginning to recover its reputation when the civil war broke out and it was once again shut off from the rest of the continent.

Another reason for Spain's traditional backwardness in this area has been a straightforward lack of funds. Unlike art and literature, music cannot thrive without money. A novel or painting is the product of a single creative person and a few reasonably cheap materials. Concerts, operas and ballets require large premises, sizeable numbers of performers and a lot of costly equipment. Yet the Spanish monarchy and aristocracy have traditionally been reluctant to patronize music. In this respect, Franco was a typically Spanish ruler. The amount of money allocated to music while he was in power was pitiful. A number of fine composers like Luis de Pablo, Cristóbal Halffter, Carmelo Bernaola and Juan Hidalgo rose to prominence during the Franco era. But they did so only by dint of immense personal sacrifice. 'Whenever I look at my *curriculum vitae*,' Luis de Pablo once said, 'I feel a strong desire – that no one should have to struggle as I have struggled ... The first time in my life that I was able to devote twenty-four hours a day to composition was in Berlin when I had a grant from the DAAD. I was thirty-seven years old.' He and most of his contemporaries have had to spend lengthy periods outside their native land and most of them are still better known and appreciated abroad than they are in Spain. Hidalgo's *Ukanga* was first performed in Darmstadt in 1957. It was not put on in Madrid until 1970. A similar fate awaited talented young performers. Jesús López Cobos once remarked that being born a conductor in Spain was a bit like being born a bullfighter in Finland. When Franco died there were only two state-aided orchestras – the *Orquesta Nacional de España* and the *Orquesta Sinfónica de RTVE* – one opera house and no classical ballet company at all. If, in the years since, Spain has managed to become a minor force in the world of music that is a considerable achievement.

Underlying this achievement is a change of attitude on the part of the government which has shown itself altogether more sympathetic to music and especially contemporary music. It has set up a *Centro de Divulgación de la Música Contemporánea* and contemporary composers have found it much easier to get their works performed in Spain. Luis de Pablo's first opera, *Kiu*, which was to have been launched in Paris, made its début in Madrid instead.

As far as orchestral music is concerned, the return of López Cobos who took over control of the ONE in 1983 has been decisive. Like France and Italy, Spain is not a country with a great orchestral tradition. Perhaps it has something to do with Latin society, which values spontaneity more than discipline and rewards individual rather than collective achievement. At all events, the conservatories of Southern Europe are designed to turn out soloists rather than rank-and-file players. A former member of the ONE once said that the problem with tuning up in a Spanish orchestra is that 'everyone has his or her own conception of *la*'. López Cobos, who has spent much of his career conducting German and British orchestras, has set his sights on inculcating what he calls 'musical discipline'. He also aims to provide concerts for the elderly and the young and put on performances of semi-serious works as a way of extending the orchestra's appeal. His main preoccupation, however, is for the future – the early eighties saw the creation of a national youth orchestra, the *Joven Orquesta Nacional de España*, but there is still a crying need to reform and improve the conservatories.

Nowhere in the Spanish arts is the contrast between talent and resources quite so great as in opera. Spain has given the world as many of its great contemporary singers as any nation on earth – Plácido Domingo, Monserrat Caballé, Teresa Berganza, Victoria de los Angeles and José Carreras all hail from Spain. Yet Spanish opera, in the sense of the number and quality of the performances staged in Spain, is relatively unimportant. Up until the twenties, Spain had two great opera houses – the Teatro Real in Madrid and the Teatro del Liceo in Barcelona. In 1925 the Teatro Real had to be closed down for structural reasons and when it re-opened it did so as a concert hall. Throughout the Franco years, the only opera available to *madrileños* was a brief programme every spring – usually, and significantly, referred to as a 'festival' rather than a 'season' – which was staged at the Teatro de la Zarzuela, the state-aided operetta house. For well over half a century, therefore, the only proper house has been the Liceo, or Liceu as it is called in Catalan.

Since, in modern times at least, Barcelona has not had a court, the Catalan upper classes have tended to use the Liceo as the next best thing. Referring to the late nineteenth and early twentieth centuries, the Catalan author Victor Alba wrote that 'to own a seat at the Liceu was almost a patent of nobility, as was membership of the Liceu circle, the club housed in the same building as the opera'. Stories about the philistinism of Liceo audiences are legion. The main reason for going there was to see and be seen (although some of the boxes contain artfully angled mirrors that bear witness to the fact that for some – widows especially – the most important thing was to see and *not* to be seen). In 1903 a decision by the management to put out the lights in the auditorium during performances prompted a letter from a group of regulars arguing that 'although the performance is an attraction that provides a reason for people to come to the theatre, the main interest is centred on the auditorium rather than the stage'. They went on to point out that it was hardly worth the ladies buying expensive dresses and jewels if no one could see them. In times gone by it was customary to dine during performances, returning to the auditorium only for the highlights. More recently it was not uncommon, whenever Barcelona was playing, to see box holders listening to the match commentary on the radio. All this made the Liceo a target not only for the Anarchists, who bombed it in the 1890s, but also for the creative and intellectual community. And since, after 1925, the Liceo *was* opera in Spain, opera suffered from the same stigma as the Liceo.

It is revealing that until very recently none of the country's contemporary composers had written an operatic score. It was only in the seventies that interest began to grow. In the eighties writing opera has become positively fashionable. The composers' respect has been earned by the opera world's determined efforts to shed its 'social' image. In recent years the Liceo has staged some magnificent seasons, full of 'stars', but more importantly striking an acceptable balance – for the first time in decades – between the traditional and the experimental.

Until very recently the only ballet companies in Spain were devoted exclusively to *ballet español*, a fusion of flamenco, classical and modern influences. There were schools of conventional Western dance, most notably the one run by María de Avila in Saragossa where Victor Ullate and Carmen Rocha were trained. But after graduating, promising young dancers who wanted to pursue a career on stage had nowhere to go but abroad.

In 1977 the Ministry of Culture finally got around to putting aside the funds for a *Ballet Nacional de España* consisting of two companies – one for *ballet español* and the other for classical ballet. Antonio Gades was recruited to head the first and Victor Ullate returned at the height of his career to direct the second. His original idea was to reunite the many talented dancers who, like himself, had been forced to work abroad. But it soon became apparent that most of them had other commitments and Ullate was left to do the best he could with the youngsters emerging from the schools and in particular the state-funded school which was set up at the same time as the *Ballet Nacional* and run by his wife. Given these inauspicious beginnings, it is to his immense credit that within the space of a mere five years Ullate managed to form a national ballet company worthy of the name. In 1983 the incoming Socialist government – apparently concerned that the two supposedly national companies were becoming the fiefdoms of their respective directors – sacked Ullate together with Antonio Gades's successor, Antonio Ruiz, and put María de Avila, Ullate's old tutor, in charge of both companies. It was an unseemly and unjust reward for the man who had single-handedly resurrected Spanish classical ballet. Ullate's parting words were 'I shall go away saddened because I do not understand a great deal of what has happened. Or rather, I do understand, but it seems impossible.'

Popular music in Spain is on the whole a good deal healthier than classical music. Julio Iglesias's 'Begin the Beguine', released in 1981, was the first single recorded in a language other than English to sell more than a million copies worldwide and Iglesias himself is now unquestionably an international rather than just a Spanish, or Hispanic, star. Another ballad singer, Raphael, has built up an immense following in Latin America. But they are only the most successfully marketed of several highly professional mainstream performers like Miguel Bosé, Camilo Sesto, Mari Trini, Massiel and Marisol.

It is in the field of rock music that Spain lags behind. The story of Spanish rock is the story of successive imitations. America produced the Everley Brothers, so Spain came up with a Duo Dinámico. Britain produced the Beatles, the Who and the Rolling Stones and all of a sudden Spain was full of groups, only one of which – Los Bravos – made any impact abroad (with a song called 'Black is Black'). In this respect, Spain is no different from most other countries in continental Europe, although it is interesting that the northern nations – and especially Germany – are more capable of producing authentic rock than the southern ones. Once again, it probably has a lot to do with the nature of Latin society. Rock is the product of a youth culture which is in turn the result of a rejection of established social values. In societies where family ties are still strong, it is impossible to create such a youth culture. The problem with Spanish rock musicians – even the most talented of them like Miguel Ríos, who has been going strong ever since the sixties, or the group Tequila who had their heyday in the seventies – is that they look and sound like, and are, nice kids with well-scrubbed faces and neatly combed hair who would not recognize a generation gap if they fell into one. But then rock is also a product of urban rather than rural society and of the working class rather than the middle class. City life in Spain nowadays requires at least some of the toughness and slickness that is needed to get by in, say, Detroit or Liverpool and the economic progress of the sixties and the political changes of the seventies have given the Spanish working class a prosperity and influence that they never had before. All this has been reflected in Spanish rock and has to some extent served to narrow the gap between Spain and the Anglo-Saxon countries.

Up until about the time of Franco's death, the centre of gravity of popular music was in Catalonia. But in the late seventies, a series of quasi-punk groups began to make their appearance in Madrid. The first to make an impression, if only because of its name, was Kaka de Luxe (which sounds just like Caca de Luxe or Luxury Shit). They were followed by dozens of others, of which the most accomplished is probably *Radio Futura*. Together they constitute what is called the *movida madrileña** which now dominates Spanish rock. By and large, the roots of the modernist groups that make up the *movida madrileña* are in the middle classes, but the last few years have also seen the emergence of authentically working-class music out in the poor industrial suburbs – so-called *rock duro* which is similar to Heavy Metal.

---

* *Movida* is the buzz-word of the eighties in Spain. It means 'stir' or 'commotion' but it also carries the connotation of 'scene' in the sense originally used by British and American gays.

However, there is an important exception to the general rule that the rock music produced in Spain is merely an inferior imitation of the songs turned out in Britain and the U.S. a few years earlier, and that is *rock con raices* (rock with roots). As its name suggests, it is a fusion of rock with regional and ethnic folk music. The phenomenon is older than the term. Back in the seventies, several young Andalusian musicians were fired by the idea of blending rock and flamenco. Two groups – Triana and Veneno – were formed and although both have since disappeared, the idea they implanted has grown. There are now groups playing *rock con raices* in Catalonia and Galicia (in which the fusion is with traditional Catalan and Galician music) and there are also several gypsy rock groups like Los Chichos, Los Gitanos and Los Chunguitos, whose blend of styles is particularly appealing.

The emergence of *rock con raices* is to some extent only a reflection of one of the most dramatic, heartening – and wholly unexpected – developments in recent years, and that is the flamenco boom. To some extent flamenco offers Spaniards much the same as it offers tourists – a dash of the unusual in an increasingly drab world. The songs are exotic, the dances are dramatic and flamenco history is dotted with performers sporting gloriously improbable names like 'The Child of the Combs', 'Frasco, the Coloured One' and 'Mad Matthew'. But the flamenco tradition also offers one of those links with the world of a younger mankind in which Spain is so rich, for it is capable of generating that feeling of ecstasy whose inculcation is thought to have been the object of all early music. A flamenco singer will not perform until he or she has drifted into something approaching a trance – a state of suppressed emotion in which the need to express themselves gradually becomes so strong that it can no longer be contained. This ecstatic element in flamenco is splendidly captured in José María Caballero Bonald's description of a gathering at a wayside inn in the midst of the undulating Andalusian countryside:

> The night draws on. Already daylight has begun to show over the trees. At the inn, there is a group of seven or eight people. They are drinking wine parsimoniously, calmly. The guitarist is tuning his instrument. All of a sudden, the notes coincide with the beginning of a song and someone utters the preliminary wails. The singer clears his throat and searches for the beat. Everyone maintains a respectful, religious silence. At length, the lyrics emerge. Hands begin to clap miraculously in time with the guitar. The singer, gazing into infinity, moves his face and contorts his body in response to the difficulties of the song and raises his hand in a gesture of majesty.

Flamenco began in the late eighteenth century among the

gypsies of the provinces of Seville and Cádiz. The word itself meant 'gypsy' in the Andalusian gypsies' own slang. At the outset therefore flamenco music was gypsy music and gypsy music has remained at the core of the flamenco tradition even though a number of southern Spanish songs such as the *fandango*, which is of Moorish origin, have been absorbed into the repertory. In the same way, many non-gypsies have become masters of the art as *cantores* (singers), *bailadores* (dancers) and *tocadores* ('players' – i.e. guitarists). The vast majority of flamenco songs are true folk songs – devised by some now forgotten villager and modified by endless repetition until they gell into the form which is considered most attractive. All attempts to transcribe the music have proved abortive, so the flamenco tradition is reliant entirely on word of mouth, instruction and example. But it also means that there is great scope for individual interpretation.

The songs, or *coplas*, vary between three and six lines in length but because each word is drawn out by wails and ululations they take several minutes to sing. The language is always very simple and direct. There are about forty different types of song. Some are intended for specific occasions, such as weddings. Of the remainder, the exuberant ones which can be danced to and which the tourist is most likely to come across comprise only a relatively small proportion. Most are agonized laments for the death of a loved one, particularly a mother (a figure who is even more important among the gypsies than among their Latin neighbours), or for the loss of freedom (for the Spanish gypsies have spent more than their fair share of time in the country's jails), for the transience of life's pleasures and the persistence of its miseries. As the flamenco critic and researcher Ricardo Molina wrote, flamenco is 'the response of a people repressed for centuries', and this may explain why it became so popular among the non-gypsy peasants of Andalusia in the nineteenth century as they too fell victim to another kind of oppression when their commons were enclosed and they were left as landless labourers.

The spread of flamenco in this century has been uneven. Twice it has seemed to be on the point of going into a permanent decline and twice its fortunes have been revived by organized competitions – those of Granada in 1922 and of Córdoba in 1956. These inspired a succession of smaller contests that rekindled interest and unearthed talent. The second revival was far less dramatic than the first but it has proved to be far more enduring.

Flamenco lost its impetus after the civil war largely because it became a political tool. Casting around for 'authentic Spanish culture', the nationalists seized on flamenco and proceeded to promote a bastardized version of it to the public. The latest renaissance is largely due to a single man, the *cantaor* Antonio Mairena, who has insisted on singing an unadorned, undiluted repertoire and been tireless in organizing and promoting flamenco festivals. But Mairena and his disciples have also been helped by economic and social factors – the recovery of 'pure' flamenco came at just the moment when hundreds of thousands of Andalusians were preparing to pack their bags and start a new life in Madrid or the industrial cities of the north. The post-Franco era has seen a particularly forceful upsurge of interest, and today flamenco has an established following in every region of the country except perhaps Galicia, Cantabria and the Balearic and Canary Islands. It has transformed flamenco from a purely Andalusian art form into one that can now fairly be described as Spanish.

This has long been true of that other pre-eminently Andalusian art form, bullfighting.* That is not, however, to say that the *fiesta nacional*, as it is often called, is in the same state of health as flamenco. Far from it. Bullfighting has been declining for several decades now, even though the increase in box-office receipts during the sixties as a result of higher disposable incomes, the influx of tourists and – not least – the phenomenon of *El Cordobés* disguised the fact for many years.

The decline can be traced back at least as far as the civil war. So many fighting bulls were slaughtered either for meat or vengeance during the conflict that the *ganaderos* (breeders) were unable, during the years immediately following the war, to provide enough bulls of the right age and quality. The taurine *reglamento* stipulates that only four-year-olds should be allowed to fight. But during the forties fattened-up three-year-olds became increasingly prevalent.

The war may also have brought about a change in the whole approach of those involved in bullfighting, because the period following it saw two developments which both reflected a desire to minimize the risks involved. Firstly, following the example set by Manolete – the great *torero*† killed in the ring in 1947 – the predominant style of

---

* Readers may find it surprising or even offensive that I should include bullfighting in a chapter on the arts. But that is how it is regarded within Spain. In 1918 a number of leading artistic and literary figures gave a celebrated banquet for the bullfighter, Juan Belmonte, precisely in order to make the point that they considered him to be a fellow-artist. The journalists who write on the subject for Spanish newspapers are known as bullfighting critics (not correspondents or reporters) and they come under the *jefe de sección de cultura* (i.e. the arts editor). For the moment, bullfighting is the responsibility of the Ministry of Interior, but there is a long-standing feeling among *aficionados* that it should be dealt with by the Ministry of Culture.

† A *torero* is a bullfighter. A *torero* may be a *picador*, responsible for lancing the bull from on horseback during the first stage of the fight, a *banderillero*, responsible for placing the two coloured darts in the second stage of the fight, a *matador* (literally 'killer') – the senior member of the team who puts the bull to death in the third and final stage – or one of the

fighting became *de perfil* (sideways on), rather than *de frente* (face on). Secondly, the post-war years saw the birth and growth of the *afeitado* or shaving of the bulls' horns. The shaving, which is done with a hacksaw, continues right down to the nerve that runs through the horn, which is then rounded off to a blunter point that will do less damage in the case of a goring. The effect therefore is not only to render the bull less dangerous, but to subject him to horrific trauma. The *afeitado* has been compared to pulling out a boxer's fingernails and shortening his reach by several inches on the eve of a fight. But it is usually done with such skill that the evidence can only be detected under a microscope.

However, the principal cause of bullfighting's woes originated not in the forties but in the fifties when the art, spectacle, business or whatever you care to call it fell into the hands of a small group of *empresarios*. The *empresarios*, who hire the rings from the local town and city councils, arrange the programme, buy the bulls and hire the *toreros*, did not set out to establish a monopoly for the sake of it, but rather to break the hold of the *apoderados* (bullfighters' managers) who were threatening to establish a monopoly of their own. But that is of little consolation to the *aficionados* who have had to watch while bullfighting has been dragged into its longest and deepest crisis.

Like all good businessmen, the *empresarios* set out to minimize their risks. To match the number of *toreros* to the number of *corridas*, they created 'stables' of fighters each subject to exclusive contracts. This should have meant that the best *toreros* were guaranteed regular work. But all too often the result has been that bullfighters who have established a relationship with an *empresario* can continue to fight long after they have lost form, while better men are blocked by the lack of a contract and the *empresarios*' monopoly of the rings.

The *empresarios* also exerted pressure on the *ganaderos* (breeders) to supply them with bulls which looked impressive, but which lacked the *casta* ('breeding', 'spirit') to present any serious challenge to the bullfighters whose salaries the *empresarios* were now paying. In an earlier age, when rearing bulls was simply a pastime of the aristocracy, the *ganaderos* might have been able to resist, but it has become an increasingly commercial activity over the years and since at that time more bulls were being bred than was necessary, the *ganaderos* were in no position to put up a fight. The post-war bulls, although small and young, had at least been fiery. As the sixties progressed they became progressively weaker and by the start of the seventies some of them were actually falling over in the ring. It was only then that action was taken,

---

matador's assistants who are called *peones*.He may even be a *rejoneador*, a mounted *matador* in the Portuguese style. But he is never, in Spanish at least, a 'toreador'.

with the introduction of measures such as branding and registering. But the predominance of the seemingly powerful but relatively manageable bull is such today that many *aficionados* fear that the strain may have been irreparably distorted.

Today, bullfighting is still at the mercy of a handful of *empresarios* – Manuel Chopera (who runs the Madrid ring, Las Ventas), Pedro Balañá, Diodoro Canorea and the Jardón brothers. When, in 1977, the bullfighter *Paquirri* tried to take a stand against the system, he was excluded from that year's San Isidro festival – the most important series of fights in the bullfighting calendar – and never again made the attempt. After the retirement of Paco Camino and *El Viti* at the end of the 1978 season, *Paquirri* – son-in-law of the legendary Antonio Ordóñez – was perhaps the only real *figura* (star) left in the ring. His death as a result of a goring in 1984 was a tragedy lamented by *aficionados* of all persuasions. However, he left behind him a *fiesta nacional* which, although it lacked a fighter of outstanding stature, was in slightly better shape than a few years earlier.

Several factors have combined to raise the standard of fights in recent seasons. Firstly, the return to the ring from retirement of a series of talented veterans. The most publicized re-appearance was that of *El Cordobés* in 1979. But he failed to catch the public's imagination as he had done in the sixties and after a succession of generally mediocre fights in mainly obscure rings he returned to his ranch. More important from the point of view of the future of bullfighting was the re-emergence of two of the great 'purists', Manolo Vázquez and Antoñete, who were both in their fifties when they once again put on the suit of lights. Their classical style of fighting proved to be a great success not only with the critics but also with the public.

Secondly, recent seasons have seen the emergence of several interesting young *toreros*, most of whom are graduates of the *Escuela de Tauromaquia* which was set up in Madrid in the early seventies by an unemployed *novillero* (junior bullfighter) called Enrique Martín Arranz whose aim was to restore to bullfighting the technical soundness and sophistication which it had lost even before the sixties. Another fighter of considerable interest is Francisco Esplá who uses passes that have not been seen in the bull ring for decades.

It could be that we are on the verge of a revival. Bullfighting has suffered crises in the past, such as during the period from 1900 to 1912. Each time it has revived and survived. But against the possibility of recovery one has to set the effects of a growing disquiet among Spaniards about the morality of their *fiesta nacional.* There has always been an active and vocal minority within Spain which regarded it as neither a sport nor an art, but simply ritualized slaughter, and in the years since Franco's death there has been an unmistakable increase in the number of people publicly objecting to bullfighting in print and on radio and television. Although none of the political parties has yet seriously considered taking a stand against bullfighting, it is noticeable that none of them is keen to be seen to be taking an interest in its problems. This is particularly remarkable in the case of the Socialists, several of whose leaders, including Felipe González himself, are from Andalusia and are known to be *aficionados*. So far – and perhaps with one eye on public opinion in the EEC – they have been content to treat bullfighting with a sort of benign neglect.

CHAPTER FOURTEEN

Religion and the Church

Contrary to the image conveyed by the sherry advertisement, Jeréz – the home of sherry – is a poor town with long traditions of Anarchism, Marxism and atheism. In the late sixties the workers at one of the great sherry houses mounted what became a prolonged and bitter strike. Among their demands was that they should be given two days off every year for christenings. One of the leaders of the strike later recalled that the head of the firm had asked them why 'a bunch of commies' should need time off to go to church. 'We said that that was different. You might not believe in God, but you had to believe in baptism otherwise your kids'd be Moors, wouldn't they?' he said.

Spain, like Pakistan, became a nation as the result of a process of religious segregation. Christianity was as essential to Spain's nationhood as Islam to Pakistan's. As the Jeréz sherry worker's remark shows, saying that you are a Christian can – even today – be as much a claim to national identity as a profession of religious belief.

And if being a Spaniard means being a Christian, in Spain being a Christian means being a Catholic. The *reconquista* had barely ended when the Reformation began and after centuries of fighting the infidel, Christian Spaniards were in no mood to put up with heretics or dissenters. Spain was the undisputed leader of the Counter-Reformation. A soldier-turned-priest from the Basque country, Ignacio de Loyola, provided the movement with its spiritual shock troops, the Jesuits, and Spanish commanders like Alba, Spinola and the Cardinal Infante Fernando led the military offensive against the Protestant nations of the north.

At home the Inquisition made sure that by 1570 there was not a single Protestant left in Spain. Abolished in 1813, during the War of Independence, the Inquisition was reconstituted the following year by Fernando VII and was only finally suppressed in the 1830s. Even after that – except under the two Republics – religious freedom was usually more national than real. Brave souls like George Borrow, author of that exuberantly idiosyncratic classic *The Bible in Spain*, set out to break the stranglehold of Popery but only succeeded in creating the odd prayer group. One result of the virtual absence of Protestantism was that disagreement with the doctrines of Catholicism, which in other parts of Europe was channelled into Lutheranism or Calvinism, tended to take the form of Freemasonry in Spain. Many of the nineteenth-century *pronunciamientos* were the result of Masonic conspiracies.

Franco, while not actually banning other forms of worship, outlawed their external manifestations. Services could not be advertised in the press or on signboards and since none but the Catholic Church had legal status other denominations could not own property or publish books. The Second Vatican Council's historical declaration on freedom of conscience forced the regime to abandon this policy and in 1966 a law was passed which, while retaining a privileged status for the Catholic Church, freed other creeds from the constraints that had been placed upon them. But it was not until the 1978 Constitution took effect that Spaniards secured an unambiguous right to worship as they pleased. Today there are no more than about 200,000 to 300,000 Spanish Protestants of whom a disproportionate number – about three in ten – come from Catalonia.

In Spain, Catholicism is not so much *a* religion as *the* religion. More than 95 per cent of the population have been baptized as Catholics and recent surveys suggest that between 80 and 90 per cent regard themselves as Catholics, although only some 55 to 60 per cent actually go to church. Of those, quite a large proportion go to church only very occasionally – usually at Easter. A study commissioned by the Bishops' Conference calculated that the attendance at Mass on a typical Sunday in 1982 was about nine million – just over 29 per cent of those able to go. The last reliable survey before that, in 1967, put the figure at 34.5 per cent, so it seems that attendance at Mass, which fell during the thirties under the Republic and then rose steadily under Franco, is now on the decline again. Still, nine million is a substantial figure. As the head of the Church's statistical department pointed out when the figures were issued, neither football nor cinema attracts as many people each weekend.

Attendance varies enormously from region to region. It has always been highest in the north – particularly in the Basque country and Old Castile – and lowest in the south. Curiously enough, this is the same pattern that exists in both Italy and Portugal. But the theory – applicable almost everywhere else – that people who live in towns go to church less than people who live in the countryside does not hold good for Spain. Or rather, it holds good only in the north. In the south attendance at Mass is higher in the cities than in the villages. Several theories have been put forward to explain why the north should be more pious than the south. One is that, because of the *reconquista*, the north had 400 more years of Christianity than the south, but this does not explain why the same phenomenon should exist in the other Catholic countries of Latin Europe. Perhaps a more plausible explanation is that in the south of all three nations the Church was far more closely linked to an oppressive 'establishment'. This might also explain the breakdown of the usual correlation between city dwelling and irreligiousness in Andalusia, since it is the peasantry who have suffered most from the depredations of a ruling class supported by the clergy.

There was a time when religiosity was almost a preserve of the right in Spain. Today, that is no longer the case. According to a recent book on relations between the Church and the PSOE, more than half the country's practising Catholics and a fifth of its daily communicants voted for the Socialists at the 1982 general election. Although the leadership of the PSOE is overwhelmingly agnostic, an increasing number of Catholics are not only voting for, but also joining, the party. A recent study by its *Grupo Federal de Estudios Sociológicos* found that over 45 per cent of members described themselves as believers. Less than 20 per cent of those who had joined during the Franco era were Catholics, but among those who had joined since then, the proportion has been increasing each year until, among the most recent entrants, it is 50 per cent.

The number of Spaniards in Holy Orders is high by any standards. In 1984 there were 21,423 parish priests, 10,905 ordained monks, 7,695 unordained monks and a staggering 79,829 nuns. But it is clear that the clergy – and in particular the diocesan clergy – will soon be facing a crisis of numbers. This is because its age structure nowadays is thoroughly anomalous. Instead of there being a steady fall in numbers from youngest to oldest, there is a huge bulge between the ages of thirty-five and sixty – reflecting the boom in vocations during the first half of Franco's rule. Above and below this bulge – which takes in more than 70 per cent of the diocesan clergy – the numbers are severely impoverished. In the case of older priests this is partly because of the effects of the civil war, which claimed the lives of more than 4,000 parish priests. In the case of younger priests it is because of the worldwide vocational crisis which began to be felt in the sixties and whose effects were felt particularly acutely in Spain.

The crisis manifested itself in two ways. In the first place, there was a decline in the number of young men applying to join the priesthood. The number of seminarists in Spain, which had reached more than 9,000 in the fifties, fell to 3,500 during the sixties and to 1,500 during the seventies. Since 1979, however, there has been a slight but steady increase. The drop in the number of seminarists had an inevitable effect on the number of ordinations – 825 in 1961, 395 in 1972 and a mere 163 in 1981. Another, more controversial system of the crisis in vocations was an increase in the number of priests giving up Holy Orders. During the sixties more priests renounced their vows in Spain than in any country except Brazil and Holland. The reason in most cases was the Church's policy on celibacy. An unpublished survey conducted while Franco was still alive in the diocese of Santiago de Compostela, the cradle of traditional Spanish Catholicism, found that almost a quarter of the parish priests there considered chastity an unrealizable virtue. 'What is really serious and worrying,' the authors of the report added, 'is that almost all those priests who judged it unrealizable are consistent in their way of thinking and behave accordingly.'

The number of 'secularizations' reached its peak in the early seventies and it had fallen by 50 per cent when, in 1978, Pope John Paul II decided not to sign any more documents releasing priests from their vows. Of the 6,000 priests throughout the world who have applied to be released from the priesthood, no less than 500 – one in every twelve – is a Spaniard. Frustrated by the pontiff's hardline attitude, they are becoming a disruptive and embarrassing element within the Church. Celibacy continues to be the main grievance and since the promulgation of the 1978 Constitution, which revived civil marriage, they have been able to get married without permission from the Church. Several have done so. In a particularly blatant exercise, at Córdoba in 1979, five priests who had been through a civil marriage took part in a ceremony of blessing at which they simultaneously exchanged rings with their five partners.

Up to now, the vocational crisis has had only a slight effect on the overall size of the clergy. This is because there are so few elderly priests. The number dying or retiring has been almost as low as the number being ordained. But as the thirty-five to sixty 'bulge' moves up the age scale it will create a serious imbalance between those entering and those leaving the priesthood that will have a significant effect on the total.

Historically, the Spanish clergy has been among the most conservative in the world. The Church that had spearheaded the Counter-Reformation was quite incapable of coming to terms with the new ideas that flooded into Spain during the nineteenth century and took refuge in a forlorn hope that the old order of things could be re-established. The identification of the Church with reaction created by implication a mirror-image alliance between radicalism and anti-clericalism. Whenever, during the late nineteenth and early twentieth centuries, the right lost its grip on the levers of power there were frenzied outbursts of violence directed against Catholicism and its representatives. Churches were burned or desecrated. On occasions, priests were killed and nuns raped. The civil war provoked the worst atrocities of all – the 4,000 parish priests who died were accompanied to the grave by over 2,000 monks and almost 300 nuns.

The atrocities perpetrated by the Republicans make it a little easier to understand the Church's attitude to the Nationalists. Spanish prelates blessed Franco's troops before they went into battle and were even pictured giving the fascist salute. In a famous broadcast to the beleaguered defenders of the Alcázar in Toledo, Cardinal Isidro Gomá y Tomás – a future Primate of Spain – inveighed against 'the bastard soul of the sons of Moscow and shadowy societies manipulated by semitic internationalism'. On the day of his victory, Franco received from Pope Pius XII a telegram of congratulation which read: 'Lifting up our hearts to the Lord, we rejoice with Your Excellency in the victory, so greatly to be desired, of Catholic Spain.'

Yet within twenty-five years of that telegram, the Spanish Church had changed from being one of Franco's most enthusiastic allies into one of his most vocal critics. This extraordinary about-turn takes some explaining. To an extent it was a reflection of the diminishing support throughout society for Franco's regime. Unlike Spain's army officers, who make great play of being drawn from among the 'people' but are in fact recruited from a quite narrow section of society, the clergy really do come from every stratum and so tend to be more susceptible to the feelings of the nation as a whole. It was partly too a question of morality. The gap between what the regime promised and what it delivered in the way of social justice grew wider every year and was quite soon demonstrably at variance with Christian ideals. In addition, the Spanish Church, like every other Catholic Church, was deeply influenced by the liberal spirit which began to emanate from the Vatican as soon as John XXIII was elected Pope and which took shape in the measures adopted by the Second Vatican Council. But perhaps the main reason for the change was, ironically enough, Franco's own victory.

Just as the Church's political conservatism had helped to forge an alliance between anti-clericalism and radicalism, so the anti-clericalism of the radicals had ensured that the Church remained conservative. The death and exile of so many Freemasons, Anarchists and Marxists effectively destroyed anti-clericalism as a force in society and gave the Church a freedom of manoeuvre which had been unthinkable previously. Among other things it encouraged the Church to fish for souls in the traditionally anti-clerical urban working class. In the early fifties, the leaders of the Vatican-inspired lay organization, *Acción Católica*, set up three new societies, *Hermandades Obreras de Acción Católica* (HOAC), *Juventud Obrera Católica* (JOC), and *Vanguardias Obreras Juveniles* (VOJ) to proselytize among the working classes, particularly the young. They were followed into the poor suburbs by a succession of idealistic young priests. Perhaps the best known of them was Fr José María de Llanos, a Jesuit from a well-to-do background, who had been a sort of unofficial chaplain to the young Falangists and was even called upon by Franco to prescribe spiritual exercises for him and his wife. In 1956 he went to live among the migrants from Andalusia who had settled at Pozo del Tío Raimundo, a patch of wasteland outside Madrid.

In the end, the urban working classes were to have a much greater effect on the Church than the Church ever had on the urban working classes. In an interview in 1981, Fr Llanos conceded ruefully that 'These people have taught me to be a Communist but I have not been able to teach them to be Christians'. He is an extreme case – not many priests became Communists – but in general the result of the experiment was to raise the social consciousness of, first, the laity and then the clergy more than the religious consciousness of the people they had set out to convert. By the early sixties, a sizeable element within the Church was at odds with the regime. This was the heyday of the *curas rojos* (red priests), like Fr Llanos, who took advantage of the privileges and immunities granted to the Church by Franco to allow strike meetings in the vestry and sit-ins in the nave. Some, like Francisco García Salve – *Cura Paco* – a priest-turned-construction-worker who was imprisoned three times under Franco, became 'worker priests' on the French model, giving up their dog-collars altogether to take ordinary jobs that brought them even closer to the working class.

The younger clergy's antipathy to Francoism was further fuelled in some areas by the regime's hostility to regional nationalism. This was especially true of the Basque country, the most devout part of Spain. There, the clergy had always identified themselves closely with demands for the restoration of traditional rights and privileges, although during the nineteenth century this had tended to take the form of support for Carlism. In contrast to what happened in the rest of Spain, the Basque clergy sided with the Republic during the civil war and paid the price for their choice after Franco's victory when sixteen of their number were executed. Understandably therefore many Basque priests were sympathetic to the resurgence of militant nationalism. Churches and rectories were favourite ETA hideouts during the early years of the movement and I have heard former sympathizers recount how they stored guns and ammunition in monasteries. Although support for ETA among the clergy dropped off as the organization became increasingly ruthless, individual links undoubtedly remained. Two of the sixteen defendants at the celebrated Burgos trial in 1970 were priests.

The revolt within the Church, particularly in the Basque country, reached such proportions that a special priests' prison had to be created at Zamora. The French journalist Edouard de Blaye calculated that by 1970 187 priests had been sent to prison. 'It is one of the paradoxes of this regime that calls itself Christian,' he remarked, 'that there are more priests in prison in Spain than in all the Communist countries of Europe put together.' At first, the radicalism of the rank and file appalled the hierarchy. The mutual suspicion which grew up between the bishops and the priests was heightened by the fact that at that time Spain had the youngest priesthood and the oldest episcopate of any Catholic Church in the world. But the two Papal Nuncios appointed by Pope Paul VI engineered a transformation of the hierarchy so that between 1964 and 1974 the average age of Spain's bishops dropped by ten years. Towards the end of the sixties, the hierarchy itself began to show signs of dissent. In 1972 the Church got a 'red bishop' to add to its many 'red priests' – Bishop Iniesta who was appointed to Vallecas, a working-class suburb of Madrid. In 1973 Bishop Palenzuela of Segovia was brought before the Public Order Court for describing conditions at the priests' prison in Zamora as 'inhuman' and in 1974 Bishop Añoveros of Bilbao was placed under house arrest for a pastoral letter in which he argued in favour of minority rights. A year later, after he had criticized the use of the death penalty, Bishop Iniesta was forced by threats from the ultra-right to flee for his life to Rome. By that time even the moderate Archbishop – later Cardinal – Tarancón, who had assumed control of the Spanish Church in 1971, needed police bodyguards.

The publicity given to the 'red' bishops and priests of the Franco era tended to give an impression that the Church had become more radical than was in fact the case. By the end of the dictatorship it consisted – in Bishop Iniesta's words – of 'a minority right wing, a minority left wing and a majority belonging to the centre'. Cardinal Tarancón who, as Archbishop of Madrid and President of the Bishops' Conference, held both the key posts in the Spanish Church, was the embodiment of this ecclesiastical centre. A friend and admirer of Pope Paul VI, he shared the late pontiff's cautious but realistic approach to the modern world. His withdrawal from administrative and pastoral activities in the early eighties caused a discernible shift in the direction of the Spanish Church. He was replaced as the head of the Bishops' Conference by the somewhat apolitical figure of the Bishop of Oviedo, Gabino Díaz Merchán and when, in 1983, Tarancón reached the age of seventy-five and was obliged to submit his resignation from the Archbishopric of Madrid, Pope John Paul II replaced him with the Bishop of

Santiago de Compostella, Angel Suquía, an admirer and supporter of the shadowy Opus Dei.

It is deeply ironic that the most successful and notorious 'export' of the increasingly progressive Church which took shape during the Franco era should have been a society as reactionary as Opus Dei. Opus Dei, the Work of God, now has between 75,000 and 95,000 members in eighty countries. Its ideology is a curious hotchpotch of copied or inherited ideas. Some of them, such as the mortification of the flesh, come straight from the Middle Ages. Its sense of mission and its curious blend of religious and military rhetoric are reminiscent of the Counter-Reformation. In its secrecy, exclusivity and hierarchical structure, it mirrors Freemasonry and in its exaltation of hard work it resembles some of the more po-faced forms of Protestantism. In both these latter respects in fact Opus Dei is perhaps another product of the absence within Spain of any serious rival to Catholicism.

Despite its official title – the Priestly Community of the Holy Cross – only about 2 per cent of Opus Dei's members are priests. But those priests who do belong to the movement wield tremendous power within it. All the members of the Opus Dei – be they priests, lay men or women – belong to one of three categories. At the top are the Numeraries, subdivided into three further categories according to their powers and responsibilities. Numeraries must have good intellects (they are usually university graduates) and be free of physical deformities. They live in Opus residences, handing over their incomes to the Director of the house who then returns to each of them as much as he or she needs to get by. Since the majority have well-paid jobs this is a highly important source of income. Numeraries take the three monastic vows of poverty, chastity and obedience. At least once a week they have to flog themselves on the buttocks with the *disciplina*, a five-thronged lash, for as long as it takes to say the prayer 'Salve Regina', and for two hours every day they must wear the *cilicio*, a chain with pointed links which is tied on to the upper thigh so that neither it nor the wounds it inflicts can be seen.

After the Numeraries come the Supernumeraries who must have the same intellectual and physical qualifications as Numeraries, but live normal family lives, although with the significant difference that they hand over a share of their earnings to the society and keep their membership secret from even their closest friends and relatives. Finally, there are the Associates (once known as Oblates) – men or women with a limited intellect or a physical blemish who, like the Numeraries, take vows and live in communities but whose job is to do the menial tasks involved in running the residence. In addition to its members, the Opus recognizes a fourth category of so-called Co-operators. These are non-members regarded as sympathetic to the organization. Interestingly, Co-operators need not even be Christians and they sometimes have no idea that they are classified as such.

In spite of the air of secrecy enveloping the organization, it is not difficult to recognize a member of the Opus. They tend to be unusually fastidious in the way that they talk and dress, and their homes almost always contain somewhere a little model of a donkey, representing the ass upon which Christ entered Jerusalem. Young Opus priests are particularly easy to spot. Unlike their contemporaries, who generally do their best not to look like priests at all, they wear cassocks and dog-collars and in imitation of Opus Dei's founder they frequently wear Atkinson's cologne. But, somewhat unexpectedly, many of them also have a back-slapping, hail-fellow-well-met, one-of-the-boys air about them and smoke strong Ducados cigarettes.

Theologically, Opus Dei represents a step into the past best illustrated by the movement's attitude to confession. In recent years, Catholics in many parts of the world have come to regard it as an anachronism. In Spain, some churches, particularly in working-class districts, no longer even have a confessional. Yet Opus Dei has been doing its best to reverse the trend and if you go to the sanctuary run by Opus Dei at Torreciudad, near Barbastro, you will find a crypt packed with confessionals. Politically, the organization's centre of gravity is well to the right of centre. Liberal members like Rafael Calvo Serer, who was editor of the newspaper *Madrid* until it was closed down by the authorities in 1971, are merely exceptions that prove the rule.

Opus Dei was founded in 1928 by a young Aragonese priest and shopkeeper's son, José María Escrivá de Balaguer y Albás. Known to his followers as *el padre* (the father), Escrivá seems to have given way in his later years to a sort of monomania. He had a special crypt built in Madrid for his father and mother (who are known in Opus circles as 'the grandparents') and he asked for – and was given – the defunct title of Marquis of Peralta. Such was the criticism this provoked, he was forced to transfer the title to his brother. María Angustias Moreno, the director of an Opus residence in Andalusia, who left the organization in the early seventies and later published a book about her experiences, wrote that 'whenever he arrived, we had to drench the house in Atkinson's cologne. He only drank French mineral water and melons had to be flown out to him when he was in America.' Six years after Escrivá's death in 1975 the Congregation for the Cause of Saints began to examine the case for his canonization.

It was not until the publication in 1939 of Escrivá's collection of maxims, *El Camino*, that the movement started to make any real impact. Unlike other Catholic pressure groups, such as the *Asociación Católica Nacional de Propagandistas* (ACNP), which exerted considerable influence within the regime in the late forties, Opus Dei was not content simply to place its members in positions of political influence. It aimed – and continues to aim – at a much more thorough 'infiltration' of society. Like the Jesuits before him, Escrivá realized the benefits to be derived from gaining a foothold in the educational world and using it to build up support among the élite. Opus Dei's efforts have been directed principally towards higher education. In 1941 José Ibáñez Martín, a friend of one of Escrivá's closest associates, was made Minister of Education. By the time he left the job in 1951, it was reckoned that between 20 and 25 per cent of the chairs at Spain's universities were held by Opus members and sympathizers. The year of Ibáñez Martín's departure also saw the foundation by the Opus of a college near Pamplona, the *Estudio General de Navarra*. In 1962 it achieved the status of a university and has since been responsible for educating many of the more intelligent members of the Spanish upper-middle classes. In addition, Opus Dei set up a business school, the IESE, in Barcelona and an administrative college, the ISSA, in San Sebastián. As the young people whose sympathies the Opus had won at university and college moved up in the world, they spread the organization's influence into every area of Spanish life. They became – and remain – powerful in the media. By the time Franco died, members of the Opus could be found at or near the top of the biggest private news agency, Europa Press, the largest commercial radio network, SER, and several publishing houses including the one that produces Spain's most popular encyclopedia, *Salvat*. But it was in the field of business that Opus Dei's members became most influential. It is known, for example, that a lot of Opus money went into building up RUMASA, the massive holding company which, until its spectacular collapse in 1983, controlled several banks, insurance companies and trading houses as well as numerous industrial and agricultural concerns.

Ironically, it was Opus's business dealings which led to the organization's most disastrous setback. In August 1969 a large textile machinery firm MATESA, which was run by a member of Opus Dei, collapsed owing vast amounts of money and Manuel Fraga, who resented the technocrats' power and influence and who was at that time Minister of Information and Tourism, deliberately let the press off the leash in the hope that they would discover enough to embarrass and discredit the organization. He was not disappointed. It was revealed that over the previous ten years MATESA had received thousands of millions of pesetas from the state to help it to export looms that were never sold. Some of the money went towards financing Opus Dei's educational activities. Some of it even found its way into Richard Nixon's campaign funds.

The MATESA scandal certainly succeeded in stripping the technocrats of their credibility although, ironically enough, it cost Fraga his job. During the last years of Franco's life, the Opus – for all its economic and social influence – exercised very little direct political influence. And that is the way things have remained. Even while the UCD was in power, only one known member of the organization managed to gain a seat in the cabinet. However, the organization's lack of success within Spain has been amply compensated for by Pope John Paul II's decision in 1982 to grant it the status of a Personal Prelature. The new status, for which Opus Dei had been pressing ever since the early sixties, means that members of the Society are no longer accountable to the local diocesan authorities. This is particularly important in Spain itself where the majority of bishops have always been deeply suspicious of it and, indeed, voted against it being granted the status of Personal Prelature. It could well be that the next few years will see a revival in the fortunes of this strange organization.

Relations between the Church and the state in Spain have traditionally been extremely close and, in spite of all the changes that have taken place since Franco's death, this is still the case. As the *reconquista* pushed forward the limits of Christian Spain, the Church acquired immense tracts of land, especially in the southern half of the peninsula. No sooner were they confiscated by the *liberal* politician Juan Alvarez Mendizábal in the 1830s than his successors felt they had to make amends. In the pact, or Concordat, drawn up between Madrid and the Vatican in 1851, the government undertook – by way of indemnity – to pay the clergy's salaries and meet the cost of administering the sacraments. This extraordinary commitment was honoured by every government until 1931 when it was renounced by the authors of the Republican Constitution. But two years later, when a conservative government came to power, the subsidy was resumed.

Franco not only continued to pay it, he also provided government money to rebuild churches damaged or destroyed in the civil war and passed a series of measures bringing the law of Spain into line with the teachings of the Church. Divorce was abolished, the sale (but not, for some reason, the manufacture) of contraceptives was banned and Roman Catholic religious instruction was made compulsory in public as well as private education at every level.

In return, the Vatican granted Franco something that Spanish rulers had been seeking for centuries – effective control over the appointment of bishops. Co-operation between the Church and the regime became even closer after the end of the Second World War when Franco needed to turn a non-Fascist face to the world. Several prominent Catholic laymen were included in the cabinet and one of them,

Alberto Martín Artajo, succeeded in negotiating a new Concordat with Rome.

Signed in 1953, the Concordat ended the diplomatic isolation to which Spain had been subjected ever since the Allied victory and Franco was happy to make whatever concessions were necessary to clinch it. The Church was exempted from taxation and offered grants with which to construct churches and other religious buildings. It acquired the right to ask for material it found offensive to be withdrawn from sale, yet its own publications were freed from censorship. Canonical marriage was recognized as the only valid form for Catholics. The Church was given the opportunity to found universities, run radio stations and own newspapers and magazines. *Acción Católica* was made an exception to the laws banning non-governmental organizations. The police were forbidden to enter churches except in cases of 'urgent necessity'. The clergy did not have to do military service and could not be charged with criminal offences except with the permission of their diocesan bishop (in the case of priests) or the Holy See itself (in the case of bishops).

It was the Second Vatican Council which first brought the terms of this cosy relationship into question. The Council, which came down unambiguously in favour of a clear separation between Church and state, invited all those governments which had a say in the appointment of ecclesiastical officials to give it up. But nothing – neither the example of Argentina, nor even a personal letter from Paul VI – could persuade Franco to surrender what he regarded – correctly – as an immensely powerful instrument of control. Because of it he was able to block the elevation of numerous liberally minded priests upon whose heads Pope Paul VI wished to place a mitre. The only way that the Church authorities could promote them was by making them auxiliary bishops (like Iniesta) or apostolic administrators (like Añoveros). By 1968 more than a third of Spain's dioceses were without a fully-fledged pastor. The first glimpse of a compromise came in the early seventies when the Spanish bishops announced that they were prepared to give up some of the privileges accorded to the Church in the Concordat. They did not renounce their claim to a state subsidy, but they did describe it as a 'necessary evil' and justified it as a payment for the Church's contributions to education and welfare rather than as compensation for the seizure of its property. Throughout the last years of Franco's life, ministers and officials were flying to and from Rome with suggested revisions of the Concordat. But all attempts to re-write it foundered on the ageing dictator's point blank refusal to give up his power over the appointment of bishops.

In 1976, however, King Juan Carlos unilaterally renounced the privilege and cleared the way for progress to be made. In August of that year, the Spanish Foreign Minister, Marcelino Oreja, and the

Vatican's Secretary of State, Cardinal Villot, signed an agreement formally restoring to the Church the power to appoint its own leaders in Spain. It was now up to the Church to fulfil its side of the bargain. In December 1979 it agreed to a partial revision of the Concordat which prepared the ground for a financial separation between Church and state. In the first place, only those church properties which were used as places of worship or which were of particular historical or artistic merit would be exempt from tax. Referring to the state's lengthy atonement for the confiscations of the last century it was agreed that 'the state can neither ignore nor prolong indefinitely juridical obligations acquired in the past'. But tacitly acknowledging that the Church was incapable of going it alone overnight, the agreement proposed a transitional period of six years divided into two three-year stages. During stage one the government would continue to pay the usual subsidy. But during stage two there would be a new system of finance. Taxpayers would be able to state on their returns whether they wished a small percentage of their taxes to go to the Church and the government would then hand over the total to the bishops. The press immediately dubbed it the *impuesto religioso* (religious tax), although since it was never conceived of as a separate charge this was a rather inaccurate label. In fact, given that whatever the individual taxpayer decided would make no difference to the size of his or her tax bill, it was more a form of words than anything else. Under the timetable drawn up in 1979 it was only when the transitional period was over and the Church was fully self-financing that Spain's Protestants, Jehovah's Witnesses and atheists would be free of the burden of having to pay for the upkeep of the Catholic Church. But in fact the timetable has not been adhered to. In 1984, five years after the partial revision of the Concordat, both parties were still stuck in the first of the two transitional stages – the government was still providing the Church with an annual grant of more than eleven billion pesetas and there was no sign of the *impuesto religioso* being introduced.

Several reasons have been put forward to explain the delay. It was said that the idea of asking taxpayers to declare whether they wanted some of their money to go to the Church was contrary to the constitutional stipulation that no one ought to be called upon to reveal their religious beliefs. Then it was said that by diverting funds to the Catholic Church alone, the government was in effect discriminating against the other denominations. But neither of these poses an insoluble dilemma. A form of words has been found to get around the constitutional issue and talks have taken place with the representatives of other faiths to decide which religions and sects have sufficient following in Spain to qualify as legal entities capable of receiving funds.

Successive governments appear to have been held back by the

fear that the Church will simply not be able to cope without the subsidy. It is hard to say whether that fear is justified. The Church has two other sources of income – the money it derives from its property and investments and the donations it receives from the faithful, which include the money put into the collection plates and boxes, the payments which are made to priests for conducting special services like christenings and funerals (which, although officially banned, continue to be paid and received in the more backward areas of the country) and legacies (many of which are tied by the donor to a specific purpose such as the building of a chapel and cannot really be counted as disposable income). It is impossible to know how much the Church gets from these sources since it has always carefully avoided publishing its accounts. Cardinal Tarancón once made it clear that it was more than half the total and some observers believe it may account for as much as three quarters. On the other hand, the Church has lots of expenses such as providing ecclesiastical paraphernalia, furnishing and maintaining churches, running seminaries and so on, which are not – and never were – covered by the government subsidy.

The overall impression one gets of the Church's finances is that they are like those of certain very old titled families – high in assets but low on liquidity. This has been particularly true since the sixties when laws were passed forbidding the Church to sell off objects of artistic or historical value. The imbalance between what the Church owns and what it can spend is nowhere more graphically illustrated than in its apparent inability to look after the treasures it owns. In the late seventies, 90 per cent of robberies carried out against the national heritage took place on church premises. During 1977 alone, thieves broke into, first, Murcia Cathedral where they helped themselves to crosses, statues and jewellery worth between 150 and 300 million pesetas and then into Oviedo Cathedral where they stole a priceless chest and chiselled the gold and gouged the jewels from two medieval crosses. In Valladolid, meanwhile, a burglar was caught leaving the Cathedral carrying the *Cronicon of Nuremburg* and seventy-three other valuable antiquarian books. Three days earlier the *Libro de las Estampas*, which had been stolen from León Cathedral in 1969, was auctioned in Germany.

The Church's apparent helplessness in such matters begs the wider question of just how powerful the Spanish Church really is. There is a tendency among commentators to be dazzled by the historical greatness of the Spanish Church to the extent that they ignore its contemporary limitations. The most important curb of all is in the Constitution. It did not mention the Catholic Church at all in its initial draft and it was only after a determined campaign that the bishops succeeded in getting it referred to. Even so, the reference that was included looks like what it is – an afterthought. Having specifically rejected the idea of an official religion, the Constitution goes on to say that 'The authorities shall take into account the religious beliefs of Spanish society and maintain the appropriate relations of co-operation with the Catholic Church and the other denominations.' There is no explicit affirmation that the majority of Spaniards are Catholics, nor that the state should take into account – let alone be guided by – the teachings of Catholicism.

Another important limitation on the power of the Church is the absence of a Christian Democrat party. The forces of Christian Democracy had been split into pro- and anti-Francoist factions under the dictatorship and were unable to sink their differences in time for the 1977 elections. Some Christian Democrats stood for the AP, others for the UCD, while a third group who entered the lists as Christian Democrats pure and simple suffered a crushing defeat. The fall of the UCD and the rise of the AP have served to concentrate most of them into a single party, but they remain a minority within it.

The Church, in other words, does not have either the moral authority or the political means with which to intervene directly in politics. That does not, of course, mean that it cannot intervene indirectly. The hand of the Church – and more particularly the Vatican – could be clearly discerned in the positions taken by some right-wing politicians during the debates on private education, divorce and abortion. Catholicism also exerts a subtler but no less potent influence over the affairs of the nation by influencing the way in which people think and act. The Church may no longer be able to break governments or even block legislation but, as Cardinal Tarancón was fond of saying, the Roman Catholic Church is a 'sociological reality' in Spain and this is nowhere more true or more pertinent than in the field of education.

The prevalence of instinctively Catholic attitudes is far greater than Spaniards themselves perhaps realize. Castilian is crammed with phrases drawn from Catholic practice and dogma. When, for example, a Spaniard wants to convey the idea that something or somebody is reliable, trustworthy, 'o.k.' in the widest sense, he or she will say that that person or thing '*va a misa*' ('goes to Mass'). When some terrible thing like multiple sclerosis or nuclear war is mentioned in conversation, in circumstances where an English-speaker might say 'It doesn't bear thinking about,' a Spaniard – even an ostensibly irreligious one – will often say '*Que Dios nos coja confesados*' ('Let's hope God catches us confessed'). And when the world's first test-tube baby was born that eminently secular periodical *Cambio 16* headlined its report with the words 'Born without Original Sin'.

CHAPTER FIFTEEN

THE SEXUAL REVOLUTION

The Club Privat Kira occupies the lower part of a block of flats at the top of a steeply inclined street in one of Barcelona's more modest residential areas. There are no gaily coloured awnings or flashing neon lights by which to identify it – just a discreet brass plate set to one side of the big black door.

As I waited for it to be opened, I became aware of being scanned by a camera a few feet above me, operated from inside the building. If I had gone there alone, the door would probably have remained shut forever. But I was with my wife, so – after a lengthy interval – it opened to reveal a young bespectacled accountant, Juan Contreras, who runs the club along with his wife, Ana Viana, a child psychiatrist. I explained what we were about and he ushered us into a dimly lit bar and fixed us a couple of drinks. By Spanish standards it was still quite early and there was only one other couple on the premises.

The bar itself looks much like hundreds of others in Barcelona – until you take a look at the noticeboard in the corner. 'Couple seek bisexual girl' reads one message. 'Bisexual man seeks couple' says another. The bar is the first of four areas into which the club is divided. The second is a dance floor. The third is lined with built-in sofas. The fourth and final area, which is up some steps, consists of three unfurnished rooms of varying sizes, the floors of which are covered wall-to-wall with mattressing. The four areas are arranged in sequence so that it is impossible to reach the fourth without passing through the second and third, so the patrons of the Club Privat Kira progress from one to the next like acolytes in some ancient, sacred ritual. The idea is that couples who meet and take a fancy to each other in the bar, can swap partners on the dance floor, and then – if they wish – go on to petting on the sofas and/or lovemaking on the mattresses.

The Kira is not strictly speaking a club at all. 'Having members means having to keep lists of names and people don't like that. There were some clubs with members but they all went bust,' said Juan. Like its predecessors, the Kira – which was founded in 1981 – seems to exist in a legal twilight, tolerated rather than authorized by the authorities. This gives the police an ample margin of discretion and provided the neighbours do not object, as they have done to similar clubs in other parts of the city, the police seem content to live and let love. 'Legally, we ought to close at 3 a.m.,' says Juan, 'but there have been times, when things were going really well, when we've stayed open until 9 a.m.'

By now, the bar was beginning to fill up with couples in their thirties and forties. 'Who knows?' said Juan, 'maybe tonight will be a good one.' He invited us to stay on a little longer, but in the best tradition of Fleet Street journalists, we made our excuses and left.

The Club Privat Kira is exceptional only insofar as customers can actually copulate on the premises. There are at least a half a dozen bars in Barcelona where couples can go in the knowledge that they will meet others keen to swap partners. A few years back, there was also a mysterious, nameless company operating in the city which arranged masked balls for the same purpose. What Anglo-Saxons call 'swinging' and Spaniards *intercambio de pareja* is confined, within Spain, to Catalonia. The only bars and clubs dedicated to it have all been set up in Barcelona and the majority of the Kira's customers are Catalans rather than 'immigrants' from other parts of Spain. A 'sophisticated' attitude to infidelity has always been one of the characteristics of Barcelona society. Taking a young lover is quite common among middle-class Catalans of both sexes and, according to Juan Contreras, some of his older customers have been 'swinging' for twenty or thirty years, although under Franco it had to be done privately.

Of all Spain's cities, Barcelona has long been the most liberated or degenerate, depending on your point of view. It probably has a lot to do with the fact that Barcelona is a port. There are an estimated 45,000 prostitutes in Barcelona, most of whom live and work in the *barrio Chino*, the maze of alleyways and tenements depicted by Jean Genet in *Journal du Voleur*. It is no coincidence that at the nearby monument to Dr Fleming there is always at least one bunch of flowers, left there by someone eternally indebted to the inventor of penicillin. The *barrio Chino* has been a red light district ever since the last century and has given its name to the similar areas which exist in other Spanish cities.*

---

* In a historic lapse of taste, a board game called *El Chino* was marketed in Spain in the early eighties. Players moved pieces representing pimps, whores and transvestites. Those unlucky enough to catch venereal disease had to be moved to a square marked 'clinic'.

But whereas the red light districts elsewhere tend to be discreetly hidden from view, Barcelona's *barrio Chino* is right next to the Ramblas, Barcelona's main thoroughfare, so the whores and pimps are rarely out of sight – or earshot – of families strolling through the flower and pet markets or taking a quiet drink at one of the Ramblas's many pavement cafés. I am sure that this must have had a significant effect on the city's moral climate.

Today Barcelona is the Hamburg of Southern Europe. You can buy hard porn off the news-stands or watch live sex at the night clubs. At the Sala Lib, there are cabins called *tocómetros* and *besómetros* with holes in them through which project anonymous hands and lips waiting to caress the client. At the Club Bagdad they used to have an act involving a donkey until the *Sociedad Protectora de Animales* turned up one day and took it away. And if you stay sipping your drink on the Ramblas until about two in the morning, you will have a front-row seat for a parade of transvestites and transsexuals as bizarre as any in the world.

But in this respect, Barcelona differs from the rest of Spain in degree rather than in kind. The years since Franco's death may have seen only tentative or gradual changes in other spheres of Spanish life, but in matters sexual there has been a revolution, which the Spaniards themselves dubbed the *desmadre sexual.** The homeland of Torquemada and Loyola now boasts a chain of plush, government-licensed 'S' cinemas where you can watch *Garganta Profunda* (*Deep Throat*) and other uncensored sex films from morning till night. Most of the big Spanish cities have striptease shows. Several have bars with topless – Spanish – waitresses. Even Burgos, that dour, grey bastion of Catholic orthodoxy, has its own sex shop. Objecting to sex in almost any form short of child molestation has become as much of a taboo as sex itself once was. Something that foreigners new to Spain find particularly curious is the way in which prostitutes and brothels advertise their services openly in 'respectable' publications. *El País* is the equivalent in Spain of the *Washington Post* or the *Guardian*. Yet if you turn to the classified advertising section you will find, for example, 'Mayka. Girls. Boys. Hotel or home. 24 hours. Credit Cards.' As for television, if you had tuned in to watch TVE's pop music show *La caja de ritmos* on a Saturday afternoon in April 1983, you would have found yourself listening to a song called '*Me gusta ser una zorra*' ('I like being a whore'). The first couple of verses ran like this:

---

* *Desmadre* is not a word you will find in the dictionary. It means something between a binge and a debauch, but there is no word in English which quite conveys the same sense of uninhibited revelry.

So you come to me speaking of love
And telling me that life is hard
Well, let me tell you what I think
Look, you fool, can't you understand?
I like being a whore (repeated several times)
You bastard!

I'd rather masturbate alone in bed
Than sleep with someone who speaks about the future
I'd rather fuck with businessmen
Who give you the money and step into oblivion
I like being a whore (repeated several times)
You bastard!

The occasional excesses of Spain's sexual revolution are a measure of the intensity of the repression which preceded it. Alone of the countries of Southern Europe, Spain has been subject in recent years to a special, double oppression.

In the same way as the other Catholic countries of the Mediterranean, she has been subject to the doctrines of a religion which, ever since St Paul, has been deeply suspicious of physical enjoyment of any kind. To the monks and nuns in charge of many of Spain's private schools, the penis was the 'diabolic serpent' and the vagina 'Satan's den'. There is of course a direct link between attitudes of this sort and the Spaniards' traditional enthusiasm for the mortification of the flesh. As Monsignor Escrivá, the founder of Opus Dei, wrote: 'If you know that your body is your enemy and the enemy of God's glory, why do you treat it so gently?'

Sex was strictly for the purpose of procreation within wedlock. Pre-marital contact between the sexes was kept to a minimum by the strictures attached to courtship or *noviazgo*. Incredible as it may now seem, the Church had great difficulty in agreeing to any form of physical contact between *novios*. As late as 1959 the Spanish bishops' 'Norms of Christian Decency' stated unequivocally that '*novios* walking along arm-in-arm cannot be accepted'. A Capuchin friar, Quintín de Sariegos, writing in the early sixties, had reconciled himself to the fact that *novias* would not only touch their *novios*, but might even kiss them. But he offered this advice – 'Whenever you kiss a man, remember your last communion and think to yourself "Could the Sacred Host and the lips of this man come together on my lips without sacrilege?"'

What really distinguished Spain from other Catholic countries like Italy and Portugal, however, was that for almost forty years the Church was able not merely to advocate, but to enforce, its ideas with the assistance of a regime that depended upon it for its legitimization.

The Church was involved in official censorship at every level and was particularly responsible for deciding on matters of sexual propriety. As the decree which created Francoist Spain's board of film censors, the *Junta Superior de Orientación Cinematográfica*, put it: 'on moral questions, the vote of the representative of the Church shall be especially worthy of respect'. The cinema was of particular concern to the Church. Fr Angel Ayala, the founder of the Catholic pressure group, the ACNP, described it as 'the greatest calamity that has befallen the world since Adam – a greater calamity than the flood, the two World Wars or the atomic bomb'. In spite of its representative's privileged status on the *Junta*, the Church was not apparently convinced that the Francoist authorities were sufficiently rigorous in their approach and four years later it set up its own *Oficina Nacional Permanente de Vigilancia de Espectáculos* whose officials watched the films passed by the *Junta* after they had been censored and gave them a rating on a scale that went from one ('suitable for children') to four ('gravely dangerous'). Although it had no official standing, the Church's 'moral classification' was invariably printed alongside each film in the listings section of the newspapers.

But not even that was enough to satisfy the more zealous members of the clergy. Sometimes, after one of those 'gravely dangerous' films had slipped through the net, parish priests would take it on themselves to put up a notice in the foyer of the local cinema which said: 'Those who watch today's programme are committing mortal sin.' One bishop, outraged by the authorization of a film to which he objected, went so far as to arrange for groups of pious ladies from *Acción Católica* to wait at the entrance of the cinema. Whenever someone approached the box office, the leader would cry out: 'Say an Our Father for the soul of this sinner!' and the others would fall to their knees in prayer. It cut down the audiences no end.

Under the Church's guidance, censorship attained extraordinary heights of puritanism. Professional boxing matches were kept out of newsreels on the grounds that they meant showing naked male torsos. Photographs of the bouts did appear in the press, but with vests painted in by the *retocadores* (retouchers) who were employed by every newspaper and magazine up until the fifties. Among their other duties was to reduce the size of women's busts. In later years, producers at TVE had to keep a shawl handy in case a starlet turned up for a show with a dress that was too *décolleté*. A similar horror of the female mammary glands led TVE's censors to cut from a Jean-Luc Godard film a glimpse of a magazine advertisement for brassières and to reject *Moana*, Flaherty's classic documentary about Polynesia, on the grounds that it included too many shots of bare-breasted native women.

In the forties and fifties it could be argued that the moral climate had at least some foundation in the nature of society. Sexual repression may have been severe, but then society was very traditional. During the sixties and seventies, however, the gap between what was considered acceptable by the authorities and what was considered acceptable by the public grew markedly. Official attitudes changed, but not as quickly or as much as those of society at large. In 1962 the Ministry of Information and Tourism, the department primarily responsible for censorship, was taken away from Gabriel Arias Salgado, the religious bigot who had run the ministry since its inception eleven years earlier, and given to the more pragmatic and secular Manuel Fraga Iribane. The changeover ushered in a period in which some of the more absurd restrictions were lifted. Even so, it was not until 1964, for example, that the censors allowed a woman in a bikini (Elke Sommer as it happened) to appear on the cinema screens. On the other hand, migration from the countryside to the towns, rising prosperity and increased contact with the outside world as a result of tourism and emigration transformed the sexual customs and attitudes of the Spaniards themselves. According to a survey carried out in the last year of Franco's dictatorship for the current affairs magazine *Blanco y Negro*, 42 per cent of Spanish girls had lost their virginity by the age of twenty.

After Franco's death, it was the publishing world which first breached the established taboos. In February 1976 a Spanish magazine called *Flashmen* (sic) carried a photograph of a model in which her bare nipples were plainly visible. Whether by accident or design, it was overlooked by the censor and thereafter *Flashmen* and others of its ilk set about pushing back the frontiers of the acceptable inch by inch and curve by curve. Most of the nude models in the early days were foreign girls, but a previously obscure revue artiste called Susana Estrada won eternal fame by becoming the first Spanish woman in modern times to appear bare-breasted in the pages of a Spanish magazine.

The situation as far as films were concerned was somewhat anomalous, as were so many things at that time. The import of hard-core films for private viewing was banned but the import of soft-core productions for general release was permitted. For several years therefore there were no soft-core films being made in Spain although hard-core one-reelers were being churned out by the dozen by an outfit called Pubis Films. It was not until 1978 that the situation was reversed. It was then that the ban on imported films for private viewing was relaxed and the domestic film industry came up with *El maravilloso mundo del sexo* – a film so embarrassingly dreadful that the boyfriend of one of the starlets walked out on her half way through the première. In other respects 1978 was a turning point. It was the year that Spain got its first sex shop, *Kitsch*, which was opened in Madrid in February and closed by the authorities five months later. It was also the year that the fashion for topless bathing – which was to change forever the Spanish attitude to nudity – reached the holiday *costas*. At first, the *Guardia Civil* did their best to stamp it out – sometimes by charging offenders with not being in possession of their personal documents.* But by the beginning of the following season they had come to realize that it was an impossible task. Ever since then, they have tended to turn a discreet, blind eye and going topless has even become fashionable among Spanish girls. It is difficult, as one watches them walking around all but naked, to believe that their mothers were probably chaperoned.

The years since Franco's death have also witnessed a number of less obvious but more important changes in the law that have helped to narrow – although not, as we shall see, to close – the gap between what actually happens and what is officially condoned.

The first of these was the legalization of contraception. In practice the ban on contraception was never quite total. Condoms could always be obtained, albeit with some difficulty, in red light districts and street markets. The invention of the Pill opened up further possibilities, because – in addition to its purely contraceptive effects – it can be used to treat certain hormonal disorders, such as severe pre-menstrual tension. During the last years of the dictatorship many doctors were prepared to prescribe the Pill on remedial grounds for women who wanted it for contraceptive purposes. By 1975, according to a confidential report drawn up by the *Instituto de Estudios Laborales y de la Seguridad Social* and leaked to *Cambio 16*, the Pill was being used by more than half a million women.

But the demand for contraceptives was still vastly greater than the supply. If, by the end of Franco's rule and in spite of official exhortations to the contrary, the average Spanish family had only 2.5 children, it was mainly due to self-restraint – *coitus interruptus*, *coitus reservatus* and a good deal of simple abstinence.

The fear of an unwanted pregnancy inevitably robs sex of its pleasurability, especially for the woman, who actually has to bear the child. A succession of learned inquiries carried out in the latter years of the dictatorship suggested that between 60 and 80 per cent of married Spanish women were frigid in the sense that they routinely obtained no pleasure from sexual intercourse. In *Las españolas en secreto: Comportamiento sexual de la mujer en España*, Dr Adolfo Abril and José

* Just as it is an offence for Spaniards to go out without their identity card, the *Documento Nacional de Identidad*, it is also – strictly speaking – illegal for foreigners to walk around in Spain without their passports.

Antonio Valverde noted that 'no more than 20 per cent of the (female) population is able to use the word "orgasm" properly, another 30 per cent has heard or read the word "at some time" and the rest – half the (female) population – half of all Spanish women – have never heard the word and do not of course know what it means'.

There is also evidence that the poverty of heterosexual relations under Franco stimulated an abnormal level of lesbianism. In 1971 a Catalan doctor, Ramón Serrano Vicens, published a study based on interviews he had carried out over a period of thirty years with more than a thousand women who attended his surgery. Two thirds of the unmarried women he interviewed admitted to having wanted at some time to have sexual contact with other women – and half of them had actually done so. This could help to explain one of the most curious aspects of the *desmadre sexual* which followed Franco's death – the frequent declarations of bisexuality by singers, actresses and others in the public eye, who were keen to have their fans believe that not just some but all women were bisexual by nature.

The articles in the Penal Code which made the sale of contraceptives illegal were revoked in 1978, but little was done after that to ensure their safe and reliable use. While the UCD remained in power there was no sex education in the schools and the only family planning centres to be set up were financed not by the central government but by local authorities (invariably those run by the left). There is still, therefore, a lot of ignorance about contraception, and it even extends to doctors, especially the older ones. This is particularly dangerous with regard to the Pill, which is now the most popular form of contraception in Spain.

The difficulty of obtaining safe and reliable contraception explains a phenomenon which foreigners find particularly mystifying about the Spaniards – the prevalence among them of abortion. This is perhaps the area of Spanish life where reality and the law are still furthest apart and where the difference in attitudes between young and old is most pronounced. 'Back-street abortions' have long been commonplace in Spain, particularly among working-class women, and although it has never been possible to arrive at an exact figure, a report prepared by the Spanish equivalent of the Attorney-General's office, the *Fiscalía del Tribunal Supremo*, in 1974 while Franco was still alive put the annual total at 300,000. Since then, according to most estimates, the figure has risen to around 350,000. If those estimates are correct, it means that in Spain there is one abortion for every two live births – the closest ratio anywhere in the Western world. Moreover, recent years have seen the growth of a thriving trade in overseas abortions, especially among middle-class girls. The favourite destination is London which attracts some 5,000 young Spanish women every year. In fact, Spaniards account for one eighth of *all* abortions in England and Wales and half those carried out on foreign women.

The prevalence of abortion contrasts dramatically with the stiff penalties for practitioners. Under Spanish law, they can get from six months to twelve years in prison on a single count. In 1979 the case of eleven Bilbao women charged with carrying out abortions became a *cause célèbre*. In the days leading up to their trial 300 women occupied one of the main court buildings in Madrid and were violently evicted by the police. More than a thousand women – including several well-known actresses, lawyers and politicians – published a document announcing that they had had abortions and a similar number of men – including other well-known personalities – signed another document declaring that they had helped to arrange abortions. Whether as a result of this pressure or not will never be known, but when the case came to court it was thrown out by the judges on the unprecedented grounds that the defendants had acted out of necessity. Their verdict did not, however, put an end to the prosecutions. Shortly afterwards, another abortionist was sentenced to twelve years and a girl who had had an abortion in London was fined.

Nevertheless, the outrage felt among middle-class intellectuals at these sentences tends to distract attention from the fact that a clear majority of the Spanish electorate is opposed to abortion on demand, although polls show that the level of opposition is much higher among older voters than among younger ones and that in the youngest age groups, the 'pros' and 'antis' are more or less evenly balanced. On the other hand, abortion in special cases, such as after a rape or when the foetus is seriously deformed or the mother's life is in danger, commands more support – that of about two thirds of the electorate in fact – and the Socialists in their winning manifesto promised to introduce a bill legalizing abortion in these three circumstances. Even so, it was obviously going to be a political hot potato and the Socialists gave the distinct impression of intending to put off the introduction of a bill for as long as possible. The pressure which forced them to take action came from a most unlikely quarter – the courts. During the first few weeks of the Socialist government, the Provincial Court in Barcelona handed down a succession of judgements in which the judges, while reluctantly passing sentence on defendants who had clearly been involved in abortions, criticized the government for its failure to change the law.

At the end of January 1983 the government decided to bring forward its plans for legislation and, as a way of heading off criticism from the right that their bill went too far and from the left that it did not go far enough, they announced a series of measures designed to reduce the need for abortions – the distribution of more family planning information through the state health service, a campaign to eradicate congenital deformity and increased assistance to single mothers. Seemingly unconvinced of the government's resolve, the Barcelona courts kept up the pressure and in March an attorney acting not for the defence but for the prosecution found an even better way of holding the law up to ridicule. As it then stood the only mitigating circumstance which could be taken into account in abortion cases was where the defendant had undergone an abortion 'to hide her dishonour'.* It was such an archaic formulation that it had long since fallen into disuse, but when this particular attorney found himself in the position of having to prosecute a women who was charged with having an abortion, he argued – tongue in cheek doubtless – that she was just such a case. At all events, the judges accepted his plea and reduced her sentence to one month. It was clear that unless something was done, every liberally minded judge in the land would soon be handing out nominal sentences to defendants in abortion cases on the grounds that they had been defending their honour and that this in turn could make Spain look ridiculous internationally. In fact the original case went unnoticed outside Spain but by the end of the year the Socialists' bill had passed through both chambers of the *Cortes*. It became law in 1985 but its implementation has been seriously jeopardized by the refusal of some doctors and nurses to carry out the operation on grounds of conscience.

Up to now, we have been dealing with the restriction of sexuality *per se*. But there is another kind of sexual repression and that is the repression of one sex by the other, which in Western society has invariably meant that of women by men. In the Hispanic countries, this particular form of repression has traditionally been more pronounced than elsewhere and it is no coincidence that the first word coined to describe it should have been a Spanish one.

The word *machismo* did not in fact originate in Spain but in Mexico. Nevertheless, the phenomenon of *machismo* is a product of Mexico's Spanish heritage. Spain – in common with other Southern European societies – lived for centuries by a code of moral values at the core of which was a peculiar conception of honour. It was regarded not, as it was in Northern Europe, as a subjective measure of self-esteem, but as an objective, almost tangible, asset that could be lost both by one's own actions and those of others, particularly one's relatives.

A wife could strip her husband of his honour by cuckolding

---

* Defence of one's honour was also a mitigating circumstance in cases involving the murder of an illegitimate child. It applied not only where the child had been murdered by its mother but also in cases in which it had been put to death by her father (with or without the mother's consent).

him and a daughter could forfeit her father's honour by losing her virginity before marriage. If the girl were betrothed there was a good chance of getting the marriage held earlier than planned, at which point the loss of honour could be minimized, but if she had had sex without even getting engaged, the sanction was horrific because the only way in which the family could save itself from dishonour was by removing the cause, which in this case was the girl herself. Expelled from home, single mothers have usually been unable to find any respectable employment in these societies where it has always been difficult enough for women to acquire a training let alone a job. As a consequence many have been forced into prostitution. In this way, Latin society has divided women into whores and madonnas not just in theory but in practice. For the father of the child, on the other hand, the fact of having had sex before marriage – whatever the circumstances – was as much a distinction as a disgrace.

This was consummately unjust on more grounds than one, since men had less excuse for pre-marital dalliance. Unlike women, they could always resort to prostitutes. But then the reason why frustrated young men were able to afford the services of a prostitute was that they were cheap and the reason why they were cheap was because they were numerous, and that was because their numbers were constantly being replenished by cohorts of unmarried mothers who had themselves been unable to withstand the pressures imposed by the taboo on pre-marital sex. Thus, the Latin way of sex has always had a sort of iniquitous internal logic.

In Spain the discrimination inherent in such a system was given an especially keen edge by the peculiarity of her history – the sustained contact with Islam, a religion which has always held women in low esteem, and the seven centuries of conquest and settlement that were needed to remove Islam from the peninsula and which inculcated among the Christians a special respect for masculine virtues.

The division of women into the stereotypes of whore and mother and the elevation of male attributes are both deeply embedded in the Castilian language and especially its slang. For example, *de cojón* (literally 'of testicle') means 'magnificent'. The usage of phrases involving women is even more telling. *Hijo de puta* (son of a whore) is a serious insult, yet *de puta madre* ('Whore-motherish') means 'great', 'superb', 'fantastic'. The allegation, in *hijo de puta*, that one's own mother might be a whore is intolerable, but the abstract notion of a woman combining both erotic and maternal qualities is nevertheless thought to be highly appealing.

This whole complex of social and moral values was sustained and encouraged under Franco's dictatorship. As a way of promoting the growth of a population which had been severely reduced by civil war, Franco instituted a system of incentives for large families – but the prizes were given to the fathers, not the mothers. Although divorce and contraception were outlawed within a matter of months of the end of the civil war, there was no law to ban brothels until 1956 and even then it was never implemented. At a time when Franco's censors were busy covering boxers' chests and trimming actresses' busts, they were quite content to give their *imprimatur* to a novel, *Lola*, whose heroine was a prostitute-spy. Very nearly two thirds of the men interviewed in the first comprehensive investigation of Spanish sexual attitudes and customs, carried out in the mid-sixties, had had their earliest experience with a professional and in the last year of the dictatorship it was estimated that 500,000 women were working as prostitutes – one in twenty-seven of the adult female population.

How then have women fared under the monarchy? Well, in one important respect things have got worse for them. Rape, which was almost unknown in Spain before the mid-seventies, seems to have become much more common. In 1976 there were only 287 rapes reported in the whole of Spain. By 1983 the figure had risen to 1,071. As in the case of other crimes, the total is still quite low by the standards of other Western countries but the rate of increase is nevertheless worrying, even if it is partly the result of a greater readiness on the part of the victims to go to the police.

However, the increase in rape is a notable exception to the general rule. On almost every other front, *machismo* is in full retreat. Successive governments have undoubtedly helped to change the atmosphere. Shortly after the first general election, the Ministry of Culture produced a series of television advertisements designed to draw attention to the sexual inequality in Spanish society. The most memorable of them opened with a handsome young (male) executive striding down a street towards a group of women of about his own age. As he drew near, the women looked him up and down and then broke into whistles and catcalls, interspersed with suggestive remarks. The effect was hilarious – although none the less effective for that.

Opinion polls suggest that young Spaniards of both sexes are, if anything, rather less sexist than their counterparts in the rest of Europe. In the winter of 1976–7 an extensive survey was carried out at the behest of a multinational advertising agency among young city-dwellers in nine European countries. Asked whether they agreed that 'a woman's place is in the home', only 22 per cent of the young Spaniards said 'yes', compared with 26 per cent in Britain, 30 per cent in Italy and 37 per cent in France. The only countries which returned a lower figure than Spain were the Scandinavian ones.

But while the number of women going out to work has increased substantially in recent years, women still account for a marginally smaller proportion of the workforce than in the other OECD countries. This is because their numbers drop sharply when they reach their mid-twenties – the habit of staying at home after getting married is still deeply ingrained. It is likely to remain so while women continue to be disadvantaged at work. There is still no law to prevent bosses paying women less money for doing the same jobs as men and there are appreciable differences in most sectors of the economy, although by and large they are far greater in factories than in offices.

Nevertheless, the years since Franco's death have seen a number of important moral victories. The UCD's term of office saw a woman appointed to the cabinet for the first time in Spain's recent history and women have also been let into such bastions of rampant *machismo* as the Academy of the Spanish Language, the *Guardia Civil* and the *Policía Nacional*. The first time that women were free to apply for entry to the *Cuerpo Superior de Policía*, one of them – Sagrario Martinez Sanmillán – came out top of the 3,500 applicants. There are now several women jockeys, including one professional; two league football clubs have chairwomen; and one of the First Division men's basketball teams has a female trainer. There is even a woman governor of a men's prison.

But perhaps the greatest advances have been made in the field of civil and family law, where in less than a decade the status of women has undergone a rapid and dramatic improvement.

CHAPTER SIXTEEN

Family ties

It has been said that towards the end of Franco's rule the only European country in which there was a comparable degree of institutionalized discrimination against married women was Turkey and that on several counts the status of wives in Turkey was actually higher. The assumptions underlying the Spanish Civil Code were summed up in Article 57 – 'The husband must protect his wife and she must obey her husband.' At the crux of their legal relationship was the concept of *permiso marital* (marital permission). Without her husband's say-so, a wife could not embark on any sort of activity outside the home. She could not take a job, start a business or open a bank account. She could not initiate legal proceedings, enter into contracts or buy and sell goods. She could not even undertake a journey of any length without her husband's approval.

Under the Spanish system, the property owned by a married couple is divided into three categories – that which the husband has brought into the marriage, that which the wife has brought into the marriage and that which they have acquired since (their so-called *bienes gananciales*). But whereas the man did not need his wife's permission before selling, lending or mortgaging the property he had brought into the marriage, she required his. Not only that but the wife had no control whatsoever over their *bienes gananciales*, even when she had been partly – or entirely – responsible for earning them. As if that were not enough, the wife did not have proper control over her children either, because – unlike the husband – she did not enjoy what was called the *patria potestad* or paternal authority.

Leaving the family home for even a few days constituted the offence of desertion, which meant – among other things – that battered wives could not take refuge in the homes of their friends or relatives without putting themselves on the wrong side of the law. And although adultery by either sex was a crime, punishable by between six months and six years in prison, there were different criteria for men and women. Adultery by a woman was a crime whatever the circumstances, but adultery by a man only constituted an offence if he committed it in the family home, if he were living with his mistress or if his adulterous behaviour was public knowledge.

The first significant reform of this system was approved shortly before Franco died. In 1975 Spain abolished *permiso marital* – fifty-six years after Italy and thirty-seven years after France. The laws against adultery were revoked in 1978 and those articles of the civil code which put women at such a disadvantage with regard to their children and the family finances were replaced in 1981. The same year also saw what, for many Spaniards, was the most important single change brought about by the advent of democracy – the re-introduction of divorce.

Under the dictatorship, there were two kinds of marriage – civil and canonical. But if only one of the partners was a Catholic* they had to have a canonical marriage. Not the least of the injustices of this system was that Protestants and non-Christians who wanted to marry a Spaniard had no choice but to undergo a Catholic ceremony, often against the dictates of their consciences.

Since there was no divorce – the Republican divorce law passed in 1932 had been revoked by the Nationalists six years later while the civil war was still in progress – the only way that a marriage contracted in Spain could be dissolved was by means of an annulment. The circumstances in which a marriage can be annulled in accordance with the laws of the Roman Catholic Church are, on the face of it, highly restrictive. The marriage has to have been unconsummated and non-sacramental and the grounds for an annulment only extend to such contingencies as one of the partners being physically unable to have intercourse, being under age at the time of the marriage or not giving his or her genuine consent.

These strictures did not, however, prevent several thousand Spaniards obtaining an annulment during the years before the introduction of divorce. Ordinary members of the public could not help but notice that the people who got the annulments were invariably rich and either famous or influential. Suspicions were increased still further when some of those who had obtained annulments on the grounds of impotence remarried and had children! Perhaps the most extraordinary case was that of the singer Sara Montiel who had not one, but two marriages annulled to become one of the very few Spanish women up to that time to marry three times.

---

* The law defined as a Catholic anyone who had been baptized in a Catholic Church. In 1969 it became possible for baptized Catholics to renounce their faith by notifying the civil and ecclesiastical authorities.

As of 1971 annulments became even easier to obtain, provided that you had a large amount of money at your disposal. This was because of Pope Paul VI's decision to grant certain dioceses, some of whose ecclesiastical courts had rather laxer standards of evidence than the Spanish ones, the power to annul the marriages of expatriates. A number of Spanish ecclesiastical lawyers set up offices in the Puerto Rican quarters of New York, for example, simply for the purpose of accrediting the residence there of Spanish couples seeking to have their marriages dissolved. Dioceses in which the authorities could be counted upon not to look too closely at the grounds for annulment were found in Haïti, Zaïre, the Central African Republic, Gabon and Cameroon. It is clear, however, that officials employed by the Spanish ecclesiastical courts were also involved in the racket since the annulments granted abroad had still to be ratified in Spain.

Several hundred annulments came from tribunals in the Zaïrean dioceses of Sakania and Lubumbashi, neither of which – as the Vatican subsequently confirmed – had a court authorized to grant annulments. The scandal came to light through the efforts of an ecclesiastical lawyer called Ignacio Careaga whose persistence caused him to be banned from practising by the legal adviser to the Archbishop of Madrid. It was only through the good offices of a conservative Cardinal, appalled by what was happening, that Careaga was able to lay his evidence before the Apostolic Signatura, the Catholic Church's Supreme Court of Appeal in matters of matrimonial law. Shortly before the start of the Spanish Bishops' Conference in 1979, a message arrived from the Vatican asking the bishops to confirm or deny the existence of corruption within the Spanish ecclesiastical judiciary. After a reportedly tumultuous debate, they came up with this extraordinary pronouncement – 'While in no way admitting as absolutely true and objective many of the accusations which have been made about the actions of some courts, we are not unaware that in some cases the procedures themselves or certain circumstances of time and place have led to serious defects in the judicial witness which the Church ought to provide for the world.' The Zaïrean annulments were subsequently declared worthless by the Vatican and a number of well-to-do Spaniards who had paid anything from 800,000 to 2,000,000 pesetas to obtain them in order to get remarried found that they had become bigamists overnight.

For those unhappily married Spaniards who lacked the grounds or resources for an annulment the only solution was a legal separation. But the process of obtaining one was a nightmare. In the first place, there was no guarantee of any kind that the courts would grant a separation at the end of it all. The parties and their lawyers had to prove, rather than merely state, that their marriage had fallen apart and the aim of the judge and the court officials (especially the so-called *defensor del vinculo* or 'defender of the link') was to contrive a reconciliation. Secondly, blame had to be apportioned before a case could be settled. Witnesses had to be called, statements had to be taken. More often than not private detectives had to be hired and on occasions even the police got involved, bursting in on couples *in flagrante delicto*. Nor was the question of guilt simply a matter of personal pride. Whichever party was found guilty not only forfeited custody of the children but also the right to alimony.

In normal circumstances it took between two and three years to obtain a separation, but it could take up to eight years. The expense was therefore considerable – in the mid-seventies it cost about 300,000 pesetas. In theory it was possible for couples with low incomes to apply for a separation and have the cost borne by the authorities, but cases of this sort were virtually worthless to the lawyers and, in practice, they were postponed indefinitely.

When the dictatorship came to an end, there were about a half a million people whose marriages had broken down and who were legally separated, but many, many more living in misery with partners whom they were unable to leave. Not surprisingly therefore, some 71 per cent of Spaniards, according to an official survey carried out in 1975, were in favour of divorce.

Its opponents argued that the effect would be to leave thousands of middle-aged women lonely and impoverished as their husbands set off in pursuit of younger wives. But a timely study of the workings of the 1932 Act – Ricardo Lezcano's *El divorcio en la Segunda Republica* – showed that more than half the petitions during the first twenty-two months that the act was in force were submitted by women. In no less than sixteen provinces – of which, interestingly, the vast majority were rural – *all* the petitions came from women.

By the time that the drafting of a divorce bill began, in 1977, the question was not whether Spain would have a divorce law, but what kind. In contrast to what had happened in Italy, it seemed that the Spanish Church had not come to terms with the idea. A bill passed through the cabinet without incident in January 1980 and was submitted to parliament later than year.

However, the *proyecto Cavero* (Cavero Bill), as it was called after Iñigo Cavero, the Christian Democrat Justice Minister, was considerably less progressive than the mood of the nation. If it had become law, petitions for divorce would have had to be channelled through the old judicial separation procedure with its insistence on a verdict. There was no provision for divorce by mutual consent and the judge was given the power to refuse a divorce if he deemed it to be prejudicial to the interests of one of the partners or to those of the children. The *proyecto Cavero* also suffered from a number of serious technical shortcomings. For example, a wife awarded alimony would have been able to demand it from her ex-husband's heirs – a monstrous injustice whose sole purpose, it seems, was to reduce the government's bill for widows' pensions.

In the summer of 1980 Suárez reshuffled his cabinet and handed the Justice portfolio to Francisco Fernández-Ordóñez, the Social Democrat who had already provided Spain with the foundations of a modern tax system. One of his earliest moves was to withdraw the *proyecto Cavero* from parliament and order the drafting of an entirely new bill. This new bill, inevitably dubbed the *proyecto Ordóñez*, halved the period in which a divorce could be obtained to between one and two years. There was no provision for allotting blame and in effect if not in name it offered divorce by mutual consent.

The Christian Democrats in the UCD were less than happy with it. The Speaker of Congress, Landelino Lavilla, who was one of the leaders of the Christian Democrat wing of the party, succeeded in postponing any further discussion of the bill in parliament until after the UCD's national conference, which was due to be held in January of the following year, in the hope that by then the Christian Democrats would have regained their ascendancy within the party. During the run-up to the conference, their attitude hardened still further and it was and is generally felt in Spain that the intensification of their campaign against the bill reflected the hostility towards it of the new Pontiff, Pope John Paul II.

The long-awaited UCD conference was pre-empted by Suárez's decision to resign – a decision which was at least in part the result of the pressures to which he had been subjected by the constant warring between Christian and Social Democrats over divorce. The choice of Leopoldo Calvo Sotelo as Suárez's successor and the shock of the abortive coup both helped to shift the UCD to the right, but not enough for Fernández-Ordóñez to be removed from the Ministry of Justice.

The bill survived its first debate in Congress more or less intact, but then the leadership of the UCD agreed under pressure from the Christian Democrats that it should be amended in the Senate so as to restore the judge's power to refuse divorce in certain circumstances. However, in the final, historic and tumultuous debate in Congress – on 22 June 1981 – the amendment was removed with the help of the votes of at least thirty UCD deputies who defied the party line. The session broke up in disorder with one Centrist deputy declaring prophetically that 'We may be a coalition but never a party – the models of society which the Christian Democrats and Social Democrats have are just too different.' It was the beinning of the end of the UCD. Within less than eighteen months, it would be deserted by its founder and decimated by the electorate. The issue which, above all others, sealed its fate was divorce.

So, when the dust settled, what sort of divorce law was Spain left with? The answer is, a really quite liberal one. You can get a divorce in Spain by one of two methods – directly or indirectly. In the first case, you have to establish that you have been living apart for at least two years if the separation was mutually agreed, or for at least five years if it was not. In the second case, you have to start by obtaining a legal separation. This can now be done in one of two ways – by citing one of the grounds for legal separation laid down by law, such as adultery, cruelty or desertion, or – provided the marriage has lasted for a year – by simply making a joint approach to the courts. One year after the granting of a legal separation – regardless of how it was obtained – either partner is free to petition for divorce. In other words, whichever path is used, it is possible to get a divorce two years after the break-up of a marriage – a longer period than in some Northern European countries perhaps, but a considerably shorter period than in Italy where couples must first obtain a legal separation and then wait for another five years. And because of that final, dramatic vote in parliament the judges in Spain do not have the power, which they do have in France, to refuse to grant a divorce so long as the petition fulfils one or other of the conditions laid down by law.

Spain's new divorce law came into effect on 7 July 1981 and, as was to be expected, a lot of the earliest petitions came from couples who had completed separation proceedings before divorce was made legal. The vast majority of these had been married by the Church and so the documents to show when they were separated were in the hands of the ecclesiastical courts. It is altogether typical of the Spanish Church's attitude since the departure of Cardinal Tarancón that more than a year after the new law came into effect requests for information addressed by the civil courts to the ecclesiastical tribunals were still being turned down on the grounds that the Bishops' Conference 'still has the subject under consideration'.

PART THREE:

A Divided Nation?

CHAPTER SEVENTEEN

Centrifugal forces

You may have noticed that cars with an international car registration plate bearing the letter E (for España) often have another plate or sticker with, for example, the letter G on a white background with a blue band across it or C on a red and yellow striped background. What they represent are one or other of the traditional regions of Spain. G stands for Galicia and C for Catalonia, and there are others bearing the initial letters and regional colours of each of the other areas. They are not recognized by anyone, least of all the Spanish authorities, but that has not stopped them selling like hot cakes ever since the return of democracy.

Nothing could illustrate better the division of loyalties that so many Spaniards feel. More, I would say, than any other people in Europe, the Spaniards tend to put their loyalty to their region on a par with, or even ahead of, their loyalty to their country. Regional sentiment bedevilled attempts to build a strong unitary state in Spain during the sixteenth and nineteenth centuries. And it is separatism in the shape of ETA and its supporters which now poses perhaps the greatest threat to the survival of democracy.

To some extent, the strength of regional feeling in Spain is simply a manifestation of the Mediterranean tendency to subjectiveness. Southern Europeans, far more than Northern Europeans, will tend to favour whoever is closest to them, physically or socially, regardless of their merits. This is why face-to-face contact is so vitally important in business dealings and why corruption in the form of favouritism towards friends and relatives is so common. The same, I think, applies to places. Traditionally, a Spaniard's greatest affection has always been reserved for his or her native town or district which the Spaniards themselves, in a telling phrase, often refer to as their *patria chica* or little fatherland. Next comes their province, then their region and, last of all, the nation.

With the exception of high-ranking officers in the armed forces and those who are politically well to the right, the nation is the entity for which Spaniards usually feel least affection. 'In general,' wrote Fernando Díaz-Plaja in *The Spaniard and the Seven Deadly Sins*, 'the Spaniard has an instinctive dislike of belonging to associations . . . So the state, the one organization which one cannot help but belong to, is viewed with mistrust. The state is an abhorrent body which is not regarded as the necessary link between the individual and society, but as a conglomeration of interventionist forces attempting to regulate the life of Juan Español* for the sole purpose of doing him down.' Even so, the strength of regional nationalism in Spain cannot be explained entirely or even principally as a reaction to the power of the state. A number of other factors – geographical, historical and cultural – have combined to divide Spaniards from each other and to produce in many of them the conviction that the region comes first and the nation comes second – and, in extreme cases, nowhere at all.

By European standards at least, Spain is a big country. If you leave out Russia, the only country in Europe bigger than Spain is France. It is very nearly half as large again as a reunited Germany would be and, at slightly less than 200,000 square miles or rather more than 500,000 square kilometres, it is almost twice the size of Italy and four times the size of England. Yet throughout its history, Spain's population has been modest. As a result, it was – and is – a country of widely spaced communities. Since earliest times their isolation from one another has been made more acute by a dearth of navigable rivers and, because of the poverty which was Spain's lot, road and rail links developed only very slowly. It was not, for example, until 1974 when the *puente aereo* – the air shuttle between Madrid and Barcelona – was opened that one could travel between the country's two largest cities with any ease. Right up until the late seventies, when a lengthy stretch of motorway was built, the journey by car took about nine hours of solid driving.

The *meseta* which one might think would have drawn the country closer together has, if anything, had the reverse effect. Apart from being a formidable obstacle to communication between the peoples of the periphery, it is itself riven by a succession of mountain ranges – 'those East–West ramparts,' as Laurie Lee called them, 'which go ranging across Spain and divide its people into separate races'.

Spain's geography may not have exactly favoured unity, but it did not make it unthinkable. France is almost as varied and marginally bigger, yet the French today are a remarkably homogeneous people. What ensured that Spain would remain so divided was the course of its history.

---

* Juan Español is to Spain what John Bull is to England.

Like much of the territory bordering the Mediterranean, the Iberian peninsula was visited by Phoenicians, settled by Greeks and finally conquered and occupied by the Romans. When Rome's power declined, the peninsula – in common with most of the rest of Europe – was invaded by tribesmen from the North and East of the continent. At the start of the fifth century, three German peoples – the Alans, Vandals and Sueves – crossed the Pyrenees. The Alans were all but wiped out when the Visigoths, a Christian people loosely allied with Rome, who had carved out a kingdom for themselves with its capital at Toulouse, raided the peninsula in a short-lived attempt to return it to the Empire. The Vandals moved on to North Africa, leaving behind them only the name of the territory they had occupied for less than twenty years – Vandalusia, later corrupted to Andalusia. This left only the Sueves and by the middle of the fifth century they were on the point of taking over the entire peninsula when it was once again invaded by the Visigoths. This time, the Visigoths came to stay. Soon after their invasion of the peninsula they lost most of the territory they controlled on the other side of the Pyrenees and from then on their kingdom became a predominantly Iberian enterprise.

The task of bringing the entire peninsula under Visigothic rule took more than a century. Successive monarchs had to contend not only with the Sueves, who had retreated into the north-west, but also with an army of Byzantines who – in return for helping a Visigothic pretender on to the throne – helped themselves to a large chunk of territory in the south-east. The Sueves were finally overcome in 585 and the last bit of the Byzantine colony was annexed in 624. The Visigothic monarchs continued to be plagued by uprisings among the native population, and in particular by the Basques. But there again so had the Romans. If anything, Visigothic Iberia was rather more united than the other realms that were emerging in Europe after the collapse of the Roman Empire. Both the Visigoths and the majority of their subjects practised Christianity and spoke a form of Latin. Moreover, in the middle of the seventh century the Visigothic monarchy imposed upon the entire country a code of laws applicable to all.

Doubtless, Visigothic rule would not have lasted forever, but there is no reason why – barring a bolt from the blue such as the one that ended it – it could not have survived for a few centuries longer. And when it did fall, it is quite possible that the peninsula would have survived to this day as a single political entity in the way that France has. At the very least, the Visigoths would have been able to bequeath to their successors a land which was in the process of evolving a common language and way of life so that if – like Germany and Italy – Iberia had then disintegrated into a plethora of tiny states, a strong sense of national identity could have survived.

But Iberia was not to follow the same path as the other great geopolitical entities of Europe. Her fate was being decided 3,000 miles away on the shore of the Red Sea where a man who believed himself to be God's messenger was preaching the doctrine of Holy War. Mohammed's followers burst out of Arabia after his death in 632 and by the end of the seventh century their descendants had conquered the whole of North Africa. The first Moslem incursion into Iberia was in 710 when a small reconnaissance force landed at the southernmost point of the peninsula. The following year a former slave, a Berber by the name of Tariq ibn-Ziyad, led an army of about 7,000 ashore at a point close to the huge rock which dominates the entrance to the Mediterranean (the Moslems named the rock Jabal Tariq, or Tariq's Mount, and eventually clumsy Christian tongues changed it to Gibraltar). It took no more than two years for Tariq's small force to subdue the whole of what is now Spain and Portugal. But after crossing the Pyrenees and penetrating to the very heart of France where they were defeated by the Franks, the Moslems withdrew into the southern three quarters of the peninsula. Most of the indigenous inhabitants fell under the rule of the Moslems, but some of them fled across the Pyrenees or took refuge in the line of hills and mountains that stretches along the top of the peninsula from Galicia to Catalonia.

The Moslem invasion shattered the tentative unity that had been achieved by the Visigoths. When the Christians began to fight back, they did so not in unison but grouped into tiny statelets that soon acquired distinct traditions. The first was formed by Visigothic noblemen who had retreated to the mountains of Asturias. Supported intermittently by some of the Basques, the Kings of Asturias expanded westwards into Galicia and southwards until, in the tenth century, they were able to establish their capital on the *meseta* at León. This Asturo-Leónese kingdom was responsible for giving birth to two counties in the strict sense of the word – Castile and Portugal – which subsequently grew into kingdoms themselves. Another miniature state was set up by the Basques in Navarre while further to the east – but still within the foothills of the Pyrenees – a number of little counties were created of which Aragón, soon boasting its own monarchy, emerged as the most powerful. Finally, on the Mediterranean coast, an army composed largely of the descendants of men and women who had fled across the Pyrenees, fought its way back into Catalonia where another network of counties then emerged.

The arrival of the Moslems also put paid to any hope of a single language. Cut off from one another in the mountainous north and brought into much closer contact with the languages of the pre-Roman peoples who lived there than would otherwise have been the case, the descendants of the Latin-speaking refugees who had fled from Tariq's conquering army evolved no less than five separate new languages – Galician, Bable (the language of Asturias), Castilian, Aragonese and Catalan. In the south, the Christians living under Moslem rule developed yet another tongue – Mozarabic. With the exception of Mozarabic, all these languages have survived to the present day, although Bable and Aragonese are nowadays spoken by only a tiny number of people in remote rural areas. Together with Basque and such curious linguistic relics as Aranés (a variety of Gascon Provençal which is spoken in the Aran Valley of northern Catalonia), they constitute a rich heritage – and a source of persistent friction. Today nine million of Spain's thirty-five million inhabitants speak a vernacular language in addition to, or instead of, the official language of the state.

It is noticeable that all but one of the early Christian states started life in the mountains, and mountain regions – Switzerland is a prime example – tend to favour the development at an early stage in their history of representative systems of government. The indigenous inhabitants of the mountains of northern and north-western Iberia were no exception. When they moved south in alliance with descendants of the refugees from the Moslem invasion they took with them their institutions and customs, albeit in a progressively diluted form. In the north-east, the political and social system was much closer to the feudal model developing elsewhere in Europe, but even certain sections of Catalan society were able to win from their rulers political freedoms in exchange for their financial or military contributions. For most of the Middle Ages, therefore, the inhabitants of the Iberian peninsula enjoyed far greater individual freedom and carried far greater individual responsibility than their contemporaries in other parts of Europe. As a consequence, Spaniards today tend to look back at the medieval period when the regional states were at the height of their power not as a time of disunity so much as one of freedom and equality.

The *reconquista* was neither continuous nor co-ordinated. The petty Christian states spent quite as much time fighting each other as they did fighting the Moslems. Outstanding monarchs tried and occasionally succeeded in uniting two or more states either by treaty or conquest, but time and again they were persuaded by factional interests to re-divide their territories in their wills. In fact, the process whereby the various kingdoms came to form a single state lasted far longer even than the *reconquista*. In 1137 the County of Barcelona – which by then had absorbed most of the other Catalan mini-states – was joined by marriage to the Kingdom of Aragón. Together the Catalans and the Aragonese went on to conquer Valencia and the Balearic Islands during the thirteenth century. Castile – which was in the process of recovering a large chunk of Andalusia – and León – which by then took in Asturias, Galicia and Estremadura – eventually came together in 1230 having united and divided twice in the preceding hundred years. The conquest and settlement of Murcia at the end of the thirteenth century was a joint venture by the Crown of Castile (the name given to the state formed by the unification of Castile and León) and the Crown of Aragón (the name given to the state formed by the federation of Aragón and Catalonia). The Navarrese meanwhile, whose most outstanding sovereign, Sancho III, had come closer than any of Spain's medieval rulers to uniting the Christian domains, had for several centuries been looking northwards. At its point of greatest expansion, Navarre took in a large stretch of what is now France and its rulers became entwined by marriage with several French noble and royal families to the extent that it came within a hair's breadth of being incorporated into France.

By contrast, the members of the royal families of the three other kingdoms – Portugal, Castile and Aragón – had so often intermarried that it became inevitable that sooner or later two of these states would be united by inheritance. In the event, it was later rather than sooner, for it was only in 1474 when the ineffectual Enrique IV of Castile died without leaving a son that the opportunity arose. The two claimants to his throne were Isabel, his half-sister, and Juana, the woman he claimed was his daughter but who was alleged by opponents to be the illegitimate offspring of an affair between Enrique's wife and a courtier. The nub of the matter was that Juana was married to Alfonso V of Portugal while Isabel was the wife of Fernando, heir to the throne of Aragón. Whichever of these two won the throne would determine whether the peninsula was to be dominated by an alliance between Castile and Portugal or one between Castile and Aragón. It took a war to settle the issue. But by 1479 – the year in which Fernando succeeded to the throne of Aragón – Isabel's forces had overcome Juana's. Technically, Castile and Aragón remained separate. Under the agreement worked out between Fernando and Isabel each was to reign as sole monarch in his or her own country while ranking as no more than a consort in the realm of the other. But, in practice, Isabel concerned herself with the domestic affairs of both countries while her husband looked after their foreign affairs.

One of Isabel and Fernando's most celebrated joint ventures was the ten-year campaign which culminated in the surrender in 1492 of the Kingdom of Granada – the last Moslem stronghold on the peninsula. The fall of Granada marked the end of the *reconquista*. It had lasted for almost 800 years and it had had a profound effect on the characters of both the Spanish and the Portuguese, although – as more than one historian has pointed out – the fact that Portugal was fully reconquered more than 200 years before Spain meant that it left a much greater impression on the latter than on the former. The legacy of almost eight centuries of conquest and colonization can be seen in many aspects of Spanish life, such as the almost casual acceptance of violence and bloodshed, and in the two most contradictory aspects of the Spanish character – their immense respect for firm leadership and their uncompromising faith in their own judgement and ability. It also, I believe, gave rise to a trait which is characteristic of other frontier societies, like those of North America and South Africa – an inordinate love for the land that has been captured and settled.

The gradual spread of the Christian peoples through the peninsula had cleared the way for a corresponding expansion of the Romance languages that had begun life in the highlands of the north. Some prospered more than others. In the west, Galician had given birth to Portuguese. In the east, Catalan had spread to the Balearic Islands and to much of Valencia. But it was Castilian which had become preeminent – to the point that it would come to be known in most of the rest of the world as 'Spanish'. Spaniards who speak one of the other languages tend to believe that Castilian gained its ascendancy by dint of force – by conquest in medieval times and by repression and coercion more recently. This is only partly true. An equally important reason for its expansion has been that it is a superbly efficient and flexible means of communication which, whenever it has come into contact with another language, has tended to be adopted solely on its merits. In the centre of the country, it had made inroads into the Kingdoms of León to the west and Aragón to the east, displacing Bable and Aragonese respectively long before Castile acquired any political clout in either area. Its linguistic excellence also won it a foothold in the Basque country centuries before anyone tried to force the Basques to abandon their native tongue. It was undeniably force of arms which allowed it to spread through Andalusia. But it is significant that when Castilian clashed head on with Catalan in Murcia, following a campaign in which the Castilians and the Catalans both took part, it was Castilian – albeit sprinkled here and there with Catalan words and phrases – which emerged as the language of the region.

Events following Isabel's death in 1504 underlined the shakiness of the alliance between Castile and Aragón. For one thing, she had added a codicil to her will barring the Aragonese and their confederates, the Catalans and the Valencians, from trading with the New World discovered by Columbus in the same year that the Christian Spaniards conquered Granada. Isabel's only son and his posthumous son had both died before she had, so the Crown of Castile passed to her daughter, another Juana who – being mentally incapable of ruling – had to have a regent. Since Fernando had remarried and gone to live in Italy, the task fell to Juana's husband. It was only his sudden death in 1506 that caused Fernando to become involved once more, as regent, in the affairs of Castile. In this capacity he was responsible for the incorporation of the third of the medieval peninsular kingdoms when, in 1514, he masterminded the annexation of most of Navarre.

Fernando died two years later. Although it was Isabel who had consciously aspired to the unification of the peninsula, it was he who had done most to bring it about. Appropriately, he left his own kingdom, Aragón, to Juana's son Carlos. Rather than follow in his father's and grandfather's footsteps by becoming regent in Castile, Carlos insisted on being made King.

His accession in 1516 is traditionally regarded as marking the unification of Spain. But that is only true with hindsight. The goal had always been – and remained – the re-unification of the whole of Iberia and that was not achieved until 1580 when Carlos's son, Felipe II, annexed Portugal after its King had died on a madcap expedition to North Africa, leaving behind him no obvious heir. What then happened was that the process of unification suffered a reverse – as it had many times in the past. This time it was not the result of a will but a war. In 1640 the Catalans and the Portuguese, both of whom had been chafing at Castile's insensitive centralism, rebelled against Madrid. The Catalans were finally beaten into submission in 1659, but the Portuguese survived as a separate nation ruled by a new dynasty until in 1665 they confirmed their independence by defeating the Spaniards at the Battle of Montes Claros.

Spain and Portugal were never again to re-unite, although the dream of re-unification through a loose confederation of the traditional regions was to persist until this century. That the six states which emerged in the north of the peninsula should have evolved into two nations – one of them made up of five of those states and the other consisting of the remaining one – was a matter of the purest chance. Had a battle here or there gone the other way, had this or that son not died in infancy, had this or that mother not perished in childbirth, the division might have been altogether different. Contrary to what the more rabid of Spain's centralists claim, there is absolutely nothing 'sacred' about the unity of Spain, because there was nothing pre-ordained about its shape.

The Habsburg and Bourbon monarchs who ruled Spain from the beginning of the sixteenth until the end of the eighteenth centuries were aware that their realms were circumstantial conglomerations of states that had once been independent and this was reflected in the fact that, with the exception of Felipe II, they styled themselves *Rey de las Españas* (King of the Spains). It did not mean, however, that they were happy with the situation in which they found themselves, which was that several regions enjoyed political faculties and economic privileges that seriously limited the power of the central government and made the construction of a modern state virtually impossible.

The choice of Madrid as a capital was a response to this dilemma. Up until the reign of Felipe II, the Spanish court had moved from place to place. But in 1561 he decided that the machinery of government ought to remain in one place. In an effort not to boost the power and status of any one region, he hit on the idea of putting his court in the geographical centre of the peninsula. Madrid is almost totally devoid of natural advantages. It does not have a harbour. It does not stand by the shores of a lake or at the meeting place of two rivers. The reason why human beings settled there is because of an escarpment which offers commanding views across the surrounding plain. Throughout the Middle Ages the military importance of that escarpment made Madrid a valuable prize for Moors and Christians alike. But with the end of the *reconquista*, Madrid would almost certainly have withered into insignificance had it not been for Felipe's initiative. Like Bonn and Brasilia, Madrid is an 'artificial' rather than an 'organic' city and it has never therefore had much of a hold over the country's affections.

The change of dynasty from Habsburg to Bourbon was marked by a lengthy and bloody war – the so-called War of the Spanish Succession lasting from 1702 until 1713 in which the traditional regions of Spain were again split into two opposing camps, each of which supported a rival claimant. It also marked a shift in the Crown's approach to its more restive subjects. Whereas the Habsburg Felipe IV had refrained from taking reprisals against the Catalans after they rebelled in 1640, the Bourbon Felipe V who emerged as the victor from the War of Succession punished the Catalans, Aragonese and Valencians who had supported his opponent by annulling their laws and institutions and thus creating within the Catalan-speaking part of Spain an undercurrent of discontent that has persisted to this day.

The Spaniards' reaction to the occupation of their country by the French in 1808 underlined something which foreigners, and indeed many Spaniards, find difficult to understand – that for most Spaniards patriotism and a form of regionalism or nationalism that borders on separatism are not mutually exclusive. In what came to be known as the War of Independence, Galicians, Basques, Castilians, Aragonese, Catalans and Andalusians turned on the interloper with a ferocity which proved that, however distinct they might feel themselves to be from one another, they felt a good deal more different from foreigners. Yet they did so in a characteristically independent way. The vacuum left behind by the overthrow of the monarchy was filled, not by a provisional central government set up in opposition to the administration installed by the French, but by a plethora of local *juntas* (committees), most of which ran their own tiny armies.

France's short-lived occupation introduced the relatively small Spanish middle class to a number of ideas about government that were then regarded as progressive. As I mentioned earlier, one of these was that the monarch ought to be subject to a constitution. Another was that a modern state ought to be uniform. It could not tolerate feudal rights and privileges. The result was that the cause of centralism in nineteenth-century Spain was taken up by the bourgeois proponents of a constitution – the *liberales* – while the defence of traditional local laws was left to the supporters of absolutism, who were mostly to be found among the most reactionary sections of the aristocracy and the peasantry. Unhappily for Spain, a dispute over the succession enabled these two opposing groups to identify themselves with rival claimants to the throne. Twice during the last century, the ultra-reactionary Carlist pretenders waged unsuccessful but highly disruptive wars against a monarchy which – although not progressive by instinct – was forced to turn for support to the *liberales*. The Carlist cause appealed above all to the pious, reactionary and fervently independent Basque peasantry and when Carlism was finally defeated in the 1870s, the central government penalized the Basques – including a large section of the community which had stayed loyal to the central government – by abolishing their traditional rights and privileges.

As Spain entered the final quarter of the nineteenth century, therefore, the central government had succeeded in alienating precisely those regions – Catalonia and the Basque country – where conditions existed, or were about to develop, that would foster the growth of modern nationalism. In the first place, the Basques and Catalans had a language and a culture of their own (this factor alone was sufficient to stimulate the growth of an effective nationalist movement in Galicia). Secondly, these were the two parts of Spain which industrialized first and which were therefore the earliest to nurture a substantial middle class of the kind which, in every part of the world, has been eager to support nationalist aspirations. Among the Basque and Catalan middle classes, a sentimental hankering after traditional values mingled with a feeling of superiority with regard to the hated Castilians. This feeling stemmed largely from the quite reasonable belief that Madrid was incapable of understanding the problems of advanced industrial societies such as theirs. But it was also in part the result of an instinctive desire to dissociate themselves from Spain's decline.

Unfortunately for Madrid both the Basques and Catalans live hard by the two main routes into France and in each case there are people of their own race on the other side of the border. Rebel Spanish Basques and Catalans have never found it difficult to find refuge or supplies, especially since it has often proved convenient for Paris to turn a blind eye to the activities of the Basques and Catalans under French rule as a means of distracting the Spanish government and exhausting its resources.

The defeat of Carlism put paid to any chance that regional aspirations might be fulfilled by the accession of an absolute monarch. From then on, the Basques' and Catalans' best hopes lay with the overthrow of the *liberal* monarchy by opponents at the other end of the political spectrum. Spanish radicals had already developed an affection for federalism which came to the fore when they ruled the country for less than a year during the First Republic (1873–4). When the monarchy was once again overthrown in 1931, the pressure for home rule was immense. The Catalans were granted a Statute of Autonomy in 1932 and the Basques and the Galicians were on the verge of gaining a limited form of home rule when civil war broke out again in 1936.

Although General Franco and his allies described themselves as Nationalists, what they meant was that they were Spanish nationalists – wholly opposed to the regional nationalism which they regarded as one of the principal reasons for the turmoil that had bedevilled the Second Republic. During the early years, not only was it forbidden to teach the vernacular languages but serious efforts were made to stop people from speaking them. They could not be used on official premises or at official functions. Stickers were even put up in telephone booths telling callers that they had to conduct their conversations in Castilian or – to use the parlance of the regime – 'speak Christian'. A ban on the publication of books in vernacular languages did not last long, but a similar prohibition on their use in the press, and on radio and television remained in force until Franco's dying day.

Indeed, such was the intransigence of Franco's centralism that it succeeded in creating nationalist regionalist groups in areas such as Estremadura and Murcia where no one had previously questioned their Spanishness. Ironically, although not perhaps surprisingly, it was regional nationalism in its most radical and violent form which ensured that Franco's style of government would not survive him when, in 1972, his Prime Minister and chosen successor, Admiral Carrero Blanco, was blown to pieces by terrorists drawn from among the most fiercely independent minority of all – the Basques.

CHAPTER EIGHTEEN

The Basques

The most obvious difference between the Basques and their neighbours in France and Spain is their extraordinary language which the Basques themselves call *euskera* or *euskara*, depending on which dialect they speak. Although, over the years, it has absorbed individual words from both French and Spanish, the basic vocabulary and structure of the language bears absolutely no resemblance to either.

A phrase taken at random from a text-book, 'The table is laid – you can bring in the food,' comes out in Basque as '*Mahaia gertu dago. Ekar dezakezue bazkaria.*' The syntax is no less exotic. The definite article 'the' is not a separate word but a suffix. Nouns used with numerals remain in the singular. Auxiliary verbs vary according to the number of objects as well as the number of subjects and what we would call prepositions are in Basque suffixes and prefixes, which alter according to whether the word to which they are attached represents something animate or inanimate. The author of the first Basque grammar entitled his work *The Impossible Overcome*. One sixteenth-century Sicilian author was convinced that the Basques' strange tongue enabled them to communicate with the monsters of the deep.

It seems always to have been assumed that Basque was a language of great antiquity. In the Middle Ages, when it was believed that the various languages of the world were the product of God's intervention at the Tower of Babel, a number of scholars argued that it was the language which Noah's grandson, Tubal, was said to have taken to Iberia and that in ancient times Basque must have been spoken throughout the peninsula. Long after the Biblical explanation of the origin of languages had been called into question elsewhere in Europe this theory was stoutly defended within the Basque country itself, largely because of the immense authority there of the Church. Some Basque authors went as far as to claim that theirs had been the original language of

Europe or even the world. There is no doubt that Basque was once spoken over a much larger area than it is today – an area which almost certainly included the entire Pyrenees, since it is known to have been spoken in parts of Aragón and Catalonia during the Middle Ages. But it was never the language of all Iberia, much less that of Europe or the world.

Modern scholarship has, however, shown that it is indeed an extremely old language. The touchstone of modern philology was the discovery towards the end of the eighteenth century that many European and Asian languages – subsequently given the name Indo-European – came from a common source. Throughout the nineteenth century, Basque resisted all attempts to find it a place in the Indo-European family and philologists have eventually had to reconcile themselves to the conclusion that Basque predates the migrations from the East which brought the Indo-European languages into Europe some 3,000 years ago. But there is also evidence that it may be much older even than that. It has been suggested, for example, that words like *aitzkor* (axe) and *aitzur* (hoe) derive from *aitz* (stone) and date from the time when tools were made of stone.

Recent research has concentrated on trying to find a link between Basque and other pre-Indo-European languages, such as those still spoken in the Caucasus and among the Berbers of North Africa, using a method invented by the American linguist Morris Swadesh, whereby a hundred-word passage in one language is compared with a hundred-word passage in another language to discover the percentage of similar words. Up to 5 per cent is regarded as no more than coincidence. But it has been found that there is a 7 per cent overlap between Basque and two of the three Caucasian languages, Georgian and Circassian, and a 10 per cent overlap between Basque and certain Berber languages, which suggests that there could well be a distant link.

While linguists have been puzzling over the singularity of the Basques' language, doctors and scientists have been discovering that they have other, less evident, peculiarities. To understand these, one has to make a brief detour into the world of serology, the study of blood.

On occasions, when the blood of two individuals is brought into contact, it coagulates. This is because the blood of at least one of them contains what is called an antigen. There are two types of antigen – A and B. Some people have both and they are classified as type A/B. Other people's blood contains only one antigen and they are classified as either A or B. But there is also a third category (O) whose blood contains no antigens at all. There are two reasons why all this is of importance to anthropologists. Firstly, antigens are hereditary – no one can have either A or B in their bloodstream unless at least one of their parents had it in his or hers. Secondly, the proportion of each blood type in the population varies significantly from place to place. As one moves across Europe from East to West, for example, the percentage of As increases while the percentage of Bs decreases. The Basques conform to this pattern, but to an exaggerated degree. The percentage of As is higher and the proportion of Bs lower than one would expect for a people perched on the Atlantic coast.

In 1939 an American researcher opened up new fields for exploration when he discovered a substance in the blood of the Macacus Rhesus monkey which was also found to be present in the blood of some humans. According to whether or not their blood contained the new substance, people could thereafter be divided into Rhesus positive (Rh+) and Rhesus negative (Rh−). It was found that in Europe the percentage of Rhesus negatives was higher than in other parts of the world and that throughout the continent it was a more or less uniform 12 to 16 per cent. The relevance of this to the Basques was discovered, not by researchers in the Basque country, but by an ordinary general practitioner working thousands of miles away in Argentina who was concerned with an entirely different problem – eritroblastosis. This is an often fatal illness wich affects newly born children whose blood is incompatible with that of their mothers. In most cases, the problem arises because the mother is Rh− while her child is Rh+, having inherited the substance from its father. The general practitioner, Dr Miguel Angel Etcheverry, noticed that an unusually high proportion of these unfortunate mothers were, like him, of Basque descent. To test his suspicion, he took samples from 128 Argentinians with four Basque grandparents and discovered that fully one third of them were Rh−, which was an abnormally high proportion even for a group of European descent. After his findings were published in 1945, a series of studies in the Spanish Basque country all produced figures in excess of 30 per cent and one, carried out in the French Basque country, put the proportion of the population who did not have the Rhesus substance in their blood at 42 per cent – the highest figure recorded anywhere in the world. As far as blood grouping was concerned, therefore, the Basques were emerging as exceptionally 'European' (by virtue of their Rhesus count) and very 'Westerly' (by virtue of their antigen pattern).

Throughout history, the Basques have been thought of by their neighbours as being bigger and stronger. A great deal of measuring and weighing by anthropologists, especially during the early part of this century, proved this to be the case. The Basques were found to be, on average, two to three centimetres taller than the average in France and Spain and, although they tended to be more muscular, their limbs – and in particular their hands and feet – were inclined to be quite delicate.

The anthropologists also established that the typical Basque had a distinctive 'hare's head', broad at the top and narrow at the bottom, and that he or she was likely to have a high forehead, a straight nose and a distinctive bulge over the temples.

By themselves, these findings proved nothing. But when they were put alongside the archaeological discoveries of that period, they became very interesting indeed. Shortly after the First World War, two Basque researchers, Telesforo de Aranzadi and José Miguel de Barandiarán, had begun excavating a number of dolmens dating from around 2000 B.C., the time of the Indo-European invasions. The bones they found in them suggested that the people who had lived in the Basque country at that time had the same physical characteristics as the Basques of today. But even more interestingly, a skull found in the mid-thirties by Aranzadi and Barandiarán in a cave near Itziar in Guipúzcoa dating from the late stone age – about 10,000 B.C. – also displayed several typically Basque traits, suggesting that the Basques of today could be the direct descendants of Cro-Magnon man.

Taken in conjunction with the absence from Basque folklore of any sort of migration legend, the linguistic, serological, anthropological and archaeological evidence all points towards the same, remarkable conclusion – that the Basques are the last surviving representatives of Europe's aboriginal population. Secure in a homeland of steep-sided hills and valleys much of which was covered in dense forest, they seem to have had only the most limited contact with the peoples who entered Europe two millennia before Christ and who brought with them their Indo-European languages and their distinctive blood group distribution, characterized by a high proportion of B and Rh+. Thereafter, isolated from those around them by language as well as geography, the Basques began to inculcate that resistance to outside influence – and especially outside rule – which is the hallmark of their history.

The Basques enter written records with the arrival of the Romans. The Latin authors noted that there were four tribes in what is now the Spanish Basque country – the Vascones, the Vardulos, the Caristios and the Autrigones. Interestingly, each of the areas in which a particular Basque dialect is spoken today coincides roughly with an area occupied by one of these tribes. Navarrese is, or was, spoken in the area once inhabited by the Vascones. Guipuzcoan corresponds to that of the Vardulos, Biscayan to that of the Caristios and the part of the Basque country outside Navarre in which Basque has long since ceased to be spoken was once the land of the Autrigones.

In the seventeenth century, the theory was put forward that the Vascones were the only genuine Basques and that they imposed their culture on the other tribes in the period following the Roman occupation of Iberia. The theory gained wide acceptance and Biscay, Guipúzcoa and Alava came to be known as the *provincias Vascongadas* (Vasconized provinces). The theory has since been discredited, but you will still see the phrase used in old-fashioned newspapers like *ABC*.

One of the most enduring myths about the Basques is that they were never subject to Roman rule. Spaniards will earnestly assure you even now that the reason why the Basques are so fiercely independent is that they were never given a taste of Roman discipline. It is true that the Romans had to contend with persistent rebellions in the Basque country, but their grip on the area was firm enough to enable them to build roads and settlements there and even run the odd iron mine. Basque soothsayers were renowned throughout the Empire.

The collapse of Roman rule marked the last time that all the Basques were subject to the same administration, although that is not to say that the Basques on both sides of the Pyrenees had formed a single administrative entity either before or during Roman rule. After the legions departed, it was left to the Romans' 'barbarian' successors to try to impose their will on the area – the Franks strove to control an area roughly corresponding to the modern French Basque country and the northern part of Navarre while the Visigoths attempted to govern what is now Guipúzcoa, Biscay, and Alava. Neither succeeded fully.

In 605 the Franks set up a dependent Duchy of Vasconia, which at one stage stretched from the Garonne to the Ebro. It was shaken by a succession of violent revolts until, in 824, a Frankish army returning from an unsuccessful campaign against the Moslems was ambushed by Basques in the Valley of Roncesvalles. The ensuing battle was immortalized in the *Chanson de Roland*, although its author depicted the attackers as Moors not Basques. Soon after Roncesvalles, the Basques in the south of the Duchy declared themselves independent. The state they founded, which at first controlled no more than a small area around Pamplona, was destined to become the Kingdom of Navarre. It subsequently expanded to take in much of the French Basque country and a large area, non-Basque in speech and custom, to the south of Pamplona.

The Visigoths, meanwhile, were forced to wage repeated wars against the Basques of Alava, Biscay and Guipúzcoa but never seem to have actually ruled them except for brief spells. The Visigothic nobles who founded the Kingdom of Asturias inherited the Visigoths' claim to the western Basque country. But they and their successors, the Kings of Castile and León, had to contend not only with the Basques' stubborn refusal to be ruled, but also with the rival ambitions of the new Kingdom of Navarre. Next to nothing is known about the provinces of Alava, Biscay and Guipúzcoa during this period, but it was clearly a pretty wild place. It was the last area of Southern and Western Europe to be converted to Christianity, probably in the ninth or tenth centuries. Local legends suggest that pockets of paganism survived for quite a long time afterwards and as late as the twelfth century nominally Christian Basques were harrying pilgrims on their way to the shrine of St James at Compostela. It was also the last region of Europe to acquire towns – the last to be civilized in the strict sense of the word. The earliest inland settlements in Guipúzcoa were not founded until the second half of the thirteenth century and those in Biscay were not established until the latter half of the fourteenth.

Treaties were drawn up solemnly allotting this or that province or the entire area to either Castile or Navarre, but to all intents and purposes power was held locally. The Alavese were ruled by nobles, but Biscay and Guipúzcoa retained a kind of primitive democracy in which the heads of all the families in a valley either elected or formed a council that sent representatives to a provincial assembly. The provincial assembly decided who should be responsible for taking decisions about the affairs of the province when the assembly was not in session. At different times, this power was delegated to councils of notables or to elected or hereditary lords (there was an aristocracy in both provinces but its power seems to have been more economic and social than political).

Although the Basque country was a poor area, serfdom disappeared there more swiftly and completely than elsewhere in Spain, and by the end of the Middle Ages the liberties enjoyed by ordinary Basques would have been the envy of their counterparts elsewhere in Europe – they could bear arms, they were free to hunt and fish and they were entitled within their native district to make use of what were usually extensive common woodlands and pastures.

The Kings of Castile acquired sovereignty over the western Basques only very slowly and gradually. The Guipúzcoan notables in the thirteenth century and the Alavese aristocracy in the fourteenth century both voted to offer the Castilian Crown the overlordship of their respective provinces, while the lordship of Biscay passed to Castile by inheritance in 1379. Navarre, on the other hand, remained fully independent until 1512 when Fernando, the King of Aragón and Regent of Castile, who was at that time waging a war against the French, demanded that the Navarrese allow his troops free passage through their realm. The Navarrese refused and Fernando invaded and annexed their kingdom. In 1530 the newly united Kingdom of Spain relinquished the bulk of what had been Navarrese territory on the other side of the Pyrenees and the Spanish Basque country took on more or less its present shape.

Although nominally integrated into the Spanish state, the

Basques held back a good deal of power from the central government. In Guipúzcoa and Biscay they retained intact their system of local administration. The Guipúzcoan assembly could veto laws submitted by the Spanish sovereign with the words 'we obey but do not comply' and the Biscayan elders insisted that as soon as a monarch succeeded to the throne, he or she or a representative had to go to the province and swear to uphold its laws beneath the tree in Guernica where their assembly met. The Navarrese, for their part, enjoyed the privilege of being ruled by a viceroy – the only one outside the Americas – and were allowed to retain their own local legislature, executive and judiciary. They also had the right to mint their own money – as late as the nineteenth century the Navarrese were striking coins depicting King Fernando VII of Spain as King Fernando III of Navarre. These political rights, together with a number of valuable economic and social privileges such as immunity from Spanish customs duties and exemption from military service outside their native province, were embodied in codes of traditional law known as *fueros*.

Nationalists tend inevitably to emphasize the extent of the Basques' independence under the Castilian Crown, but remain silent about their close links with the Castilian people. Yet one of the reasons why the Basques enjoyed such a privileged status was precisely because they had been associated for so long and so intimately with the Castilians, even though it had always been on their own terms. Basques helped the Castilians to establish their earliest settlements on the *meseta* and subsequently played a prominent role in many of the decisive battles of the Castilian *reconquista*. Under the Habsburgs, the Basque country provided Spain with some of its finest administrators, two of its greatest explorers – Pedro de Ursua and Lope de Aguirre whose doomed search for Eldorado provided the inspiration for Werner Herzog's film *Aguirre, Wrath of God* – and two of its most celebrated religious figures, St Ignacio Loyola and St Francisco Xavier.

Another distinguished Basque from Spain's Golden Age was Sebastián Elcano, who took command of the first expedition to circumnavigate the globe after its commander, Magellan, had been killed in the Philippines. The Basques had for centuries had close links with the sea. They seem to have learnt how to fish from the Normans and, until the eighteenth century, they were also renowned whalers. Some of their terminology was picked up by the whalers of the Azores who passed it on to the seamen from Massachusetts who used the Azores as a supply base in the last century. The word for a sperm whale, cachalot, is ultimately of Basque origin. But although the fishing villages of the Guipuzcoan and Biscayan coast have always played a large part in the life and lore of the region, its soul lies inland where, between the end of the *reconquista* and the start of the Carlist Wars, there evolved a highly idiosyncratic society, the last traces of which can still be detected in the Basque country of today.

Its outstanding characteristic is the relatively low proportion of the population concentrated in villages and the correspondingly high proportion scattered over the countryside in homesteads. This pattern is thought to have developed in the stable and prosperous sixteenth century at the same time as the characteristic Basque farmhouse – called *caserío* in Spanish and *baserri* in Basque – began to take shape. The earliest *caseríos* consisted of a ground floor containing accommodation for both humans and animals and a top floor where grain was stored. In later designs the people slept upstairs, but the cooking and eating continued to take place downstairs next to the stables. With their steep roofs, the *caseríos* look very like Alpine chalets. Most of them are held on tenure (although the number of owner-occupiers has been increasing since the fifties) and they almost always stand on the land which their occupants farm. The farms are small (about six hectares on average) and invariably include a wide variety of crops and livestock. They are as a result extremely uneconomic. Traditionally, the *caseríos* housed a larger social grouping than the nuclear family – a couple, their children, an unmarried brother or sister, the parents of either the husband or wife and one or two servants, all living under the same roof.

The status of women has always been relatively high and it could well be that this is a last distant echo of the matriarchies which are thought to have existed throughout northern Spain in prehistoric times. The rural Basque country is also one of the few areas in Europe where there has never been more than a minimal division of family wealth. In much of the region this was achieved by transferring the *caserío*, the land attached to it and the family's entire wealth to the first-born (in some parts, regardless of whether the eldest child was male or female). Elsewhere, the parents chose whichever child appeared most capable.

Like many historically poor peoples, the Basques are renowned for the excellence of their cuisine and for eating to excess whenever they have the opportunity. The traditional Basque drinks are beer, cider and an acid 'green' wine called *txacolí*, but in recent times they have had increasing access to the excellent wines of the Rioja. Drunkenness does not incur quite the same fierce social disapproval that it does in the more southerly parts of Spain.

Another distinctive trait of traditional Basque society is the important role accorded to sport. The Basques have invented numerous games. The most famous is *pelota*, a game not unlike squash, which dates back at least to the sixteenth century when it was played by between eight and ten players wearing gloves and when, long before the development of professional sport in the rest of the world, there were semi-professional *pelota* players touring the Basque country giving demonstration matches. Since then, it has undergone numerous changes and evolved several variants. The name of one of them, *Jai-Alai*, is sometimes used to describe the sport as a whole. The arm basket or *txistera* which is used in one form of the game – and which allows players to throw the ball at the wall at extraordinary speeds – is not as traditional as is sometimes assumed. It only made its appearance in the middle of the last century. Some of the other sports which still thrive in the Basque country are caber-tossing, woodcutting, stone-lifting and *sokatira* (in which oxen are made to drag huge lumps of stone over short distances – often across town squares). There were also once games similar to golf (*perratxe*) and cricket (*anikote*), but they have died out. Not surprisingly in view of where they live, the Basques are celebrated hill-walkers and rock-climbers and their mountaineering clubs have traditionally been a breeding ground for extreme nationalist sentiment.

Perhaps because of the importance attached to sport, gambling has always played a big part in Basque life. It is not unusual to see a blackboard in a Basque bar smothered with wagers struck between the customers. Even the folk culture of the area has a competitive edge, exemplified by the *bertsolariak* or poetry competitions – in which the participants improvise in accordance with a given metre, each taking his cue from his rival's poem. But then the way in which most of the arts are expressed or practised in the Basque country is quite different from in the rest of Spain. Basque art is unusually symmetrical, for example. The music has none of the sinuousness of flamenco and it employs several instruments unique to the region. One is the *txistu*, a kind of flute with two finger-holes at the top and one at the bottom which is played one-handed, allowing the musician to beat a drum with his other hand. Then there is the *trikitrixa*, a small accordion, and the *alboca*, which is made from a bull's horn and sounds like the bagpipes. The songs are unusual within Spain in that each note corresponds to a syllable and the dances, which include equivalents of the Greek glass dance and the Scottish sword dance, are more athletic than sensual, the object being to prove one's agility rather than one's grace.

To an even greater extent than the rest of Spain, this isolated, innocent society was quite unprepared for the new ideas that were to enter the country during the nineteenth century – and in particular the Napoleonic concept of a centralized state whose citizens should all be subject to the same laws. The Basques soon learnt to equate this new way of thinking with antipathy to the *fueros*. They were first abolished by Napoleon himself after the invasion of Spain, and then by the *liberales* when they seized power for a brief period in the 1820s. On each occasion they were re-established by the reactionary Fernando VII and so it was natural that when his brother, Don Carlos, raised the standard of absolutism, the Basques should be tempted to rally round it. But Don Carlos's fanatical Catholicism, which so appealed to the rural peasantry, appalled the urban bourgeoisie and throughout the Carlist Wars the bulk of the middle class in towns like Bilbao sided with Madrid against Carlism.

As a way of punishing the Basques for supporting the Carlist rebellion, the *fueros* of Biscay and Guipúzcoa were again revoked in 1841 following the First Carlist War, only to be restored subsequently. But at the end of the Second Carlist War in 1876 the government decreed the abolition of the *fueros* of Guipúzcoa, Biscay and Alava – but not those of Navarre – in a move that was never to be rescinded. All that remained of the Basques' traditional privileges in the three western provinces was a special tax collection system called the *concierto económico*. But the problem with using the abolition of the *fueros* as a punishment was that it affected all Basques and not just those who had supported Carlism. In fact, the class whose economic prospects were most severely affected was the urban lower-middle class, who had tended to support the central government. Within a few years of the abolition of the *fueros*, moreover, the Basque country was to embark upon a period of rapid industrialization in which this newly disaffected lower-middle class was to play a key role.

The origins of the industrialization of the region are to be found in its ample supplies of iron and timber and the abundance of fast-running streams and rivers. The period of fastest growth was between 1877 and 1902 when the industrialization was largely confined to Biscay. It was not until the end of the period that industry began to seep into Guipúzcoa. Although there were and are several large factories in the area, the outstanding characteristic of Basque industrialization has been a multitude of small workshops both inside and outside the cities. Whereas the upper-middle-class owners of the factories, together with the owners of the big banking and insurance concerns which grew up alongside them, tended to align themselves with the Spanish economic oligarchy, often acquiring titles of nobility in the process, the lower-middle-class bosses of the workshops came to regard industrialization as a process from which they had gained less than they had lost. It did not make them particularly rich, yet it caused an influx of hundreds of thousands of workers from other parts of Spain – *maketos* they called them – who threatened the survival of Basque society in its traditional form.

The man who systematized their fears and resentments into

the political ideology which we know as Basque nationalism was one Sabino de Arana Goiri. Born in 1865 Arana was the son of a Carlist whose political sympathies had earned him a period of exile in France. Arana first entered the ideological battlefield at the age of thirty, appropriately enough with an article on the spelling in Basque of the word 'Basque'. His earliest writings were all about philology and etymology. In fact, one of his less fortunate legacies was to distort and complicate written Basque in an attempt to cleanse it of what he considered to be Hispanicisms. In his efforts to avoid any taint of centralism, he also invented a series of Basque christian names to replace Spanish ones so that Luis, for example, became Koldobika. His most useful contribution was to provide the Basques with a word for the land they inhabited. There had always been a word for the Basque-speaking region – *Euskalerría* – but it had the disadvantage of excluding all those areas populated by Basques where Castilian had taken hold. Arana filled the gap with a neologism, *Euskería*. He later changed his mind and opted for *Euskadi*, which means 'collection of Basques', and this is the word which has been used by Basque nationalists ever since to describe the nation they hope to create.

It was not until 1892 that he published his first full-length political work. As a political theorist, Arana was profoundly reactionary. He wanted to return the Basque country to a state of pre-industrial innocence in which society would be guided by the dictates of religion and the choice between socialism and capitalism would be irrelevant. At the core of his doctrine was an undisguised hatred for the immigrants – 'They came up here bringing with them their bullfights, their flamenco songs and dances, their "refined" language so abundant in blasphemous and filthy expressions, their fighting knives and so many, so many splendid means of "civilization",' he once wrote in bitterly ironic vein. What Arana sought was a kind of apartheid. In his writings he inveighed against 'mixed' marriages and in the community centres or *batzokis* which he founded to spread the nationalist faith it was forbidden to play Spanish music or discuss Spanish politics. The rules of the first *batzokis* demonstrate the depth and intensity of Arana's racialism – members were divided into three categories according to the number of their Basque grandparents and only those whose four grandparents had Basque surnames were entitled to hold executive office.

Arana's involvement in practical politics lasted from 1893 when he made a formal declaration of his ideals at a dinner given by a group of friends – the so-called Oath of Larrazábal – until his death in 1903. This period saw the launching of a nationalist newspaper and the birth of the earliest nationalist groups, but nothing approaching the formation of a party. At first, Arana and his supporters were ignored by Madrid but by 1895 the authorities were sufficiently concerned by their activities to gaol Arana for a few months. Four years later, the administration initiated a serious clampdown on regional nationalists of all kinds and Arana decided to change tack, with the result that during the latter years of his life his public demands were for autonomy rather than independence. He thus left an ambiguous legacy, but one which has enabled separatists and autonomists alike to find a home within the Basque Nationalist Party (PNV), the party founded by his followers seven years after his death.

For Basque nationalists, *Euskadi* consists of the French Basque country, which is traditionally (but not officially) divided into the three districts of Soule (Zuberoa), Labourd (Laburdi) and Basse-Navarre (Benavarra), and the four Spanish provinces which have a Basque population – Alava, Guipúzcoa, Biscay and Navarre. Nobody in Spain questions the Basqueness of the first three provinces. Paradoxically, since Navarre was the only state ever to be created by the Basques, it is the province which has become the subject of controversy. This is partly because Navarre has always contained a large number of non-Basques, but it is also partly due to the failure of nationalism to strike roots there – at least until recently. The Navarrese, as we have seen, did not lose their *fuero* at the same time as the other provinces, so they already enjoyed a considerable measure of autonomy. Moreover, Navarre – in common with Alva – was a predominantly agricultural region, lacking the sort of industrial middle class which provided the PNV with much of its support in the two coastal provinces.

When, in 1932, the Republican government asked the town councils of the Basque country to decide whether they wanted their respective provinces to form part of a self-governing *Euskadi*, the Navarrese chose to stay out. Alava also opted out shortly afterwards. The 1936 uprising widened the gulf between these two inland provinces on the one hand and Guipúzcoa and Biscay on the other. Given the deeply reactionary outlook of the Basque peasantry and the quasi-fascist ideology of the middle-class nationalists, there can be little doubt that – other things being equal – a majority of all four provinces would have come out in support of Franco's rebellion. Indeed that is what did happen in both Alava and Navarre. But by opting for autonomy Guipúzcoa and Biscay had thrown in their lot with the legally constituted government of Spain. They remained loyal to the Republic and the Republic returned the favour by granting them a provisional statute of home rule after the outbreak of the civil war in October 1936.

Guipúzcoa and Biscay were to pay dearly for their choice both during and after the war. Perhaps the most horrific single act committed by either side during the conflict was the systematic pulverization in

April 1936 of Guernica – a town which, as has been seen, had a special place in the affections of the Biscayans in particular and the Basques in general. As soon as Guipúzcoa and Biscay had been subdued, moreover, Franco passed a special 'punitive decree', abolishing not only their provisional statute of home rule, but also the *conciertos económicos* of the two provinces – the last vestiges of the *fueros* that had been abolished sixty years earlier. Alava, on the other hand, was allowed to retain its *concierto económico* and Navarre was allowed to keep its *fuero* with all that that entailed. During the thirty-six years that Franco ruled Spain, Navarre remained an outstanding exception – an island of autonomy within a sea of uniformity boasting its own legislature and government.

Having been publicly singled out for punishment, it is not surprising that Guipúzcoa and Biscay should be the only provinces of Spain in which there was sustained and violent opposition to the regime. The letters ETA – standing for *Euskadi Ta Askatasuna* (Euskadi and Freedom) first appeared during 1960, daubed on the walls of towns in the two coastal provinces. The movement which lay behind them had coalesced during the late fifties around a clandestine publication called *Ekin* (Action) set up by university students. In 1961 ETA carried out its first terrorist operation when some of its members tried to derail a train taking Francoist veterans to a rally in San Sebastián. The police response was savage. A hundred or so people were arrested. Many were tortured and some were charged, tried and sentenced to up to twenty years in gaol. But the leaders of ETA escaped to France. Thus began a cycle of terrorism and repression which has continued to this day.

The history of ETA is of a succession of internal conflicts. In 1966 the movement split into two groups, ETA-Zarra (Old ETA) and ETA-Berri (Young ETA). The latter forsook violence and eventually became the Movimiento Comunista de España. In 1970 ETA-Zarra divided into ETA 5th Assembly and ETA 6th Assembly. ETA 6th Assembly also gave up the armed struggle and re-named itself the Liga Comunista Revolucionaria. Then in the mid-seventies there was yet another parting of the ways when ETA 5th Assembly gave birth to ETA-Military and ETA-Politico-military. Finally in 1981 ETA-Politico-military was grievously weakened when it split into ETA-pm (7th Assembly), whose members dissolved their organization the following year, and ETA-pm (8th Assembly). The disputes which prompted these splits are too arcane and complicated to explain in detail here, but each time it has been the more violent, less intellectual group which has survived intact. The end result of this process is ETA-Military whose motto, it has been said, is 'Actions Unite. Words Divide'. Although they have acquired a certain Marxist–Leninist patina, the *Milis* as they are called are more interested in killing Civil Guards than in wrangling over ideology. By the time the Socialists came to power in 1982, the men and women – now mostly in their thirties – at the top of ETA-Military could justifiably claim to lead the most skilful and experienced terrorist organization in Europe. They were not suffering the *caídas* (police round-ups) that had rocked the organization at the rate of two or three a year in the seventies and their resolve was undiminished.

The movement's internal organization dates from ETA's Third General Assembly in 1964. The Basque country was divided into five regions or *herrialdes* run by full-time organizers. The membership was divided into part-time *legales* (militants whose sympathies are unknown to the police and who lead ostensibly normal lives), full-time *liberados* (men and women whose 'cover' has been blown and who live on the run or in exile) and a third, in-between category of *liberados legales* who work full-time for ETA, often as recruiting officers, but whose profession remains unknown to the authorities. Originally an ETA commando or *irurko* consisted of a small number of militants, usually three, each of whose real names was known to one of the others. But even this system did not prevent the police from penetrating the organization and in the late seventies ETA-Military's operational commander, Miguel Angel Apalategui – often known simply as *Apala* – began to apply the concept of *comandos dormidos* (sleeping commandos). The members of such a group lead outwardly normal lives while being trained for a single, pre-determined action. But they have no idea when or where it will take place until a matter of hours beforehand. After the operation has been carried out, they return to their homes and jobs as if nothing had happened.

Although ETA was founded by university students and professional people, the active end of the organization rapidly came to be dominated by Basques from the *caseríos*. This is particularly true of the *Milis*. The region which has provided them with more *gudaris* (soldiers) than any other is the Goierri, a Basque-speaking redoubt in Guipúzcoa and an area of strange contrasts between industry and agriculture where it is not unusual to see a *caserío* and a small factory or workshop side by side. The rise of ETA has, in other words, seen the re-incorporation into the nationalist struggle of the peasant farmers who fought for Carlism. For all its revolutionary rhetoric, ETA-Military – like the Provisional IRA – has always had a strong streak of conventional Roman Catholic morality and from time to time the *Milis*, like the Provos, mount campaigns against what they regard as decadent activities – threatening to murder drug pushers, for example, or planting bombs in bars and discos or in cinemas showing sex films.

The spread of violent, radical nationalism in the Basque country coincided with an altogether more peaceful process of cultural re-affirmation, particularly insofar as the language was concerned. Basque had been ceding terrain to Castilian – literally as well as metaphorically – for centuries, not because of repressive measures ordered from Madrid but because Castilian, being the dominant language of the peninsula, was more useful to those who had to maintain contacts with the outside world. It thus became the language of the upper and middle classes and of those such as the Alavese who were not cut off from their neighbours by mountains. But that is not to say that the repression of Basque when it was ordered by Franco was ineffective. Indeed, it was far more savage and enduring than anything put into effect in either Catalonia or Galicia and caused a good deal of linguistic self-censorship among the Basques themselves. Basque not only disappeared from the media, it virtually vanished from the streets as well. I have a friend from San Sebastián who is as Basque as it is possible to be, but who speaks not a word of her mother tongue because her parents, who were both Basque speakers, forbade her to speak it.

The late fifties, however, saw the start of a renaissance. It was then that the first *ikastolas* were founded. An *ikastola* is a primary school at which the lessons are given in Basque. In the early years many of them were run from private homes and while Franco was still alive they never had access to public funds. But although the authorities viewed the *ikastolas* with immense suspicion, going as far as to get the police to obtain lists of their staff and backers, they never had an argument for banning a movement which, however subversive, was undeniably helping to supplement the lack of state schooling which was characteristic of the entire Spanish education system at that time. Subsequently, many thousands of adult Basques embarked on the arduous task of learning their mother tongue, among them Carlos Garaikoetxea, who was to go on to become the first President of the Basque country's home rule government.

Teachers reckon that it takes between 300 and 500 hours of study for a Castilian speaker to get to the point where he or she can chat easily. For several years, moreover, the revival of the language was hindered by the existence of no less than six – arguably seven – dialects (four in Spain and two or three in France). But in 1968 the Academy of the Basque Language completed the task of codifying a standard literary Basque called *euskera batua*. By the time that the Basque country acquired a provisional home rule government in 1979 about a fifth of the 2,500,000 people living in the Spanish Basque country (including Navarre) could speak Basque and the total was rising at the rate of about 30–40,000 a year.

Soon after the Socialists came to power in 1982, one of ETA-Military's leaders was asked by *Le Monde* whether in view of the immense political changes that had taken place in Spain they might consider altering their policies. 'Even if it were to convert itself into a model of democracy,' he replied, 'it won't change things as far as we are concerned. We are not, nor have we been, nor shall we ever be Spaniards.' That may be true of him and his fellow gunmen, but – for better or for worse – it is no longer true of the population of the Basque country as a whole. Almost a century of economic growth interrupted only by the civil war saw Biscay and Guipúzcoa, which were the poorest provinces in Spain in 1877, climb to first and third places respectively on the table of income per capita in 1973. Throughout that period, non-Basques in search of work flowed into the Basque country in an almost uninterrupted stream. The sixties, moreover, saw the process of industrialization extended with even greater rapidity, first to Alava, and then to Navarre. By 1970 a higher proportion of the population of Alava was employed in industry than in any other province in Spain. All the other Basque provinces – including Navarre – were in the top ten.

In Navarre for the most part the new businesses recruited their workforces within the province, but in Alava they took them from outside, increasing the population by almost 50 per cent in ten years. By the end of the sixties, 30 per cent of the inhabitants of the Basque country had been born outside it. Today less than half the population are Basque in the sense that both their parents were born there and even that proportion includes many whose grandparents came from other parts of Spain. Genuine Basques probably account for less than a quarter of the 2,750,000 people who live in the four provinces of Guipúzcoa, Biscay, Alava and Navarre.* The agricultural population of the region has meanwhile been reduced to a mere 40,000 and their distinctive way of life has all but vanished. Some young people live in *caseríos* and work in factories or offices, but the majority go to live in the cities when they marry, returning only at weekends.

In spite of the viciously hostile reception their forebears received, the 'immigrants' have integrated well. One reason for this is that more than half of them come from León and Old Castile, which are not as wretchedly poor as some of the southern regions, and they tend to originate from within the rural lower-middle class. By and large, they are better educated and more skilled than the typical migrant to Catalonia and although, for obvious reasons, fewer migrants learn Basque than learn Catalan, the rate of intermarriage between 'natives' and 'immigrants' has always been higher in the Basque country than in the Catalan provinces. A lot of the more recent migrants arrived to take up

---

* A further 250,000 live in the French Basque country of whom a much higher proportion are ethnically Basque.

jobs as technicians, officials and foremen, so that nowadays there is very little difference between the average earnings of Basques and those from outside. A second reason for the relatively harmonious relations between 'natives' and 'immigrants' is that both were equally affected by repression under the dictatorship. Of the eleven 'states of exception' declared by Franco, four were nationwide. But of the remaining seven, no less than six applied to Guipúzcoa or Biscay or both. It has been estimated that by the early seventies a quarter of the entire *Guardia Civil* was stationed in the Basque country. Tear gas does not discriminate between natives and immigrants. Nor did the police when they stopped people in the street, often submitting them to humiliating searches. A Bilbao or San Sebastián car number-plate was enough to get you pulled off the road a half a dozen times between the Basque country and Madrid.

By the time Franco died, the inhabitants of the Basque country, whatever their racial origins, felt deeply alienated from other Spaniards. Among children it showed up in a survey carried out by the Biscay Chamber of Commerce in 1977. Schoolchildren were asked what they most felt themselves to be. Eliminating the 'Don't knows', the answers among native children were – 'Basque' 80 per cent, 'Spanish' 8 per cent, 'European' 12 per cent. The response from the immigrant children was – 'Basque' 48 per cent, 'Spanish' 28 per cent, 'European' 24 per cent. Among adults it showed up in the much higher than average abstention rates registered in the Basque country in the referendum held to endorse the political reform bill in the general elections that followed.

That, of course, was exactly what ETA and its followers wanted. Immigration had made it increasingly difficult to justify separatism on racial grounds alone, but repression suffered by all sections of the community enabled the separatist left which supported ETA to argue with some credibility that the Basque country was subject to a unique double oppression by both capitalism and centralism. According to the view put forward by these revolutionary nationalists, or *abertzales* (patriots) as they are called, economic and social liberation can only be attained through national independence. Although the Basque Nationalist Party – which long ago abandoned the racialist aspects of its founder's creed – remains the dominant force in Basque political life, the *abertzales* regularly account for between a fifth and a quarter of the votes cast in the Basque country – a far higher proportion than, for example, support Sinn Fein in Ireland.

The economic recession has helped ETA and the *abertzales* a good deal during a period in which the more liberal attitudes emanating from Madrid would otherwise have seriously eroded the support they enjoy within the community. The Basque economy is now in dire straits.

The recession has had a particularly disastrous effect in an area where outdated, small-scale production methods are the norm. Between 1973 and 1979 Biscay and Guipúzcoa dropped from first and third places on the table of income per capita to ninth and sixth place respectively. Several of the biggest iron and steel works around Bilbao have gone bankrupt and by the start of the eighties, unemployment in the Basque country – which was virtually unknown previously – was higher than the national average which was itself well above the European average.

The effect of all this has been that a lot of the jobless workers, most of whom are 'immigrants', register their protest at their fate by voting for the *abertzales.* In a poll carried out shortly before the 1981 general election, four out of ten unemployed workers said that they would give their vote to Herri Batasuna, ETA-Military's political front, even though it had no policy on unemployment. Indeed, such was and is Herri Batasuna's contempt for the ballot box that they did not even bother to present a programme of any kind.

CHAPTER NINETEEN

The Catalans

You begin to notice the difference the moment you arrive at Barcelona's Prat airport. Its huge expanses of marble and glass are kept spotless. Well-groomed executives march to and fro across the concourse with a serious, purposeful air. On your way into the city you will see that every other hoarding sports an advertisement for this or that *caixa*, or savings bank. And if you have already spent some time in Spain, it will strike you that the Catalans spend less time over their meals than other Spaniards, and that there are more self-service restaurants in Barcelona than in the other major cities. The Catalans' legendary industriousness has always meant that Barcelona has been among the most prosperous cities in Spain.

Its prosperity, taken in conjunction with its location – close by France on the shores of the Mediterranean – has meant that it has consistently been the most cosmopolitan of Spanish cities. Most of the ideas that have shaped Spain's modern history – republicanism, federalism, anarchism, syndicalism and communism – have found their way into Spain by way of Catalonia. Fashions – whether in clothing, philosophy or art – have tended to take hold in Barcelona several years before they gained acceptance in Madrid. And although their greater sophistication has not necessarily helped the Catalans to produce better art or thought than other Spaniards, it only takes a few days in Barcelona before Madrid begins to look backward and isolated, its inhabitants incapable of comprehending the problems of an advanced 'European' society like the Catalans'. It is but a short step from there to the view, which is undoubtedly held by many Catalans, that the rest of Spain has acted as a brake on their advancement.

In an ideal world, one feels, the Catalans would not mind swopping places with the Belgians or the Dutch. There is a poem by Catalonia's greatest modern poet, Salvador Espriu, which captures perfectly the ambivalence of his fellow-countrymen's attitude to Spain:

> Oh, how tired I am of my cowardly
> old, so savage land!
> How I should like to get away
> to the North,
> where they say that the people are clean,
> and decent, refined, rich, free
> aware and happy! (. . .)
> Yet I am destined never to realize my dream
> and here I shall remain until death,
> for I too am wild and cowardly.
> And, what is more, I love,
> with a despairing sorrow
> this my poor,
> dirty, sad, hapless homeland.

It is significant, however, that Espriu ends up resigning himself to his lot. Catalan dissatisfaction has always tended to be expressed as resentment, indignation and a demand for a substantial say in the running of their own affairs, rather than in terms of outright separatism. Madrid politicians are fond of saying that the difference between an ambitious Basque politician and an ambitious Catalan politician is that the first dreams of being Prime Minister of an independent *Euskadi*, whereas the second dreams of being Prime Minister of Spain.

One reason why the separatist instinct is weak in Catalonia is that the Catalans, though they tend to have somewhat fairer skin and lighter hair, would not and could not claim to be racially different from other Spaniards. But it is also a reflection of the Catalans' most highly prized virtue – *seny*. There is no exact translation of *seny*. Perhaps the nearest equivalent is the northern English term 'nous' – good old common sense. Respect for *seny* makes the Catalans realistic, earnest, tolerant and at times a bit censorious. Yet it sits uneasily with their frequently tumultuous history.

Barcelona has come under full-scale military attack by the forces of the central government on numerous occasions, usually as a consequence of uprisings and revolutions. The popularity of anarchism among the workers of Catalonia turned Barcelona into the most violent city in Europe during the early part of this century, and at the height of the civil war the Catalan capital was the scene of a bloody street war between conflicting Republican factions.

This is how the Catalan writer and academic, Victor Alba, squares the circle – 'The opposite of *seny* is *arrauxment*: an ecstasy of violence. But *arrauxment* is seen as an ultimate consequence of *seny*.

Because they [the Catalans] are convinced that when they act impetuously they are being sensible . . . When a thing is not the way it ought to be, when a situation is not "sensible", the common-sense thing to do is to oppose it abruptly, violently.' Another explanation I have seen put forward is that the Catalans fall into two very distinct groups – those who are *sorrut* (antisocial) and those who are *trempat* (spontaneous, likeable, *simpático*) – and that the violent changes of direction in Catalan political history are the product of their uneasy co-existence.

A similarly paradoxical pattern can be identified in Catalan culture. For the most part, it is rather prim and humdrum. But from time to time it throws up an outstandingly original figure. In the Middle Ages, there was Ramón Llull, the multilingual Majorcan missionary who opposed the Crusades and put forward the theory that the earth was round, and Anselm Turmeda, a renegade Franciscan who converted to Islam and is regarded as a saint in North Africa. More recently, Catalonia has produced Salvador Dali and two architects whose works stand out like a string of beacons amid the stolidly bourgeois edifices of Barcelona – Antoni Gaudí, whose giant, eccentric cathedral, the Sagrada Familia, was started in 1882 and is likely to take until about 2020 to complete, and Ricardo Bofill, who has been responsible for, among other things, converting a cement works into an office block that looks like a medieval castle.

What unites this curiously heterogeneous and contradictory people is their language. Their pride in it is well-nigh limitless and they speak it at every opportunity. When two Catalan speakers and a Castilian speaker are talking together, the Catalans will address the Castilian speaker in Castilian, but as often as not they will address each other in Catalan – something that profoundly irritates other Spaniards.

Written down, Catalan looks like a cross between Spanish and French, but spoken it has a ruggedness which is lacking in either. It is unusually rich in monosyllabic words – to the point that Catalan poets have constructed entire poems out of them – and the syllables of multi-syllabic words are particularly strongly stressed. The diphthongs 'au', 'eu' and 'iu' crop up with great frequency so that to a foreigner it sounds a bit like Portuguese.

Just about the worst gaffe you can make when speaking to a Catalan is to refer to his or her language as a dialect. Catalan is no more a dialect of Castilian than Castilian is a dialect of Catalan. Or, to put it another way, both – like French or Italian – are dialects of Latin. The first recognizably Catalan words were found in documents written in the ninth century, although the language is thought to have begun evolving in the seventh or eighth century. It spread in the wake of Catalonia's imperial expansion to an area much bigger than the four provinces of

Gerona, Lérida, Tarragona and Barcelona which comprise the Principality of Catalonia itself. It is also spoken along a 15–30-kilometre-deep strip of Aragonese territory bordering the Principality, in about two thirds of the region of Valencia, throughout the Balearic Islands, in the Republic of Andorra and in that part of the French department of Pyrénées Orientales historically known as Roussillon. It is also spoken in Alguer, a walled town on the west coast of Sardinia, which was captured and populated entirely by Catalans in the fourteenth century and, until the early 1950s, it could still be heard in San Agustin, Florida, a town conquered by Menorcans in the eighteenth century. Catalan is the native language of something like 6,500,000 people, which makes it more widely spoken than several better-known languages such as Danish, Finnish and Norwegian.

As it spread, differences began to arise between Catalan as it was spoken in the western and eastern parts of the Catalan-speaking world. The dividing line runs from a point just to the east of Andorra to a point just to the west of Tarragona. The internal fragmentation of the language does not stop there. Both dialects can be further divided into sub-dialects – at least three within eastern Catalan (central, Roussillonaise and Balearic) and two within western Catalan (north-western and Valencian), according to the pronunciation of the 1st person singular of the 1st declension indicative. 'I sing' is pronounced 'cant*u*' in Barcelona and most of Catalonia proper, 'cant*i*' in Roussillon, 'cant' in the Balearic Islands, 'cant*o*' in Lérida and along the Aragonese fringe, and 'cant*e*' in Valencia. There are even what might be called sub-sub-dialects of both Balearic and Valencian – three of them in each case corresponding to Majorca, Menorca and Ibiza and to the northern, central and southern parts of Catalan-speaking Valencia. It is typical of the rampant localism of Spain that many of the inhabitants of the Balearic Islands and Valencia object to their language being called Catalan at all. So as not to offend local sensibilities, attempts have been made in the past to get people to call it *bacavés* (a neologism derived from the initial letters of *Ba*learic, *Ca*talan and *V*alencian).

Catalonia was the most thoroughly Romanized region of Iberia and had only the briefest of contact with the Moslems. It was, moreover, the only area to be repopulated on a large scale by *reconquistadores* from outside the peninsula. The Franks' contribution to the settlement of Catalonia was only the first of the many links which were to be established between the Catalans (who were themselves originally called *francos* by other Spaniards) and the people living in what is now France. The Catalans have always been far more receptive to French ideas and attitudes than other Spaniards who tend in fact heartily to dislike the French.

The period of Catalonia's greatest glory lasted from the twelfth to the fourteenth centuries, during which time the Catalans were allied with the Aragonese. Their confederacy was a precociously sophisticated union in which the two very different partners were each allowed to retain their own laws, customs and language under the same crown. As early as the beginning of the thirteenth century, Catalonia had a *Corts* or parliament consisting of three chambers – one for the nobility, one for the bourgeoisie and another for the clergy. The sovereigns of the confederation subsequently undertook to call the *Corts* once a year and not pass any laws without its consent. The *Corts* set up a committee of twenty-four members (eight from each chamber) whose job it was to collect taxes. In 1359 this body – the *Generalitat* – took over responsibility for the way that the money was spent as well as the way that it was collected, thus becoming what was arguably the world's first parliamentary government. As one medieval chronicler remarked, the rulers of Catalonia and Aragón were 'not the masters of their subjects, but their co-rulers'.

By the middle of the fourteenth century the Catalan–Aragonese confederation ruled not only the Balearic Islands and the city and region of Valencia but also Sardinia, Corsica and much of present-day Greece. A member of its Royal Family sat on the throne of Sicily and it controlled the gold trade with the Sudan. Today the world has all but forgotten Catalonia's golden age, but the memory of her power and influence lives on in the folk sayings of the Mediterranean. In Sicily, recalcitrant children are told to 'do what I say or I'll call the Catalans' and in Thrace you can do no worse than to wish on your enemy 'the Catalan vengeance'. A number of naval and financial terms in Castilian derive from Catalan, including probably the word *peseta*.

A banking collapse in 1381 caused by the cost of financing too many imperial wars, the rise of the Ottoman Empire and the loss of the gold trade sent Barcelona into decline even before the discovery of America shifted the geographical advantage from the Mediterranean to the Atlantic. When the city's fortunes finally took a turn for the better – in the nineteenth century – it was due not so much to commerce as to industry, and in particular the cotton business.

It was during the nineteenth century that the Catalans rediscovered themselves through their language. After the unification of Spain, the ruling class throughout the country had adopted Castilian as a mark of their status. Catalan became the language of the peasantry and the culture associated with it died out. But in the last century it became the medium for a literary revival which succeeded in enhancing the status of the language sufficiently for it to be re-adopted by the middle and upper classes, thereby regaining its respectability and influence.

The Catalan *Renaixença*, as it is called, began in the most curious manner. In 1833 a minor poet, Bonaventura Carles Aribau, published a poem in Catalan called 'Ode to the Fatherland'. He had intended it simply as a birthday present for his patron, another Catalan called Gaspar Remisa i Niarous, who was at that time head of the Royal Treasury. But the poem was published in a Barcelona newspaper and made a great impact on the intellectual community. Aribau, a dedicated centralist, never again published anything of importance and spent the rest of his life working for the government and the monarchy in Madrid. But the renewed interest in Catalan which he had stimulated grew inexorably. In 1859 an annual poetry competition called the Floral Games was inaugurated and in 1877 it brought to light one of Spain's greatest modern literary figures, Jacint Verdaguer. Several other outstanding writers emerged from Catalonia during the late nineteenth and early twentieth centuries – the playwright Angel Guimerá, the novelist Narcís Oller and the poet Joan Maragall.

The same period saw also the standardization of the language itself. In 1907 an *Institut d'Estudis Catalans* was founded and four years later the scientific section of the institute asked the philological section to prepare a report on how the spelling of Catalan might be standardized. This seemingly modest request begged a multitude of questions about grammar and vocabulary, many of which were resolved when the report was published in 1913 with the title of *Normes Ortográfiques*. The researcher who had made the most decisive contribution to the *Normes* was an engineer-turned-philologist called Pompeu Fabra. Soon afterwards he set about compiling a full-scale dictionary. Published in 1932, it is the cornerstone of modern Catalan.

The *Renaixença* provided the raw material and the driving force for the political movement which appeared towards the end of the last century known as Catalanism. Catalanism was a broad church, embracing all those who believed in Catalonia's separate identity and who were keen to see it recognized, whether in the form of autonomy or nationhood. The father of Catalanism, Valentí Almirall, author of *Lo Catalanisme*, was essentially a regionalist. But within a few years his ideas were given a sharper, more nationalistic edge by Enric Prat de la Riba, who provided the movement with its first political programme and whose Catalan Union supplied it with its earliest political organization. Except during its earliest years, Catalanism was never represented by a single party. It provided the inspiration for parties of the right and the left and for parties of all classes, of which by far the most influential was the conservative upper-middle-class Lliga. But what Catalanism lacked in cohesion, it more than compensated for in the depth and breadth of its appeal with the community and this point was never lost on Madrid.

The first attempt to solve 'the Catalan problem' was made shortly before the First World War when the Spanish government authorized provincial administrations to pool their functions with those of their neighbours to form *Mancomunidades.* The four Catalan provinces were the only ones in Spain to take advantage of the opportunity. The Catalan *Mancomunidad* lasted for barely a decade until it was suppressed by Primo de Rivera. It was not a particularly successful experiment. The degree of autonomy it offered was extremely limited and at one stage it had to go into debt because of a lack of financial support from the government.

In the brief period between the fall of Primo de Rivera and the resignation of Alfonso XIII, the parties of the Spanish Republican left signed a pact with the main regional nationalist parties – the so-called Pact of San Sebastián – promising that, if and when they came to power, they would grant home rule statutes to Catalonia, Galicia and the Basque country. But on 14 August 1931 – two days after the local elections which persuaded the King to flee the country – nationalists in Barcelona pre-empted orderly progress towards home rule by proclaiming a Catalan Republic as part of an Iberian Federation, even though no such thing existed, nor was envisaged. They were subsequently persuaded by the leaders of the central government to change the name of the administration they had set up to the Government of the *Generalitat* in memory of the medieval institution of the same name. An assembly elected by Catalonia's town councillors subsequently drew up a draft statute which won overwhelming endorsement in a referendum (562,691 votes for, 3,276 votes against with 195,501 abstentions). A considerably watered-down version of the draft statute (which gave the Catalans control over health and welfare, for example, but not education) was approved by the *Cortes* on 9 September 1932. But the financial powers transferred to the *Generalitat* in the ensuing months were severely restricted.

Two years later the demagogic anti-Catalanist, Alejandro Lerroux, succeeded in forcing the *Generalitat* to accept right- as well as left-wing members. This was anathema to the left, who believed that the right could not and would not support the Republic and the President of the *Generalitat*, Lluis Companys, proclaimed 'the Catalan state of the Spanish Federal Republic'. The Civil Governor of Barcelona, himself a Catalan, declared war on the new government, and the offices of the *Generalitat* and the city hall both came under bombardment before Companys surrendered along with his entire government. The *Cortes* suspended the Catalan parliament and appointed a Governor-General to carry out the functions of the *Generalitat*. In 1935 the members of the *Generalitat* were each sentenced to thirty years in gaol, but benefited from the amnesty for political prisoners which was proclaimed when the left-wing Popular Front came to power as a result of the elections in February 1936.

The statute of autonomy was restored and in the period immediately after the outbreak of civil war, the *Generalitat* was able to grab many of the powers which had been denied it between 1932 and 1934. As Franco and his troops steadily gained the upper hand and the Republicans were pushed back into a progressively smaller area, the capital was moved from Madrid to Valencia and then from Valencia to Barcelona, so that it was in Barcelona that the Republic met its end. Companys fled to France only to be arrested after the German invasion by the Gestapo. They handed him over to Franco who ordered him to be executed in secret. It later emerged that the President of the *Generalitat*'s last words – shouted out a matter of seconds before the execution squad opened fire – were '*¡Visca Catalunya!*' ('Long live Catalonia!')

Franco's victory unleashed a campaign against the Catalan language unparalleled in the region's history. Publishing houses, book shops, and public and private libraries were searched for Catalan books and those that were found were destroyed. Pompeu Fabra's priceless collection was burned in the street. The names of villages and towns were Castilianized, the Street of the Virgin of Monserrat (the patron of Catalonia) became the Street of the Redeemer and the Library of Catalonia was renamed the Central Library. In the mid-forties permission was granted for the publication of books in Catalan and the staging of plays in Catalan. But it remained banned from radio and television, the daily press and in schools. The *Institut* maintained a curious, half-tolerated, half-clandestine existence under Franco. It held weekly meetings, held courses on the language, literature and history of Catalonia in private houses, gave receptions and went as far as to publish books and pamphlets, some of which were even bought by the government for display at international exhibitions.

Throughout the first two decades of Franco's rule, Catalonia was the principal source of opposition to his regime. In 1944 the Communists made a disastrous attempt to invade the country through the Valle de Arán, and between 1947 and 1949 the anarchists staged a bloody but futile campaign of shootings, bombings and hold-ups in Barcelona. The failure of these attempts to overthrow Franco's regime by force ushered in a period when opposition was characterized by mass public protests. Most of the more successful ones took place in Catalonia. The pattern was set in 1948 when opponents of Franco's rule succeeded in getting 100,000 people to attend a ceremony celebrating the enthronement of the Virgin of Monserrat. In 1951 the first city-wide general strike in post-war Spain was held in Barcelona which was also the scene of mass public transport boycotts in 1951 and 1956.

But being the focus of opposition and promoting it are two very different things and the truth is that the role played by Catalan nationalists in fighting Franco was by and large a pretty tame one. There was a Catalan Liberation Front, but it never had a fraction of the support nor made a hundredth of the impact of ETA. Barcelona's students were in the forefront of the search for an independent student movement but once it had been formed the leadership was exercised from Madrid. The most dramatic acts of resistance to come out of Catalonia were symbolic ones, such as when the audience at the *Palau de la Música* sang the unofficial national anthem of Catalonia in front of Franco when he was on a visit to the area in 1960.

In short, the Catalans' response to Franco owed a good deal more to *seny* than to *arrauxment* and this, I think, has somewhat diminished their status and influence in a democratic Spain. Moreover, the virtual absence of violent nationalism has meant that the inhabitants of Catalonia were not subjected to the same relentless oppression that helped to homogenize the population of the Basque country and so the differences between 'native' and 'immigrant' have not been erased – or disguised – in Catalonia to the same extent as in the Basque country. If Catalonia has not occupied a centre stage since Franco's death, it is partly because today's Catalan nationalists are having to struggle to create a sense of nationhood in an area which is manifestly less different from the rest of the country now than it has been at any time in its history.

Immigrants have been pouring into the Principality from other parts of Spain for almost a century. The growth of industry, first in and around Barcelona and then in the other provincial capitals of Catalonia, created a demand for labour that the Catalans were quite unable to satisfy by themselves. About half the population of Catalonia today is of immigrant stock and it has been estimated that there will be no 'pure' Catalans left by the year 2040.

What is more, not only has the percentage of immigrants grown but so has the catchment area from which they are drawn. And as it has grown, it has taken in areas which are less and less like Catalonia and whose population is therefore less and less sympathetic to Catalanism. The earliest migration was of rural Catalans to Barcelona in the early part of the last century. By the end of the nineteenth century, the immigrants came from Majorca and Valencia. At the beginning of this century, they came mostly from Aragón, with which Catalonia has close historic ties. In the 1920s the newcomers were predominantly from

Murcia, which – although Castilian speaking – was partly conquered by Catalans. But the influx after the civil war and during the *años de desarrollo* consisted of an increasing proportion of Andalusians. Since this was by far the largest and longest 'wave', the Andalusians now form the biggest single group of immigrants in Catalonia. With their gracious but passionate temperaments and their love of flamenco, the Andalusians are not merely not Catalan but the heirs to a very potent alternative culture.

This is only one of several reasons why it is proving more difficult to assimilate the most recent wave of immigrants than it was to integrate those who arrived before the civil war. The immigrants of the twenties arrived at a rate of between 25,000 and 35,000 a year, their numbers peaking in the period 1927–9 because of the need for labourers to complete two major public works, the Barcelona Metro and the 1929 *Exposición Universal de Montjuic*. At the time, it must have seemed as if they would never be absorbed. The 'Murcians' as they were all called – even though a sizeable minority originated elsewhere – were a disorderly and uncouth crowd. Crimes of passion, previously almost unknown in Catalonia, became quite common. Even after they could afford to buy better food, many stuck to the lunch of bread and onion which had sustained them in the fields of the poor south. 'Murcian' acquired a pejorative connotation – first in Catalonia and then in the rest of Spain – which it has never lost. In the late seventies, *Cuadernos para el Diálogo* published a survey in which interviewees had been asked questions like 'Which region would you most/least like your son/daughter-in-law to come from?', the object being to discover which regions had the lowest and highest standing in the eyes of other Spaniards. The poor old Murcians came bottom on every count.

The attitudes and the behaviour of the 'Murcians' appalled the native Catalans who dubbed them *Xarnegos* (a word probably derived from *Xarnec*, a pejorative expression for someone who is half Catalan and half French) and accused them of 'coming to take the bread out of our mouths'. This wholly unfair accusation was based on the fact that a tiny minority of immigrants had been imported as strike-breakers – by Catalan businessmen. During the civil war, the denizens of the immigrant quarter of Torrasa put up a famous notice at the entrance to their suburb which read 'Catalonia stops here. This is the start of Murcia', and in one area the anarchists pre-empted Franco by putting up posters forbidding people to speak Catalan in the streets. Nevertheless, by then, most of the immigrants of the twenties had begun to digest influences that would turn them into Catalans. In typically Catalan fashion, their assimilation took place by way of the language.

In the thirties it was not difficult to learn – in fact it would have been hard for a Castilian speaker not to have picked up – a working knowledge of Catalan. The immigrants came to live in districts where the shopkeepers spoke Catalan, went to work in factories and on sites where in all probability the foreman spoke Catalan. There was Catalan on the radio and for those who could read there was Catalan in the press. Their children learnt Catalan at school. By the time a further wave of immigrants began to arrive, the 'Murcians' of the twenties were in a position to look down on the benighted newcomers from the standpoint of a common language and shared experiences. Today the elderly 'Murcian' whose support for Catalan nationalism is more passionate than any native and who has christened his eldest daughter Monserrat is a recognized stereotype in Catalan society.

But the most important reason why the post-war immigrants have been so difficult to assimilate is their sheer numbers – a quarter of a million in the forties, nearly half a million during the fifties and almost a million during the sixties. The tidal wave swept over Barcelona and into the rest of Catalonia. When Spain's 'economic miracle' came to an end almost one in five of the population of the other three provinces was of immigrant stock. Because of their numbers, the immigrants of the forties, fifties and sixties often live in areas where only the priest, the doctor and perhaps the schoolteachers and the shopkeepers are Catalans by origin. The new immigrants represent a far higher proportion of Catalonia's total population, which is now nearing six million, than their predecessors ever did and since the return of democracy numerical strength has acquired a political as well as a social significance. The new immigrants sense their importance and it enables them to resist Catalanization longer.

The repressive measures taken by Franco's government and the influx of this new wave of immigrants presented a dual threat to the Catalan language which, by the time the dictatorship ended, was facing a crisis. According to a report published by the Spanish government in 1975, the proportion of the population who could speak Catalan was 71 per cent in the Principality, 91 per cent in the Balearic Islands and 69 per cent in the three provinces of Valencia. The percentage who actually did speak it at home was somewhat lower in all cases. In Catalonia proper the figure was reckoned to be about half. But another survey carried out at about the same time showed that within Catalonia itself there was sharp division between the provinces of Lérida, Tarragona and Gerona where the figure was 90 per cent or above and Barcelona where, because of the high proportion of immigrants, the number of people who spoke Catalan at home was only 39 per cent. This and subsequent research highlighted two specific malaises which, if allowed to continue, would sooner or later – it was clear – finish off the Catalan language.

The first was that, since Catalan had not been taught in schools, it could not be written in the press and was not used by officialdom, a lot of people who could speak Catalan were nevertheless illiterate in it. The proportions of the population who could read and write the language were 62 and 38 per cent respectively in Catalonia itself, 51 and 10 per cent in the Balearic Islands and 46 and 16 per cent in Valencia. And even those Catalans who were literate in their own language were so accustomed to a world in which documents, books and newspapers were in Castilian that they found it tiring to read and write in Catalan. The second problem – which only became apparent as the result of a survey published in 1978 – was that, contrary to what one might expect, fewer people spoke Catalan at home than spoke it at work, in the shops and so on. This, the survey found, was because where a native had married an immigrant the couple almost always ended up speaking Castilian, which the Catalan-speaking partner had learned properly at school, rather than Catalan, which the Castilian-speaking partner had picked up unsystematically. It was clear that unless something was done the children of these marriages would grow up using only Castilian. Contrary to everything that had been assumed, Catalan remained the social language of Catalonia but was gradually ceasing to be the family language of its inhabitants.

CHAPTER TWENTY

The Galicians

A few years ago, one of the big Spanish banks got together a team of economists, sociologists and other specialists to write a detailed report on Galicia. The document they produced was, by all accounts, a blistering indictment of the region's backwardness and the way in which successive governments have misunderstood, mistreated or – at best – neglected it. The powers that be at the bank, and it is generally regarded as one of Spain's more progressive financial institutions, not only refused to publish the survey, they rounded up every single copy and had them burnt – 'as if we were living in the good old days of the Inquisition', one commentator remarked. The whole episode is sadly typical. Galicia, more even than the poor areas of the south, is the part of Spain that Spaniards have been most content to ignore.

Galicia was the area of Spain where the Celts most comprehensively swamped the indigenous population when they arrived in the peninsula around 1000 B.C. and the region still retains many traces of their culture. The bagpipes, for instance, are as traditional in Galicia, where they are known as the *gaita*, as they are in Scotland or Ireland.

Galicia also has its own language, which the Galicians themselves call *galego* and other Spaniards call *gallego*. If Catalan looks like a cross between French and Spanish, then Galician looks like a cross between Spanish and Portuguese. But, once again, it needs to be stressed that it is very definitely a language and not a dialect – whatever some Spaniards may say. Between 80 and 85 per cent of Galicia's 3,000,000 inhabitants speak Galician – a higher percentage than for either Basque or Catalan. There are three dialects – western, central and eastern – the first of which is further divided into northern and southern sub-dialects. During the seventies attempts were made by both the Royal Galician Academy and the Galician Language Institute at the University of Santiago de Compostela to standardize the spelling and grammar. But neither succeeded in winning universal acceptance for the norms they proposed. Nevertheless, a sort of standard Galician is beginning to emerge naturally, as the language spoken in the major cities becomes more and more homogeneous. The threat to the survival of the language does not derive from its diversity but from other factors. Whereas Catalan is 'the language of the people' in the sense that it is spoken in every stratum of society (except by the 'immigrants'), Galician is the language of the people, only in the sense that it is spoken by the 'masses'. With the exception of a few generally rather self-conscious intellectuals, the members of Galicia's small but influential upper and middle classes speak Spanish. There is therefore an identification in the public mind between social advancement and speaking Castilian which, as Galicia develops and progresses, could lead its inhabitants to abandon their native tongue. Already, in aspiring working-class families the children are brought up to speak Castilian.

Whether because they share with the Irish, Welsh and Bretons a common ancestry or because they live in a similarly windswept, rain-sodden land on the edge of the Atlantic, the Galicians have many of the characteristics associated with Celtic races – a genius for poetry, a love of music, a fascination with death and a tendency towards melancholy.

But the last of these traits could as easily derive from the dreadful hardships to which the Galicians have been subjected during the course of their unhappy history. 'Spain's Voltaire', the Benedictine monk Benito Feijóo who visited the area in the middle of the eighteenth century, has left his account of the typical Galician peasant:

> Four rags cover his body or perhaps, given the number of tears in them, it would be better to say *un*cover it. His accommodation is as full of holes as his clothing, to the extent that the wind and the rain enter it at leave. His food consists of a bit of black bread accompanied by some kind of milk product or some sort of root vegetable, but in such tiny quantities that there are those who have scarcely ever in their life risen satisfied from the table. Add to these miseries the tough, relentless manual labour which lasts from the first rays of dawn until the onset of night and anyone will be able to see that the life of these wretched peasants is more arduous than that of the criminals whom the courts send to the galleys.

Famines were quite frequent and whenever they occurred, as the local records bear witness, the streets of the major cities echoed to the laments and entreaties of semi-naked walking skeletons.

The last great famine was in 1853–4, but even today Galicia is the scene of tremendous hardship. If it is not the poorest region of Spain (that unwanted distinction falls to Estremadura), then it is only because of the relative prosperity of Galicia's coastal cities – Corunna, Santiago, Pontevedra and Vigo. The inland provinces – Lugo and Orense – have the lowest per capita income in Spain (barely half the national average). At Piornedo in Lugo there is still a family living in a *palloza*, a building of pre-Roman design consisting of a circular granite wall and a conical thatched roof, in which the human beings eat, drink and sleep side by side with their animals. At Sabacedo in Orense the children have to walk two miles through a forest every morning and evening to get to and from the nearest main road and the school bus. Since there are wolves in the area, they are always accompanied by an adult carrying a rifle. Many of the hamlets and villages in the interior lack proper paving, so for most of the year the spaces in between the cottages – it would be misleading to speak of streets because the dwellings tend to be grouped higgledy-piggledy – are churned into a sticky mess of mud and dung a foot or more deep. Such conditions frequently give rise to disease, but since the ratio of doctors to inhabitants is only about half the national average, infections are difficult to curb and from time to time Galicia – or parts of it – is swept by epidemics.

Galicia is a victim of the dynamics of Spanish history. Unlike Catalonia, Galicia was Romanized slowly and incompletely. But, in common with the Catalans, the Galicians had very little contact with the Moslems. One of the earliest Asturian monarchs seems to have asserted his control over the coast in the middle of the eighth century, although it was only in the reign of his grandson in the first half of the ninth century that the whole region was finally restored to Christian rule. Thereafter, however, the attention of its rulers was drawn inexorably southwards by the desire to reconquer the peninsula. As power passed to the states to which the Asturian monarchy gave birth – first León and then Castile – the Galicians found themselves progressively more isolated from the centre of power.

The Galicians' frustration at being tied to a Crown whose interests were not their own manifested itself at a very early stage in uprisings organized by the nobility and it is against this background of discontent within the region that the discovery of St James's tomb should be seen. According to legend it was found by a shepherd in a field to which he was guided by a star. The field became the site of a cathedral and of a city – Sant Iago (Saint James) de Campo Stellae (of the field of the star) – upon which the Asturian monarchy and its successors showered gifts and privileges. Right up until the last century the Spanish monarch paid an annual sum to the town, called the *voto de Santiago*, ostensibly in return for the Saint's patronage. The effect was to create within an otherwise turbulent province a city with every reason to support the central government.

As early as the fourteenth century, the Galicians were left without any representation in the *Cortes*. They played no part in the *Mesta*, the sheep-farming cartel whose influence brought such benefit to the farmers of the *meseta*, nor in the trade with the Americas which was bestowed on the Andalusians, nor in the industrial revolutions which transformed the Catalan and Basque provinces. Instead, they became a favourite target for steep taxes and military levies.

The railway from Madrid did not reach Galicia until 1883 and as the region entered the twentieth century its only industries, apart from the naval dockyard at La Bazán founded in the eighteenth century, were a modest textile industry in Corunna, a few tobacco-manufacturing and food-processing businesses and some canning. Typically, the cans came from elsewhere. The region was perhaps entitled to expect preferential treatment from Franco who was himself a Galician (from El Ferrol). But although the region undoubtedly benefited from the general increase in living standards throughout Spain during the *años de desarrollo*, during which period it acquired some important new factories (notably the Citroën plant at Vigo), the main change was a more efficient exploitation of the region's natural resources – hydroelectricity and timber. Over 40 per cent of the population still work on the land – a proportion which, if it were a country in its own right, would qualify it as an underdeveloped nation.

Galicia's agriculture, moreover, is woefully backward. Unlike most of the other peoples of early northern Spain, the Galicians were unable to relieve the pressure of population growth by mass migration southwards. The Asturians were able to spread into León and ultimately Estremadura. The Basques and Cantabrians were able to spread into Castile and ultimately Andalusia. The Aragonese and the Catalans had Valencia. But Galicia's southward expansion was blocked by the creation of Portugal – a state with which Galicians had no political ties. The only other people who found themselves in this predicament were the Navarrese. But, unlike Galicia which was bounded by the sea, Navarre could and did expand northwards.

Hemmed in on all sides, the Galicians had no option but to divide the same amount of land into smaller and smaller plots. Today, the majority of farmers own only tiny amounts of land consisting of several isolated patches which they use for a variety of crops and livestock. Time is wasted travelling between plots, land is wasted beneath the walls that separate one plot from another and the size of the holdings and the variety of the crops make the introduction of machinery frequently uneconomic. What you can see in Galicia today is not that very different from strip-farming in the Middle Ages. Indeed, the Galician peasantry had until comparatively recently to pay feudal dues called *foros* – long after other such medieval legacies had disappeared from the rest of the country.

Any people who have been as badly treated as the Galicians are entitled to be mistrustful and among other Spaniards they have a reputation for caution and guile. In Castilian, an ambiguous statement is a *galleguismo* (Galicianism). In this respect if in no other, Franco was a true son of Galicia – he was famed for his cryptic remarks and always let his ministers argue out a case before he intervened.

Poverty also breeds superstition and Galicia has long been the heartland of Spanish witchcraft. The foremost text-book of Galician magic, *O antigo e verdadeiro livro de San Cipriano* – better known simply as the *Cipranillo* – has gone through countless editions, the latest of which came out in Lisbon in the early seventies. Belief in the evil eye is widespread and the region is rich in *sabias* (wise women) and *curanderos* (folk doctors). It is a legendary haunt of the werewolf, called *lobis-home* in Galician.

To an even greater extent than in the Basque country, women have traditionally enjoyed a high standing in society and a generous measure of influence. Galicia's national hero is a woman – María Pita, who distinguished herself by her bravery during the English siege of Corunna in 1586 – and several of the region's most prominent intellectuals – the poet Rosalía de Castro, the novelist Emilia Pardo Bazán and the penal reformer Concepción Arenal – have been women. It could be just another legacy of the matriarchal society which existed in northern Spain in pre-Roman times. But it must also owe something to the fact that women in Galicia have, for hundreds of years now, been forced to assume responsibilities which in other societies were taken on by the men, simply because their menfolk were away in other parts of the country or the world.

An awful lot of nonsense has been written over the years about the Galicians' propensity to emigrate. It used to be fashionable to ascribe it to their typically Celtic thirst for adventure. But as one Spanish writer remarked, 'The next time you see one of those emigrating Celts, give him a potato and you will straight away transform him into a sedentary European. What makes "the adventurous races" adventurous is lack of potatoes, lack of bread and lack of freedom.'

It has been estimated that during the past five centuries one in every three Galician males has been forced to abandon his homeland. The earliest permanent emigration was in the sixteenth century, when thousands of Galicians were settled in the Andalusian Sierra Morena in an effort to re-people areas that had been left deserted by the expulsion of the Moslems and the Jews. Thereafter the focus shifted to the big towns of Andalusia and to those of León, Castile and Portugal where the

Galicians were only too happy to take on the menial and servile jobs that the locals spurned. Domestic servants, for example, were invariably Galician. But small-scale internal migration could only palliate the pressure on land which has always been at the root of Galicia's problems. As a race, the Galicians were blocked on land both to the south and the east. To the north and west lay the ocean, and that – in a sense – is where they finally found an outlet. For almost two centuries, beginning in the second half of the eighteenth century after the restrictions on settlement in the New World were lifted, a steady stream of Galicians set off across the Atlantic to find a new life for themselves in Argentina, Uruguay, Venezuela, Cuba and the other states of Latin America. Such was their desperation – or innocence – that in the 1850s, after the Caribbean plantation owners had been forced to free their slaves, a Cuban of Galician extraction was able to find some 2,000 of his countrymen to take their places. In much of South America *gallego/a* (Galician) is synonymous with 'Spaniard'. Perhaps the most famous contemporary descendant of Galician immigrants is Fidel Castro whose surname derives from the Galician word for a Celtic hill-top fort.

But not all the emigration was permanent. Every year, up until the early part of this century, between 25,000 and 30,000 Galicians of both sexes marched in great gangs to and from the *meseta* where they brought in the harvest. Each of these gangs was made up of a set number of reapers (*segadores*) and binders (*rapaces*), and headed by a foreman called the *maoral*. As they marched along, with their sickles slung over their shoulders, these weatherbeaten nomads, who have passed into the literature of Castile as well as Galicia, must have been a fearsome sight.

The opportunities for emigration to South America dried up in the fifties at almost exactly the moment when the post-war boom in Europe began to gather momentum, creating an alternative market for cheap labour. Between 1959 and 1973 about a quarter of all the Spaniards who left to work in Europe were Galicians.

It is one of the paradoxes of Spain that whereas Catalonia, which was independent – if fragmented – for three centuries, ranks as only a Principality, Galicia, which only enjoyed a separate existence for three brief spells totalling eleven years in the ninth and tenth centuries, is conventionally referred to as a Kingdom. Galician nationalists claim to see in the popular rebellions which took place in Galicia during the later Middle Ages – and particularly the great uprising of 1467–9, organized by peasant brotherhoods called *Irmandades* – evidence of a patriotic awareness. Modern historians tend to see them more as anti-feudal outbursts, albeit impressive ones. But it is undeniable that from the earliest times there was a consciousness among Galicians of being Galician and this was recognized by Fernando and Isabel when they set up a *Junta General del Reino* composed of one representative from each of the Galician provinces to oversee the region's economic and political affairs.

The rise of Galician nationalism, like that of Catalan nationalism, coincided with a literary revival. Indeed, there was an element of imitation. The Galicians, like the Catalans, had their Floral Games – inaugurated two years later – and just as Catalonia enjoyed a *Renaixença*, so Galicia had a *Rexurdimento*. But for all that, it is arguable that Galicia's renaissance was of greater literary importance than Catalonia's. The outstanding figures of the *Rexurdimento* are the poet Eduardo Pondal, the historians Manuel Murguía and Benito Vicetto, and above all Murguía's wife, Rosalía de Castro. The illegitimate daughter of a priest, rejected by society, unhappily married and, towards the end of her life, racked by cancer, she was a quintessentially Galician figure, who suffered as much in her lifetime as her homeland has in its history. Her *Cantares Gallegos*, published in 1863, is one of the great works of Spanish literature.

It was not, however, until after the publication of Alfredo Brañas's *El Regionalismo* in 1889 that the nationalistic sentiments inherent in the *Rexurdimento* began to assume a political shape, and then only in a relatively timid form. The first truly nationalist group was the Irmandade dos Amigos da Fala, founded in Corunna in 1916 by Antonio Villar Ponte. Forced underground soon afterwards by Primo de Rivera's coup, Galician nationalism surfaced again at the start of the Republic in the form of the Partido Galleguista and it was this movement which negotiated a statute of autonomy for Galicia. The statute, which would have given the region control over agriculture, land tenure, savings institutions and social security, as well as the power to 'nationalize', was put to the vote on 28 June 1936. The turnout was almost 75 per cent and of those who voted more than 99 per cent voted 'yes'. Nineteen days later the civil war broke out and Galicia's hopes of home rule were dashed.

The vote nevertheless put the Galicians on the same footing as the Basques and Catalans as a people with a separate culture who had publicly and verifiably laid claim to self rule and this fact made it difficult for governments of the post-Franco era to deny them a comparable status. But for the moral authority that that vote accorded them, it is more than likely that Galicia's plaintive dirge would have been drowned by the raucous clamour for self rule that was beginning to be heard in the other regions of Spain.

CHAPTER TWENTY-ONE

TOWARDS A FEDERAL SPAIN

During the final months of the dictatorship and the first years of the monarchy, Spain was gripped by a craze every bit as intense as the *desmadre sexual.* Some called it *fiebre autonómica* (autonomy fever). All of a sudden, it seemed, everyone wanted home rule. Not just those with a distinct language and culture like the Basques, Catalans and Galicians, but also the inhabitants of areas whose Spanishness had never previously been questioned.

The designs of half-forgotten regional flags were unearthed and sported in defence of every conceivable cause. Regional officials of political parties, anxious to minimize the stigma of *sucursalismo*,* lobbied for as much independence as their Madrid headquarters would allow them, so that the Andalusian branch of the Spanish Communist Party, for example, became the Andalusian Communist Party, almost as if Andalusia were a separate country. As for the pressure groups which were beginning to emerge at that time, it was virtually obligatory for them to be organized on regional rather than national lines.

Spain's medieval history, which had hitherto been depicted as a predestined process of unification, was now presented as the story of several independent nations coerced into reluctant co-operation. In fact a lot of liberally and radically minded young Spaniards stopped talking about Spain altogether and began referring solemnly to 'the Spanish state'. A number of organizations which came into being during this period retain the phrase in their titles. Hence, the Spanish parents' body

* A *sucursal* is the local branch of, say, a bank. Those who support groups like the Basque Nationalist Party, which only operate within a single region, refer pejoratively to the regional branches of nationally based parties such as the PSOE, PCE or AP as *sucursales.* A politician belonging to such an organization is thus a *sucursalista* and the option he offers the electorate is slightingly referred to among nationalists as *sucursalismo.*

is called the *Confederación del Estado Español de Asociaciones de Padres de Alumnos.*

To some extent Spain's *fiebre autonómica* was merely the belated manifestation of a wider phenomenon. Regionalism had been having a heyday throughout Europe. The late sixties and early seventies had seen demands for self-government from the Bretons and others in France, from the Scots and Welsh in Britain and even from minority groups in Germany and Italy – both countries which already offered a generous measure of decentralization. But the pressure for home rule acquired a special intensity in Spain as a result of additional, entirely domestic, factors.

The fact that Franco had been such a diehard centralist, and his most effective opponents had been separatist gunmen, created a powerful association in the public mind between regional nationalism and freedom on the one hand and between national unity and repression on the other. Towards the end of the dictatorship, dislike of totalitarian rule was frequently expressed in terms of distaste for centralism, especially among the young. It was also noticeable that, outside the three regions that had had active nationalist movements before the dictatorship, nationalist or regionalist sentiment was strongest in areas that had been particularly badly neglected by Franco. Thus, there was more anti-central-government feeling in Andalusia and the Canary Islands, both of which regions had severe economic and social problems, than there was in, for example, Aragón or the Balearic Islands, whose claims to a distinct identity on historical and linguistic grounds were far better. The only real exception to this rule was the region (as distinct from the province) of Valencia – the area comprising the three provinces of Alicante, Castellón and Valencia which its inhabitants were increasingly coming to describe as the *País Valenciano* (Valencian Country). The Valencians had done comparatively well under Franco, but a strong sense of identity had grown up among them, rooted in the area's distinct linguistic heritage.

Under the dictatorship, opposition politicians of most shades of opinion had worked on the assumption that when Franco went a measure of devolution would be necessary. But what they envisaged was the reintroduction of self-government in some form for the Basque country, Catalonia and Galicia. However, during the months between Franco's death and the holding of the first general election, it became obvious that to have granted home rule only to those regions which had had statutes of autonomy under the Republic would have been seriously at odds with the mood of the times. Apart from anything else, it seemed very likely that in Galicia, where nationalism continues to be the preserve of a relatively small number of people, enthusiasm for home rule was less widespread than in several other areas, notably Andalusia, Valencia and the Canary Islands. To have granted autonomy to Galicia but not to the others would not only have been manifestly unjust, but might have caused more trouble than it was intended to avoid. And if you devolved power to the Canaries, how could you withhold it from, say, Asturias?

By the latter half of 1976 politicians inside and outside the government were beginning to contemplate seriously the possibility of a quasi-federal arrangement. In December of that year Suárez told an audience in Barcelona that devolution might be looked at 'as a rational solution to the decentralization of the administration'. By the time that democracy returned to Spain the following year, there was a consensus among politicians of all parties, except Manuel Fraga's Alianza Popular and the ultra-nationalist groups to the right of it, that when a new constitution was drawn up, every region that wanted it ought to have access to at least a limited degree of autonomy.

But a new constitution was still a long way off and, in the meantime, the unsatisfied demand for home rule in the Basque country, Catalonia and – to a lesser extent – elsewhere provided a convenient pretext for agitation. Soon after the general election of June 1977 Suárez decided that the regions with the best claims to separate treatment needed something to be getting on with. He began with Catalonia, an area for which he always felt a special affinity and from which several of his closest advisers hailed.

Unlike the Basques, the Catalans had abolished their government-in-exile as soon as it became apparent that the victors of the Second World War had no intention of invading Spain and overthrowing Franco. They did, however, retain the title of President of the *Generalitat* as a single, symbolic link with the past. In 1954 the mantle of that office settled on the broad and lofty shoulders of one Josep Tarradellas, who had been a minister in Catalonia's republican home rule government. He was still the incumbent when democracy was restored to Spain twenty-three years later.

A high-handed, self-opinionated but charismatic old man, Tarradellas refused to return to his native land until the *Generalitat* was re-established. Yet he was stubbornly opposed to the efforts being made by younger nationalists to negotiate its restoration on the grounds that – by doing so – they were usurping the rightful powers of the *Generalitat*. Sensing an opportunity to put himself in control of the situation, Suárez made contact with the ageing exile and at the end of June 1977, in a spectacular *coup de main*, flew him back to Spain to take over a 'provisional *Generalitat*' set up at the stroke of a pen. The younger nationalists were furious, but there was little they could do. Tarradellas, whom even they regarded as the very embodiment of Catalonia's survival as a nation, arrived back in Barcelona to an ecstatic reception. For a man who must have often wondered whether he would see his homeland again and who only managed to do so by outwitting an array of political opponents half his age, his first words on Catalonian soil were splendidly appropriate – '*Ja soc aquí*', which roughly translates as 'I made it!' They were to become one of the catch-phrases of the transition.

The provisional *Generalitat* was the first of a succession of 'pre-autonomous governments' set up in the regions, most of which were made up of local deputies and senators. They had no real power, but they helped to get people used to the idea of regional government before it became a reality after the introduction of the Constitution.

The devolution of power to the regions was *the* outstanding innovation of the 1978 Constitution and occupied almost a tenth of its length. The basic unit of the state envisaged by the Constitution was the Autonomous Community, which could be made up of a single province or several neighbouring provinces. There was nothing in the Constitution to say that every province had to form part of an Autonomous Community, but it did include a clause enabling the government to force provinces into one if that were considered to be in the general interest.

Each Autonomous Community was to have a President, a Governing Council, a Legislative Assembly and a Supreme Court. The exact powers of the Autonomous Communities were to be defined later in their respective statutes, but the Constitution laid down certain guidelines, albeit somewhat ambiguous ones. Firstly, it specified the areas of government which could be handed over to the Autonomous Communities of which the most important were housing, agriculture, forestry, town and country planning, sport, tourism, freshwater fishing and health and social services (although with the proviso that in several of these areas the actions taken by the regional governments would have to fit into a framework constructed in Madrid). Secondly, the Constitution listed the fields for which the central government held 'exclusive responsibility', among which were foreign affairs, external trade, defence, the administration of justice, criminal, commercial and labour law, offshore fishing, merchant shipping and civil aviation. However, in several cases, the Constitution added that this or that sphere of activity was given to Madrid 'without prejudice' to whatever powers might be granted to the Autonomous Communities. These grey areas, together with those, such as education, which were not specifically allotted to either central or regional government and those, such as the environment, which were rather vaguely divided between the two, provided a means whereby the statutes of the various Autonomous Communities could be varied substantially.

The Constitution allowed the Autonomous Communities to

raise taxes locally but it also stipulated that there should be an inter-territorial clearing fund to ensure that the inequalities between regions were not consolidated by the introduction of regional autonomy.

Except in the case of the Basque country, Catalonia, and Galicia – the so-called 'historical nationalities'* – where all that was needed was for the existing pre-autonomous governments to notify the central government, the process whereby a region achieved home rule began when a provincial council (*diputación*) decided that it wanted the province for which it was responsible to become an Autonomous Community in its own right or join with others to form one.

Thereafter, the Constitution set out two paths by which a region could attain self-government. Under the normal procedure, which was laid down in article 143, the initiative of the provincial council or councils required the backing of at least two thirds of the town councils in the area. Once this had been obtained, a draft statute could be drawn up by an assembly consisting of the Deputies and Senators of the region and the members of the provincial councils of the provinces concerned. This draft statute had then to be forwarded to the Constitutional Commission of the *Cortes* for amendment before being debated by the Congress and Senate. Once it entered into force, a period of five years had to elapse before it could be modified to include any of the powers which the Constitution initially reserved for the central government.

But the Constitution also offered another route which was available to the 'historical nationalities' and any other region where the proposal for home rule was capable of securing the endorsement of three quarters of the town councils and more than half the votes in a regional referendum. Regions seeking home rule under this option, which was mapped out in article 151, could not only lay claim in their draft statute to the powers which the Constitution deliberately refrained from allotting to either the central or regional governments, but there was also a good chance that their draft statute would not be tampered with unduly once it reached Madrid. This was because article 151 entitled a delegation from the local assembly to take part in the deliberations of the Constitutional Commission and stipulated that the text passed by the *Cortes* be approved by the regional electorate in a further referendum.

---

* This is, to my knowledge, the only way of translating the phrase '*nacionalidades históricas*', which was first heard soon after Franco's death and has since become common usage. It needs to be pointed out, however, that the word '*nacionalidad*', like its counterpart 'nationality', had always previously been used to describe a condition rather than an entity. It started to be used out of context in an attempt to satisfy the claims of the Basque country and the other regions to national status without actually having to call them nations. 'Historical nationality' may not be English, but then '*nacionalidad histórica*' is not Spanish.

Immediately after the 1979 general election, Suárez set up a new Ministry of Territorial Administration whose principal task was to oversee the transfer of power to the regions. The granting of home rule to Basques and Catalans was achieved with speed and generosity. Both Communities got control of education and won the right to plan their own economies and set up their own police forces. The two statutes, known as the statutes of Guernica and Sau, were overwhelmingly endorsed at referendums held in October 1979 and came into effect two months later. The Basques and Catalans subsequently negotiated separate financial agreements with the government. The Basque *concierto económico* and the Catalan *cesión de tributos*, both of which were signed in 1981, were as much as anything a nod in the direction of tradition. But they did restore a significant difference, which is that in the Basque country the regional government collects the taxes and hands them over to the central government, retaining what it needs for its own purposes, whereas in the Catalan provinces, as in the rest of the country, the central government collects the money and then gives the regional government its share.

Galicia's home rule statute – the Statute of Santiago – did not include the right to a police force, but in most other respects it gave the Galicians powers that were as extensive as those granted to the Basques and Catalans. However, when it was submitted to a referendum in December 1980, less than 30 per cent of the Galician electorate turned out to vote and of those who did almost one in five did so to vote 'no'. Galicia is scarcely typical. But the whole episode was nevertheless a moral victory for those – especially on the right – who regarded the devolution process as a dangerous sham.

By and large, though, it was not the 'historical nationalities' but the other regions which presented the government with its worst headaches. The first problem was to decide how the future map of Spain should be drawn. Although Spaniards had got into the habit of thinking of their country as being divided into a series of clearly defined regions, the reality was not that simple. The regions of the periphery – Asturias, Valencia, Murcia, Andalusia and Estremadura – and the two archipelagos – the Balearic and Canary Islands – were all pretty straightforward. So was Aragón. The problems started when one began to consider how to divide up the *meseta*, and some of the provinces bordering it, where regional identities – which had been quite strong during the Middle Ages – had long since been subsumed by a general feeling of Spanishness.

Traditionally this area had been divided into León, Old Castile and New Castile. But historians were far from united on which provinces belonged to which region. First of all, there were the problems created by Santander and Logroño in the north and by Ciudad Real in the south, which although undeniably Castilian had a certain individuality and were often referred to as if they were separate regions under the names of Cantabria, La Rioja and La Mancha. There again, although Spaniards frequently described León as a region, nobody could agree on where it began and ended. Was it simply the province of that name or did it – as some believed – include the provinces of Zamora and Salamanca, or even – as others maintained – those of Palencia and Valladolid as well? And even if agreement could be reached, should León – in whatever form it took – be an Autonomous Community of its own or part of an enlarged Old Castile or Asturias with both of which it had historical ties? And what of Madrid? Did it belong to New Castile or had it acquired a personality of its own so strong that it would be better off as a sort of federal district? All these issues provided a magnificent opportunity for local power-brokers to assert their influence and many of the apparently arcane debates over regional identity which dogged the devolution process in the two Castiles and León disguised attempts by minor political figures to enhance their standing.

The government pre-empted a good deal of debate by encouraging the creation of two pre-autonomous bodies on the *meseta* called Castile and León and Castile–La Mancha. But by the end of 1979 Santander, Logroño and – less foreseeably – Guadalajara and Segovia were all set on going it alone. Moreover, although the provinces usually regarded as belonging to the region of León voted to join up with the proposed Community of Castile and León, the politicians of the province of León itself were hopelessly divided over what to do.

A second and more serious problem facing Spain's experiment in devolution concerned the way in which the regions were meant to attain home rule and the powers they received as a result. Unwittingly, what the authors of the Constitution had done was to create a sort of regional virility test. For local politicians, the pressure to demonstrate their loyalty to, and faith in, their region by supporting home rule under article 151 was immense. By the end of 1979 only two of the seven regions where the issue had been decided had opted for article 143. This was precisely the reverse of the situation envisaged by the Constitution, which clearly regarded article 143 as the normal route and article 151 as an exceptional one. At the beginning of the following year, Suárez ill-advisedly tried to deter the Andalusians, who had been the first to opt for the more advantageous path to self-goverment and who were the one group whose enthusiasm for autonomy gave them a genuine claim to preferential treatment, from going ahead with their plans. The attempt backfired on him when they massively endorsed the autonomy initiative in the referendum called for by the Constitution.

The government was beginning to get the distinctly uncomfortable feeling that the experiment was getting out of hand and it was in the hope of bringing some order and discipline into the proceedings that in September the Ministry of Territorial Administration was handed to the hard man of the Suárez team, Rodolfo Martín Villa.

In a speech a few days after taking over, Martín Villa outlined his strategy. Firstly, he intended to ensure that odd provinces here and there should not be allowed to remain outside the proposed network of Autonomous Communities. Secondly, he wanted to see a limit to the powers that the Autonomous Communities could enjoy, regardless of how they achieved home rule. A few months later he proposed that the major parties ought to reach an agreement on devolution similar to the Moncloa Pacts and welcomed an idea floated by Felipe González that there should be a special law to clarify, once and for all, the ambiguities in the section of the Constitution dealing with home rule.

The abortive coup of February 1981, which was partly the result of fears within the armed forces that Spain's 'sacred unity' was at risk, hardened attitudes all round. In April the government and the PSOE began talks aimed at producing a pact of the sort that Martín Villa had suggested. One of the first results of their co-operation was the setting up of a committee of experts under Professor Eduardo García de Enterría.

Their report outlined in more detail and with greater authority many of the doubts that politicians at national level had harboured for some time. In particular, they recommended that the government should force all those regions which had not yet achieved home rule to do so under the terms of article 143. The professor and his colleagues also expressed deep concern about the legal implications of what was going on, and especially the possibility that regional law might achieve ascendancy over state law. Finally, they endorsed the opposition's idea of a law intended to harmonize the idiosyncrasies of the devolution process.

After a brief and not particularly serious attempt to involve the other two major parties, the UCD and the PSOE signed a formal agreement in July in which they set a deadline for the completion of the devolution process (1 February 1983) and set out a strategy for generalizing and homogenizing it.

In accordance with this plan, the entire country would be divided up into sixteen Autonomous Communities. The only exceptions were to be Navarre, for which a law would be passed to make its existing executive more accountable to its legislature, and Spain's North African enclaves, Ceuta and Melilla, which were given the choice of either becoming Autonomous Communities or retaining their existing special statuses (they eventually chose to become Autonomous Communities, although with a special limited status). Of the Autonomous Communities, only six would be uni-provincial – Madrid, Asturias, Murcia, the Balearic Islands, Cantabria and La Rioja (although in the case of the last two, a clause was to be inserted in their statutes allowing them to join Castile and León whenever they wished). The idea of single-province Communities in Santander and Logroño had always had a certain appeal for the Madrid-based parties who were concerned at the somewhat fanciful possibility that the Basque authorities, thwarted in their desire to incorporate Navarre, might at some time in the future try to bring Cantabria or the Rioja or both within their orbit. It was felt that the Cantabrians and the Riojans might be more easily seduced if, by that time, they were reluctant partners in an extended Castile and León. León, Segovia and Guadalajara were a different matter. There were no geopolitical advantages to be gained by their becoming single-province Communities and even though León's historical claim to a separate identity was far better than that of Santander or Logroño, it was decided that it and Segovia should form part of Castile and León and that Guadalajara should become part of Castile–La Mancha.

The agreement also stipulated that, with the exception of Andalusia, which was already so far down the road mapped out by article 151 that it was pointless trying to do anything about it, the regions which had yet to be granted a statute should attain home rule under the terms of article 143. What is more, it was agreed that none of them should get more than the minimum powers set out in the Constitution. Any other powers granted during the negotiation of the statute would have to be listed under a separate heading and put into cold storage for at least three years from the date the statute came into effect. The only exceptions to this rule were the Canary Islands and the Valencian country for which special laws would be passed giving them rather greater powers than the others.

Having reached agreement in such detail with the only party that could have created problems for it, all that the government had to do was to impose the plan on its supporters in the regions. The only real difficulties were created by the UCD bosses in Segovia who held out to the bitter end and were forced into Castile and León only by means of a special law introduced by the Socialists shortly after they came to power. Because a general election was called before the UCD had run to the end of its term of office, the deadline agreed between the government and the opposition was missed, but only narrowly, and on 8 May 1984 the first elections were held in Navarre and the thirteen Autonomous Communities that had acquired their new status under article 143.

Since then the Socialists have moved fast to ensure that the new regional governments have the legal powers and the human resources with which to do the job, although the question of how they should be financed – and to what extent – remains a bone of contention between the new regional governments and Madrid.

It has been estimated that the new Autonomous Communities will need about 100,000 of the government's employees. A lot of these are doctors, teachers and so on who are already working in the regions where they are required. The officials come from two sources. Most are former employees of the old *administración periférica* and in some cases they have even been able to continue doing the same job in the same building, with the sole difference that what was once, say, the provincial Social Security delegation for Santander is now the Social Security Department of the Autonomous Community of Cantabria. However, it is reckoned that by the time the transfers are complete, some 10–15,000 will have had to have been moved from Madrid to the provinces and although some will go willingly, the government has had to provide a range of incentives to encourage extra volunteers.

The other aspect of the strategy proposed by the commission of experts fared less well. The law originally suggested by Felipe González eventually took shape as the Institutional Law for the Harmonization of the Devolution Process, commonly known by its initials as the LOAPA. At the heart of this much debated piece of legislation was an attempt to clarify the question of whether state law should prevail over regional law. What distinguished the regions which had achieved home rule by way of article 151 from those which had attained it via article 143 was, as we have seen, whether they were entitled to lay claim to certain areas which the Constitution reserved in principle for the central government. But the LOAPA stipulated that, where there was a conflict between state and regional law in those areas, state law should always prevail, even after they had been delegated to a particular region in its statute of autonomy. The nationalists of the 'historical' regions – and particularly the Basques – argued that the effect would be to render areas which they had previously considered to be theirs shared and put them, in effect, on much the same level as the regions which had been granted autonomy under article 143. It was, they argued, an attempt to limit the scope of their statutes without having to submit the changes to a referendum, as required by the Constitution. The UCD and PSOE, for their part, pointed out that the Constitution also included a clause empowering the government to pass a law to harmonize the activities of the Autonomous Communities, even in areas where responsibility had already been handed over to the regions. The lines were drawn for a bitter and lengthy parliamentary battle in which the two big parties were continually harried by an alliance of regional nationalists and Communists.

Nor did it end with the approval of the LOAPA by parliament in June 1981 because the law's opponents referred it immediately to the Constitutional Court. It took more than a year for the court to reach its verdict, but when it was eventually delivered – in August 1983 – it was a bombshell. The judges declared that more than a third of the LOAPA was unconstitutional, including those clauses which guaranteed state law supremacy over regional law in the marginal areas where the Basques, Catalans, Galicians and Andalusians had been given powers denied to the rest. The Constitutional Court's unfavourable verdict on a bill which had been backed not only by the party in power at the time the law was passed but by the one in government at the time of the judgement offered dramatic evidence of just how independent the Spanish courts were becoming. It also provided a fitting end to a process that had had its roots in mistrust of the overweening powers of central government.

In the regions which acquired home rule under article 143, the period which followed the deal cooked up between the government and opposition in 1981 saw a dramatic decline in regional feeling. This was partly a result of the often petty disputes which had dogged progress towards autonomy. In Valencia, for example, there were almighty rows over whether the regional flag should have a blue stripe down the side and whether 'Valencian' was a variant of Catalan or a language in its own right. But the apathy that spread through several regions in the wake of the home rule pacts was also to some extent a product of the pacts themselves. Not the least of the disadvantages of acquiring home rule under article 143 was that it robbed people in the regions concerned of any chance to participate. They did not achieve home rule so much as receive it. There are signs – now that the issue has been settled and autonomy is a reality – that the level of enthusiasm is rising again. The turnouts in the regional elections of 1983 were impressively high – over 70 per cent in most cases.

For a long time the word 'federal' was taboo in Spain. There was a sort of conspiracy of silence among politicians, officials and journalists to avoid upsetting the army, which still has bad memories of the experiment in federalism undertaken during the First Republic. And because nobody in Spain dared talk about federalism, the foreign correspondents working there rarely had occasion to use the one term which really conveys to people that a nation is run from the regions as much as from the centre. The failure of Tejero's coup and the armed forces' acceptance of a left-wing government has made the Spaniards themselves more relaxed about terminology, but people outside Spain have not yet fully realized that Spain has been transformed into a sort of federation.

Within less than a decade, one of the most centralized nations on earth has been carved into seventeen regions, each with its own flag and capital. At one extreme you have Andalusia which is bigger than Austria and at the other you have La Rioja which is smaller than Norfolk. Each of the seventeen regions has its own Presidency, staffed with aides and officials, and between them they can boast more than 150 'ministers' and no less than 1,153 legislators. All this is going to be quite expensive, especially in the early days during which money will have to be found for the building of new parliament buildings and so on, although – as a senior official in Madrid said with an ironic little smile – 'it still won't cost anything like as much as the National Movement'.

In spite of the attempts to 'homogenize' the system, one of the most striking aspects of Spain's new system of regional government is the diversity of the statuses accorded to the various regions. But more by chance than design, the powers delegated to each region reflect quite faithfully the extent of its claim to a separate identity. If one were to award points to each of them on the basis of their historical, cultural and linguistic singularity and the degree of their enthusiasm for home rule in recent years, one could easily come out with a 'ranking' such as that which has emerged – with the Basques and Catalans at the top, followed at a short distance by the Galicians and Andalusians and at a longer distance by the Canarians, Valencians and Navarrese, with the rest an equal last.

But how is this large and complicated machine operating in practice? One of the most interesting aspects of the new set-up is the way in which the 'historical nationalities' have already begun to stand out from the other regions, not just in terms of the powers which they wield under article 151 (and which are anyway shared by Andalusia) but by virtue of the political colouring of their governments. The enthusiasm for Felipe González's pragmatic and moderate form of socialism, which has swept left-wing governments into power in Andalusia and all but two of the Autonomous Communities which achieved home rule under article 143, has left the 'historical nationalities' unaffected. Ever since gaining home rule, the Basque country, Catalonia and Galicia have all been ruled by the right.

In the Basque and Catalan elections held in 1980 and 1984 it was the centre-right nationalists of, respectively, the Basque Nationalist Party and Convergència i Unió who topped the polls. In Galicia it was not the nationalists who came out on top, but Alianza Popular – a Madrid-based party, albeit one founded and led by a Galician, Manuel Fraga. In the Basque country the first *lendakari* or President, Carlos Garaikoetxea, was able to count on an effective majority because of the withdrawal from the legislature of the deputies elected for Herri Batasuna, ETA-Military's political wing, which came an unexpected second in the election. In Catalonia and Galicia, however, Jordi Pujol, the canny, unsmiling banker who took over the leadership of the Catalan *Generalitat*, and Gerardo Fernández Albor, a cultured, elderly doctor who became leader of the Galician *Xunta*, both had to rely on *ad hoc* alliances – mostly with the Centrists – to keep them in power. All three benefited in the early stages from one of the idiosyncrasies of a federal system, which is that a regional politician can reap the benefits of power and authority while at the same time depicting himself and his party as the opposition *vis-à-vis* the central government.

As was perhaps to be expected, the years since the granting of home rule have seen the 'historical nationalities' turn in on themselves somewhat. A great deal of time has been spent both inside and outside their legislative assemblies in debating the promotion of their respective vernacular languages, and laws have now been introduced in all three regions which put the local language on a par with Castilian in official use. One of the more obvious effects of this has been the appearance of vernacular place names on road signs alongside the Castilian version. In the schools most teaching still tends to be done in Castilian, but Basque, Catalan and Galician will all soon be obligatory subjects in their respective regions.

By incessantly nagging Madrid, Pujol, who is known to his colleagues as 'the human locomotive' and who came to power on the slogan '*anem per feina!*' ('Let's go to work!'), has built up the *Generalitat* to the point where, with almost 80,000 employees and a budget in 1984 of some 50,000 million pesetas, it is a veritable state within a state. And not only that, but a highly efficient one. The areas over which it exercises control, such as education and health and social services, are noticeably better organized than in the rest of Spain. It was this impressive track record which enabled Pujol to win an absolute majority in the second election to be held in Catalonia in 1984.

Garaikoetxea, on the other hand, ensured that the Basques were swifter in acquiring new powers, in particular their own police force and television channel. The first locally recruited cadets entered the new Basque police college at Arkaute in 1982. It is intended that initially the new force should consist of 600 men commanded by four serving officers in the armed forces (a reflection of the Spaniards' continuing belief that policemen are best commanded by soldiers). The Basque television channel, *Euskal Telebista*, began transmissions on New Year's Eve 1983, several days before the entry into effect of legislation authorizing the Autonomous Communities to apply for franchises from the government to run channels in their areas. Garaikoetxea and his colleagues claimed that if they had not gone ahead with their plans Madrid would have carried on vacillating and prevaricating forever, but their action was nevertheless an eloquent comment on the indifference to rules and regulations which is so much a part of the Basque character. The Catalan authorities, who had been forced by the pressure of public opinion in their region to follow suit, put their channel – called TV-3 – on the air a few days later.

Oddly enough, the main criticism of both the Catalan and Basque governments is identical – that, unlike the administration run by Fernández Albor, a charismatic father figure who leaves a lot of the day-to-day politicking to his deputy, neither has succeeded in establishing itself as a truly 'national' government with a vision of its people's role and destiny. Both were accused of pandering to the interests of the indigenous middle classes which put them in power, while doing little or nothing for the immigrant working class at a time when they ought to have been trying to achieve a feeling of solidarity. This would not matter so much if either of them had had a clear mandate. But neither did. They gained power thanks to the votes of less than a quarter of the electorate and the main reason why they won such a low share of the potential vote was the high rate of abstention among immigrants in both areas – a clear indication of their disinterest in the politics of their adoptive homelands.

In Andalusia an active team, using the extensive powers conceded to it under article 151, and the ample funds conceded it by a central government led by Andalusians, has done a lot to restore a sense of pride to a region whose inhabitants often refer to themselves as the 'niggers of Spain'. In the regions which acquired home rule under article 143, where the new autonomous governments did not take over until 1983, it is too early to hazard a judgement. But there have already been some worrying indications of extravagance and even corruption. In March 1984 *El País* revealed that the salaries and expenses of four of the autonomous Presidents were higher than the Prime Minister's. A few days later, the head of the Murcian government resigned after his Financial Councillor was accused by the local newspaper of trying to pay its political correspondent and crime reporter a total of a million pesetas to 'lay off' the President. It later emerged that the government had undertaken a lavish programme of high-risk investments – including the setting up of a Murcian film production company – which, in the opinion of one of the ex-President's colleagues, would sooner or later have bankrupted the region.

If there are many more incidents like that, it is unlikely that Spain's experiment in federalism will work – not because the army will step in again, but because the electorate will not put up with it. Spain may no longer be a poor country, but it is not yet a rich one either and people, especially in the poorer areas which have in any case tended all along to be the least enthusiastic about home rule, will not want to pay a surcharge for incompetent government. Events during the years since Franco's death have stripped regionalism of much of its glamour in the eyes of Spaniards and unless they can see that they are deriving tangible benefits from autonomy they will be indifferent to its abolition.

In fact, I think, it is already true to say of all but the Basques that one of the earliest positive results of the devolution process has been to remind Spaniards, in much the same way that the disintegration of the country during the War of Independence reminded them, of how much they have in common.

What they have in common today, moreover, is far greater than what they had in common at the beginning of the last century. Modernization by its very nature has a homogenizing effect. Mass production puts the same objects into everyone's homes, just as the mass media put the same thoughts into everyone's heads. But, in addition to that, developments in Spain during the last quarter of a century have been such as to provide Spaniards – be they Basques, Castilians or Andalusians – with a stock of shared memories and experiences that unites them as effectively as any constitutional arrangement ever could.

CHAPTER TWENTY-TWO

The Spaniards

It is difficult at times to grasp the sheer scale of the changes that overtook Spaniards during the sixties and seventies. One of my neighbours when I lived in Madrid had started out as a shepherd in the province of Toledo and ended up as an electrician on the *Talgo*, the Spanish-designed and manufactured 'super train'. He had gone from poverty to prosperity, swopped the most rudimentary job imaginable for one that required a high level of technical sophistication, and moved from a cottage in the hills to a neat three-bedroom flat in a block with fitted kitchens, modern bathrooms and a swimming pool.

Different but equally dramatic contrasts can be found in the lives of more famous Spaniards. Francisco Fernández-Ordóñez, the most active and successful reformer of Suárez's premiership, had been head of Franco's state holding company, INI. Felipe González was once a member of the Falangist youth section. Victor de la Serna, publisher of the now-defunct liberal evening newspaper, *Informaciones*, fought alongside the Nazis with the Blue Division on the Eastern Front during the last world war.

Other countries have undergone periods of rapid economic progress and bursts of rapid political change. But in no other European nation, except perhaps Greece, has the one followed so quickly on the heels of the other. This may explain why, in the years immediately after Franco's death, Spain produced a movement which, as far as I am aware, has no equivalent anywhere in the world. It grew up among the generation that was born at the start of Spain's 'economic miracle'. The members of this generation, whose parents most likely migrated from the countryside to one of the big cities, reached adolescence just as the sexual customs and conventions that had prevailed in Spain for centuries were being overturned, and were approaching school-leaving age when the recession bit into the job market and the first elections were being held, so that – unlike their elder brothers and sisters – they had no obvious economic or political role to fill. There were no jobs to go to and no demonstrations to join. They affected contempt for what they called the *años rojos* (red years) and, by way of reactions, some ostentatiously conferred their sympathies on the ultra-right. But for many more, the combination of disorientation and alienation was simply too much and they became what were called *pasotas*.

The *pasotas* were – and, to the extent that they still exist, are – a truly disconcerting phenomenon. Insofar as they use drugs and try to put as much distance between themselves and the rest of society as possible, they are like a cross between hippies and punks. But there the similarities end, for the *pasotas* have none of the mystical aspirations of the hippies or the angry nihilism of the punks. In fact, the whole idea of being a *pasota* is not to participate in any way at all, but to 'pass', as in a game of cards (which is how the term *pasota* came about). The spirit of *pasota*-ism is best exemplified by the way they speak. The words are mumbled and vocabulary is pared down to a bare minimum. Things, of whatever kind, are *chismes* and situations or activities are dismissed as *rollos*.*

The gradual disappearance of the *pasotas* is an indication that Spaniards are beginning to come to grips in their own minds with the changes that have taken place over the past quarter of a century. But what have been the end results of those changes? What sort of society is it that the other members of the European Community have welcomed into the Common Market? In the first place, a distinctly idiosyncratic one – a federal monarchy with a tax-paying King whose father was alive when he ascended the throne; a welfare state in which three quarters of the jobless do not qualify for unemployment pay; a former police state where the majority of detectives belong to a trade union founded by erstwhile members of the secret police; a democracy in which the circulation of a neo-fascist newspaper has risen sixfold; and a country dedicated to the cult of the Virgin Mary where there are a half a dozen whores for every nun.

Secondly, it is a society in which the processes of economic and social change in many areas stopped halfway and where a lot remains to be done. The economic development of Spain during the sixties made Spaniards better off, but it did not – as I mentioned in the opening chapter – significantly alter the structure of the economy. This meant that when the recession set in, Spain – heavily reliant on the industries

---

* *Un rollo* (literally a roll of paper, a scroll), has long been used to mean 'a bore' and specifically 'a long-winded explanation'. The English word rigmarole carries a similar meaning and has a similar derivation.

of the past rather than on those of the future and overloaded with small-scale businesses – was unusually vulnerable. In fact, it has probably suffered more than any other Western European country. Certainly, Spain's unemployment rate has been consistently higher than that of its neighbours. However, the 'industrial reconversion' programme embarked upon by the Socialists, while it may have worsened Spain's lot in the short term, does hold out some hopes that her economy will be able to hold its own in the long term.

Anyone who has read thus far will not need to be convinced that by the time Felipe González and his supporters came to power there was a crying need for a major programme of social reforms. During their first term of office, they showed that they were capable of implementing one. This, I believe, explains why a government which came to power promising to cut unemployment but which allowed it to increase should have been returned to office. Spaniards recognize that, although much has already been achieved, still more remains to be done – and that the PSOE, for all its faults, is still the only party with a sufficiently modern outlook to introduce the radical reforms the country needs if it is to catch up with the rest of Europe. Felipe González once remarked that Spain needed forty years of socialism to compensate for the forty years of Francoism that came before. It is just possible that Spain will get it, becoming a sort of Mediterranean Sweden in the process. But if that should happen, there will be a price to pay long before the forty years is up, for the Spaniards are not Scandinavians, and even the most progressive among them seem still to be prey to the age-old Latin vice of favouritism. One of the most disquieting and disillusioning aspects of Socialist rule is the speed with which the PSOE has taken control, not just of the government, but of the administration in its widest sense, placing its members in jobs where political loyalty ought not to be a precondition for appointment. This is all too reminiscent of the nineteenth-century administrations whose insistence on monopolizing power left their opponents no recourse but to arms. It is also disturbingly similar to the policy employed by Franco. Indeed, González seemed almost to invite the comparison when, in 1984, he decided to take his holidays on board Franco's old yacht, the *Azor*.

Spain's 'economic miracle' was, as we have seen, achieved at the cost of uprooting millions of people from their native regions and transplanting them into other parts of the country. The effect has been to turn Spain into a nation of intensely urban cities dotted around an unusually rural countryside. The recently constructed parts of Madrid, Barcelona, Bilbao, Saragossa, Valencia, Seville and Vitoria have all been built upwards rather than outwards. Their dormitory suburbs throb to the harsh music and rasping slang of a new generation as street-wise as any in Europe. Yet the vast expanses of the *meseta* and the *sierra* are now more sparsely populated than at any time since the early Middle Ages. And with their ageing populations, some regions – Estremadura and the two Castiles in particular – are on their way to becoming virtual deserts. The migrational flood tides that brought this situation about have now subsided. In fact, with the recession making work progressively harder to find, there has been a tendency for the trend to reverse. During the latter half of the seventies, for example, there was a net outflow of population from the Basque country. However, as soon as the recession abates, the rate of migration will start to pick up – unless, that is, the government can find a way of providing people with the jobs they need to keep them in the countryside. This seems to me to be one of the most important challenges facing the politicians whose job it is to govern the nation between now and the start of the next millennium. Yet it is one that is barely referred to within Spain itself.

On the political front, now that the Constitution has been passed and accepted, the main task is to ensure that the *estado de las autonomías*, as the Spaniards call their new quasi-federal arrangement, works efficiently and fairly. It may be that it will require modification. For one thing, it is becoming painfully obvious that in the Autonomous Communities of the *meseta* regional feeling is so feeble as to be almost non-existent. Not so long ago, when Jordi Pujol was visiting Old Castile, he dropped into a bar in the village of Peñafiel in Valladolid and was fêted by those present in the way that celebrities tend to be. What the customers of the bar failed to notice was that the man accompanying Pujol was their own 'President', José María García Verdugo. It would not be surprising if at some time in the not too distant future, and particularly if Manuel Fraga's party were to gain power, the regions of the *meseta* were once again put under direct rule.

But that is a minor worry compared to the problem which exists in the Basque country. It is still the case that scarcely a week goes by without a woman being widowed or a child being orphaned in the cause of independence for a region whose indigenous inhabitants are now in a clear minority. The last few years have seen some encouraging signs. The most notable has been the decision of the majority of ETA Politico-military's members to give up violence – a decision to which the government responded intelligently by effectively granting them an amnesty and the opportunity to reintegrate themselves into society. However, that still leaves ETA-Military and a political front, Herri Batasuna, which is consistently able to pick up 15 per cent of the popular vote at elections. That is a formidable degree of support for terrorism in any society.

But it would be wrong simply to stress the difficulties that remain without giving due credit for those that have been overcome. The most fundamental of these was to find a way of transforming the country into a democracy by means of the laws and institutions of a dictatorship. A few years ago, one could be forgiven for having doubts about whether this could in fact be achieved, so great was the inertial weight of tradition and reaction in some areas of government and society. Pockets of resistance remain even today, but with institutions that were once as closely associated with repression as the police and the judiciary positively flaunting their democratic credentials, there can be no question but that the strategy adopted by the King back in 1975 was a sound one.

The whole system moreover is now rooted in a Constitution which, unlike Portugal's, was endorsed by all the major parties and which therefore, unlike Portugal's, is not subject to constant sniping from those who were excluded from the constituent process.

The political changes since 1975 have made Spain not only freer and fairer, but happier. It is particularly noticeable in Madrid. When I lived there during the late seventies I always thought of it as being a bit like New York – a city where you donned your emotional armour before setting foot on the street, because you knew full well that the human being nearest to you was more likely to be rude than helpful. Returning now, I find the mood of the city changed out of all recognition. People speak more softly and swear less than they used to. There is not the frenetic tension that there once was. Even the taxi drivers are cheerier.

Another thing one notices is the increasingly widespread use of *tú* for 'you' in place of the more formal *usted* (a contraction of *Vuestra Merced* meaning 'Your Grace'). The familiar second person singular has long been more common in Spain than in France – a consequence, older Spaniards will tell you, of the informal atmosphere engendered by the Republic and the *camaraderie* on both sides during the civil war. But right up until the Socialist victory of 1982 the use of *tú* was restricted to members of one's immediate family, acquaintances of one's own age, professional colleagues and the occasional very close personal friend of a different age group. Since then there has been a dramatic change. Even waiters now *tutear* their customers. Latin Americans – and particularly Mexicans who are the most scrupulous *usted*-ers of all – find it extremely disconcerting.

All of this brings me back to the point which I raised right at the start of this book when I said that the changes of recent years have not merely produced a new Spain, but a new kind of Spaniard.

The characteristic that the Spaniards themselves are most aware of is their *individualismo*. By that, they do not mean what the British and Americans mean by 'individualism' (i.e. something bordering on eccentricity). Individualists in that sense are rare in Spain. As

Professor Stanley Payne, the American historian, wrote: 'Spanish society shows perhaps the greatest degree of adjustment to subgroup conformity found in any large Western country.' What Spaniards mean by *individualismo* is self-centredness – a legacy perhaps of the *reconquista*, a hangover from the days when self-reliance was of the essence. Their traditionally egotistical outlook on life helps to explain two of the recurrent themes in the Spaniards' history – their reluctance to sacrifice any part of their own interests to the common good and their intolerance of other people's views.

The Spaniards' unsocial behaviour, which they themselves call *insolidaridad*, can be seen in the prevalence of separatism and the popularity of anarchism. The proscription of unorthodox beliefs has a history that stretches from the expulsion of the Moslems and Jews at the beginning of the modern era through the Inquisition to the persecution of the Masons under Franco.

It was *insolidaridad* which was largely to blame for the outbreak of the civil war in 1936 and it was intolerance which accounted for many of the brutal excesses perpetrated during it. In other countries such a terrible blood-letting might have been followed by an effort at reconciliation. But not in Spain. Franco and his immediate supporters did everything in their power to ensure that the wounds of the civil war remained open for as long as possible. Tens of thousands of 'reds' – at least 50,000 and possibly several times that number – were executed in the years that followed. The Biscayans and Guipúzcoans had a 'punitive' decree passed against them; the leader of the Catalans was shot, and the widows of those who fell on the Republican side during the conflict were denied pensions – not merely during the period following the war, but until after Franco died.

It is this aspect of the Spanish character, which reached a sort of delirious crescendo during the early part of Franco's dictatorship, which I think is changing. The *individualismo* of the Spaniards is still among their most obvious traits. They still talk loudly and emphatically, shoot the lights and dress beyond their means. Their politicians are still prepared to sacrifice their careers rather than have their word doubted. The humblest waitresses still carry themselves as if they were débutantes and the poorest shopkeeper will still stop you from hunting for the extra few pesetas with an '*es igual*' ('no matter') and a gesture that suggests he has millions of them in the back room.

But the vindictive, anti-social edge to the Spaniards' *individualismo* is progressively less evident as the number of Spaniards who reached the age of reason before the civil war account for a progressively smaller percentage of the population. It is as if the horrors of the conflict and its aftermath had inoculated the Spaniards who grew up in their wake against the habits and attitudes that had brought them about. In this respect, if in no other, the generation gap in Spain is enormous. Nothing exemplified it better than the reaction of young, radical Spaniards to the fabled Republicans, such as La Pasionaria,* who returned after Franco's death. With their intemperate language and their intransigent attitudes the *viejos republicanos* seemed to the left-wingers and regional nationalists of the seventies like creatures from another planet.† La Pasionaria herself proved such an embarrassment to the Communist Party that she was subjected to something approaching house arrest.

I find that whenever one refers back to the civil war, or even to the Franco era, these days the reaction of young Spaniards is to shrug their shoulders and say with a smile, '*Bueno, eran otros tiempos*' ('Well, those were other times').

The watchwords of the new Spain are *solidaridad* and *convivencia* (which means 'living together', 'co-existence', in other words the opposite of intolerance). *Solidaridad* is still more of an aspiration than a fact. The first attempt to curb illegal parking in Madrid – by means of what Americans call 'Denver shoes' and the British 'clamps' – met with a degree of outrage bordering on apoplexy. The day after they were introduced some 500 people staged a spontaneous demonstration in a street where municipal workmen were fixing them to illegally parked vehicles. Over the weeks that followed, several people were taken to court for trying to smash the devices off their wheels with sledge-hammers and the like. When I was last in Madrid I found myself listening to a phone-in on the subject of income tax and it was quite clear from the remarks being made by callers that they regarded it as simply a form of official robbery. The idea that everybody had to contribute a certain amount to pay for common services had obviously not entered their minds.

Convivencia on the other hand is a reality. The gestures of reconciliation during these past few years have been many and moving – the remark by Lieutenant-General Vega Rodríguez, then the Army Chief of Staff, during the annual military celebrations that the Communist civil war generals Juan Modesto and Enrique Lister had had 'certain of the military virtues which so appeal to us'; the return to Spain of Picasso's

---

* Dolores Ibarruri. Born in 1895 into a poor Basque family, she went on to become a Communist deputy and the finest, fiercest orator on the Republican side during the civil war. It was she who coined the phrase '*No pasarán*' ('They shall not pass').

† A notable exception was Rafael Fernández, who took part in the Asturian uprising of 1934. As head of the pre-autonomous government in Asturias, he went out of his way to establish contacts with the right, even including a former minister of Franco in his team of advisers.

Guernica and of the remains of Alfonso XIII; the embrace – during his tour of Mexico – between King Juan Carlos and the widow of Spain's last Republican President, Manuel Azaña. And, most important of all perhaps, the gesture made by the leaders of all four main parties after the coup attempt in 1981, when they linked arms and marched through Madrid at the head of the biggest demonstration that the city has ever seen.

As the coup attempt showed, the area of society where the spirit of *convivencia* has penetrated least, where Spain is still often seen as an idealized abstraction rather than as the sum of the virtues and defects of the people who inhabit it, is in the army. It is significant, for example, that General Vega Rodríguez's remark provoked an outcry among many of his fellow officers. .

Unfortunately, it is the army which – alone among the institutions of contemporary Spain – has the means with which to forcibly impose its criteria on the rest of society. There is only a limited amount the politicians can do about this situation. They can make the army leaner and fitter (although that in itself entails further risks) and they can give its officers more and better weapons to keep them occupied (but there again that is expensive). Apart from that, all they can do is to wait and hope that the attitudes that have been seeping through the rest of society during the past quarter of a century gradually sink into the army. In this respect, the 1981 coup was more positive than negative, because the torrent of indignation it unleashed must have proved to even the most Quixotic officers that – if Tejero and his masters had succeeded – they would not have been able to count, in the way that Franco could, on a significant measure of support from the population.

That indignation remains Spain's firmest guarantee against the return of a dictatorship. Perhaps its most subtle but effective expression, during the days that followed the coup, came in a letter to the newspaper *El País* from one Francisco Gutiérrez. 'Come to the window, General,' he wrote. 'Look. Look. You see the old people taking the sun in the square? The *novios* kissing in the porch? The builders fixing the roof of the town hall? The girl studying the violin who spends all day by the window? The *pasota* lying on the grass? They are Spain, General. When we talk about Spain we are talking about them. Spain is not the Pyrenees or the Giralda or Las Hurdes. Spain is them. People. The rest is geography.'

INDEX